Halloween and Other Festivals of Death and Life

HALLOWEEN
and Other Festivals
of Death and Life

Edited by

JACK SANTINO

The University of Tennessee Press / Knoxville

Cloth: 1st printing, 1994.
Paper: 1st printing, 1994; 2nd printing, 1994.

Chapter 10, "Wishes Come True: Designing the Greenwich Village Halloween Parade,"
was originally published in the *Journal of American Folklore* 104, no. 414 (Fall 1991):
443–65. Used by permission.

The paper in this book meets the minimum requirements of the
American National Standard for Permanence of Paper for Printed
Library Materials. ∞ The binding materials have been chosen
for strength and durability.

Library of Congress Cataloging in Publication Data

Halloween and other festivals of death and life / edited by Jack Santino.
     p.   cm.
Includes bibliographical references and index.
ISBN 0-87049-812-6 (cloth: alk. paper). — ISBN 0-87049-813-4 (pbk.: alk. paper)
     1. Halloween. 2. All Souls' Day. I. Santino, Jack.
GT4965.H32 1993
394.2'646—dc20   93-5823
                                                                  CIP

For Ian, Will, and Hannah

Contents

Figures

Introduction
Festivals of Death and Life

JACK SANTINO

One of the first things I did when I began to explore the possibility of putting together a collection of essays on Halloween was to place a call for papers in the newsletters of several scholarly associations. Early on, I received a deeply moving letter and some photographs from Grey Gundaker, who was working on her dissertation in anthropology at Yale University. I showed it to some of my colleagues, but first warned them that reading the letter might actually ruin their day. Perhaps because I have three small children, Ms. Gundaker's letter chilled me to the core, particularly when I read the following:

> Early on the morning of last Nov. 2, I pulled up at a traffic light in Tuscaloosa and saw approximately the scene in the photo enclosed. This tableau—a combination birthday celebration and Halloween party for a dead child—has haunted me ever since.
>
> In the cemetery in Tuscaloosa, I photographed ten Halloween assemblages, as well as displays on other themes: fall colors, hunting, verbal/visual puns on nicknames, etc. On some graves, the Halloween materials were added to an existing display; on others, Halloween was the sole theme. One of the most poignant sights was a small glow-in-the-dark skeleton of bendable plastic sitting in a relaxed pose on the bronze grave plaque of a young boy. Other graves (like Mathew's, pictured) were flanked by ghosts.

The activities Ms. Gundaker described were almost overwhelming to me emotionally, although on an intellectual level, they were exciting. I recognized in them the adaptation of a ritual event that celebrates life—a birthday party—with a festival that incorporates the concept of death—Halloween. I had already planned on using the phrase "festivals of death and life" in the title of this volume, and now here was a dramatic example of the confluence of the two. Ms. Gundaker did indeed develop an article from her research, and it is included herein.

There are other intriguing instances in which death and life are related to each other in the Halloween festival, including a mock wedding conducted on Halloween night officiated by the personification of Death (see fig. 0.1). (The individuals involved had a legal ceremony a few days later.) In addition, there are many traditions having to do with conjuring the initials or image of one's future spouse on Halloween night, using apples and nuts, mirrors at midnight, or steam. Access to the supernatural, in this case divination

Fig. 0.1. Death officiates at a wedding. A mock wedding held on Halloween (the couple was married later) combines a life-affirming ritual with the symbolism of death, making this truly a festival of death and life. Photograph by Peter Fellman.

of the future, made possible by the liminality of Halloween, is oriented toward life-enforcing events such as love, courtship, and marriage at a time when seasonal activities include harvesting in preparation for the dead of winter.

In the juxtaposition of a calendrical festival (Halloween) with a life-cycle rite (birthday party), images of death and life are personally manipulated. The death-and-life sequence can be seen in the progression of year's-end celebrations, in which images of ghosts and skeletons are followed, in late December, by the sacred icon of the newborn baby, of candles lit in the darkness of the winter solstice, and of evergreen. These are followed in the new year by images of spring, resurrection, fertility, and renewal: hearts and flowers, rabbits, chickens, and eggs. Halloween reflects its season almost perfectly, and its position on the calendar makes sense in terms of the overall flow of the year.

Halloween is a holiday whose time has come. Again. And again, over and over, through the centuries. Literally, it is the eve of All Saints' Day in the calendar of the Roman Catholic church. To many revelers, young trick-or-treaters, and adolescent pranksters, however, there is little connection between Halloween and the Christian feast. Rather, the celebration is often thought to be quite secular, even pagan. Paradoxically, Halloween embodies the persistence of pre-Christian and non-Christian beliefs and practices carried through to the eve of the twenty-first century in part because of the Christianization of ancient festivals. The steadily increasing popularity of Halloween among many different groups of people within society, including Jews, Christians, Satanists, contemporary witches, and adherents of New Age philosophies, should force us to rethink our notions of religion and spirituality, and of what constitutes these things. For if Halloween is indeed a folk holiday, generated by everyday people, it is with parodistic images of death, harvest, evil, and the grotesque, paraded in public and adorning private homes, that people engage in holy communion with one another.

Images of death are major components of Halloween festivities, but there is a range of ritual and festival responses to death. In order to understand our attitudes toward death, we must first understand and articulate our attitudes toward life. In *Celebrations of Death,* Huntington and Metcalf take the reasonable point of view that the way we treat the body after death is indicative of our attitudes regarding the soul and the afterlife.[1] I wonder if this sheds any light on the rise of cremation as a means of disposal of the body? In this regard, we should look at some of the ways we have formalized our approach to death, ways we have ritualized it, ways we ceremonialize it, and ways we celebrate it.

People die. A particular death is recognized with some form of a rite of passage. In some regions of the country and among some ethnic groups, these rites are full-blown, major celebrations. I am thinking here of the Irish wake or the New Orleans jazz funeral, which are given over to joyous expression: dancing and music making (the New Orleans "second line"); drinking, dancing, and storytelling (the Irish wake). We generally commemorate personal deaths—the deaths of people close to us—on an annual basis. If the person who died is important to a social group, such as a fallen leader, we ceremonialize the ritual on a large scale. The best example of this would be the state funeral, such as the nationally televised mourning and burial rituals of assassinated president John F. Kennedy.

Certain days are set aside for the collective commemoration of personal deaths, specifically Memorial Day, which began as a day of tribute to the Civil War dead, grew to encompass veterans of later armed conflicts, and has become a kind of national decoration day. It is, for instance, the day my family in Boston visits the graves of our relatives. For others, decoration days, or homecomings, are held throughout the summer and fall months. Graves are tended and decorated with flowers, and there are church services and family picnics. Younger generations meet members of the opposite sex while children play among the graves of ancestors. In these family festivals of death and life, death is recognized as a part of the family unit's cycle of life. All of the above examples—funerals, anniversaries, and homecomings—have to do with specific deaths that hold personal significance. Halloween, a festival that frames death as a concept, as an existential entity, features stylized images of death as among its primary symbols: skeletons, ghosts, skulls. Like all social and cultural expressions, Halloween has a history and occurs in a context. Many of its images of the supernatural and the otherworldly are pre-Christian, whereas others, such as Frankenstein, Dracula, and Freddy Krueger, are drawn from more recent popular culture.

Broadly speaking, festivals that emphasize death or the supernatural are universal; so are those that include "masked solicitation rituals" as one of their customary activities.[2] Among these, the ancient celebration of Samhain, the chief quarter day of the ancient Celtic calendar, figures significantly in the prehistory of the modern Halloween. Heavily influenced by, if not born in, the pre-Christian, Celtic year-end festival of Samhain, the observance of the Eve of All Hallows has flourished in the Christian era, despite efforts of the Christian church to channel people's attention toward All Saints' and All Souls' days on 1 and 2 November, respectively. Known in North America since colonial days, by the middle of the twentieth century Halloween had become largely a children's holiday. More recently, however, Halloween has exploded in the United States. Adults have begun celebrating it in such great numbers that it can no longer be considered the exclusive domain of children. If we are to judge by the masquerade parties, the many decorated houses and yards, the campus festivities, and the urban street celebrations around the country, it appears that today Halloween is very much an adult celebration. In this regard, it has come full circle.

Although it has changed a great deal over the centuries, the ancient Celtic (Irish, Scottish, Welsh) festival called Samhain is considered by many to be a predecessor of our contemporary Halloween. Samhain was the New Year's Day of the Celts, celebrated on 1 November. It was also a day of the dead, a time when it was believed that the souls of those who had died during the year were allowed access to the land of the dead. It was a time when spirits were believed to be wandering. The festival also was related to the season: by Samhain, the crops should be harvested and animals brought in from the distant fields.

It was both the first day of the new year and the first day of winter. As a point of transition in the annual calendar, a great many beliefs and rituals were associated with the day. The gates that separated the worlds of the living and the dead, of this world and the world of spirits, were opened, the barriers between this world and the next were down, and the souls of those who had died during the year were allowed entry to the otherworld. Bonfires were lit on Samhain, some say to light the way for the spirits, others say to keep them away from peoples' homes. With the belief in the wandering spirits of the dead came the custom of preparing offerings of special foods, and of dressing as these spirits and as wild animals. We can only guess at the connections people made between the harvest of crops, the slaughter of animals, and the death of human beings in the cycle of life; or between lighting fires at the onset of winter and the increasing darkness, between mimicking the wandering souls and respecting them, and between the ritualized and stylized offering of food to spirits and their representatives: real human beings who need food to live. However, as both Abrahams and Glassie have pointed out in other contexts, these connections were rational and based on common sense.[3]

These customs were widely practiced in ancient Ireland, which was converted to Christianity (by St. Patrick, among others) in A.D. 300–400. With conversion came a redefinition of the local religion and its calendrical celebrations, due in large part to a successful strategy of the Christian missionaries. The Catholic church, when sending missionaries to convert native peoples, encouraged the redefinition of traditional customs into Christian terms and concepts. Thus, in A. D. 601 Pope Gregory I instructed his priests that if, for instance, a group of people worshipped a tree, rather than cut the tree down, leave it standing but consecrate it to Christ. Instruct the people to gather regularly at the same site, Gregory wrote, but explain to them that they were no longer worshipping the tree, but He for whom the tree was consecrated. In such a way the early church adapted and accommodated the traditional religious beliefs and practices of those it sought to convert. Many of the festivals and holidays we enjoy have resulted from this policy and were derived in some part from already existing festivals and celebrations. Halloween is no exception. The first of November was declared All Saints' Day; later, 2 November was proclaimed All Souls' Day. The celebration began on the sundown prior to 1 November. Many traditional beliefs and customs associated with Samhain, most notably that night was the time of the wandering dead, the practice of leaving offerings of food and drink to masked and costumed revelers, and the lighting of bonfires, continued to be practiced on 31 October, known as the Eve of All Saints, the Eve of All Hallows, or Hallow Even. It is the glossing of the name Hallow Even that has given us the name *Hallowe'en.*

All Saints' Day is a day set aside on the church calendar to pay honor to all the saints who do not otherwise have a feast day reserved for them. About A.D. 900, the church recognized that All Saints' had not supplanted the pre-Christian customs, so in an attempt to get closer to the original intent of the festival, it declared 2 November as All Souls' Day. This day is in recognition of the souls of all the faithful departed who had died during the previous year. It is obviously much closer in spirit to the Celtic Samhain than is All Saints' Day.[4]

Through its missionaries, the church also redefined the beliefs, along with the rituals and practices, of the peoples it converted. The spirits of Samhain, once thought to be wild and powerful, were now said to be something worse: evil. The church maintained that the gods and goddesses and other spiritual beings of traditional religions were diabolical deceptions, that the spiritual forces that people had experienced were real, but they were manifestations of the Devil, the Prince of Liars, who misled people toward the worship of false idols. Thus, the customs associated with Hallow Even included representations of ghosts and human skeletons—symbols of the dead—and of the devil and other malevolent, evil creatures, such as witches were said to be.

Because of these events, Halloween is associated with All Saints' Day and, by extension, with the church calendar. With the Protestant Reformation, church holidays diminished in importance. Here is where we get into the rise of Guy Fawkes Day (or Night) as an important addition to the English holiday calendar. In England, 5 November is Guy Fawkes Day, which is celebrated in ways reminiscent of Halloween. Guy Fawkes was accused of attempting to blow up the Houses of Parliament on that day in 1605. He was apprehended, hung, drawn, and quartered. On 5 November 1606, the same Parliament declared the fifth of November a day of public thanksgiving. The act of treason was viewed as part of a "popish"—that is, Roman Catholic—plot against the Protestant government. Because Halloween was associated with the Catholic church calendar, its importance diminished, but many of its traditions shifted to the annual commemoration of the death of Guy Fawkes. Today, for weeks in advance of 5 November, English children prepare effigies of Fawkes, dummies known as *Guys.* They set them out on street corners and beg passers-by for "a penny for the Guy." The eve of the fifth is known as Mischief Night, when children are free to play pranks on adults, just as 30 October, the night before Halloween, is known as Mischief Night in many areas of the United States. On the night of 5 November, the Guys are burned in bonfires, just as the ancient Celts burned bonfires on 1 November.

To this day, services are offered on 5 November by the Church of England in thanksgiving for the safety of the seat of government and the apprehension of Guy Fawkes. The day is traditionally celebrated by exploding fireworks and lighting bonfires. The fireworks are widely thought to be inspired by the explosives that were not successfully ignited by Fawkes, and many people incorrectly assume that he was burnt at the stake in a folk etymology of the bonfire custom. More likely, the bonfires represent a transition from Halloween bonfires (and the Celtic quarter-day bonfires before them). Although Halloween is still celebrated in England, Guy Fawkes Night is the larger and more important event.

Generally speaking, Guy Fawkes Night appears to be an adaptation of Halloween customs to English society, perhaps having something to do with an identification of Halloween with the Roman Catholic church, and Guy Fawkes Night celebrations are ritual dramas that underscore English independence from the pope. In Lewes, England, for example, which hosts a very large Guy Fawkes celebration, effigies of the pope are burnt, as they are elsewhere in England, and someone dresses as the pope, parades through the streets, and is pelted with fruits and vegetables—so much so that he wears a face guard.

The history of Halloween, then, from having been influenced by the Celtic Samhain to its influence on the Protestant Guy Fawkes Day, indicates many changes in the political realities and social dynamics in England, Ireland, and the United States (among other places) over the centuries. It demonstrates the fact that in addition to being vehicles for the expression of

personal, social, and cultural identity, our celebrations reflect broad historical currents. These are only some of the many dimensions found in a closer
look at major social and cultural celebrations such as Halloween.

The first week of November is marked in many countries, especially
those with a strong Catholic influence, with festivals concerned with death
in a playful but serious way. In Catholic countries we often find some cognate of Halloween associated with All Saints' or All Souls' days. In Mexico
and other Latin American countries, the first and second of November are
the Days of the Dead—El Días de los Muertos, known in various regions as
Todos Santos (All Saints), Día de los Difuntos or Fieles Difuntos (Day of
the Departed or Faithful Departed), or Día de las Animas Benditas (Day of
the Blessed Souls).[5] In some regions, the evening of 31 October is the beginning of the Day of the Dead Children, which is followed on 1 November
by the Day of the Dead Adults. Skeleton figures—candy, toys, statues and
decorations—are seen everywhere. It is a time for great festivity, with traditional plays and food. It is also a time for decorating family graves, which is
preceded by religious services and followed by picnics. In the United States,
we seem to have split these two aspects of the festival, the solemn and the
playful, and celebrate them at separate times of the year. That is, whereas in
the Mexican and Mexican American celebrations of the Day of the Dead, symbols of the general concept of death coexist with ritual commemorations of the
deaths of loved ones, this is not the case with Halloween in the United States.

However, in a way that is reminiscent of the American Halloween, el
Día de los Muertos is an occasion in Mexico to play with death, to give it its
due, to recognize it and to incorporate it into the daily rounds. The human
skeleton or skull is the primary symbol of the day. Candy forms, called sugar
skulls, are sold in the streets, as are toys and figures of skeletons performing
mundane tasks. Especially popular are figures of dancing skeletons. Unlike
the American Halloween, in Mexico people build home altars, adorned with
religious icons and special breads and other food for the dead. It is a time
for churchgoing and for cleaning and decorating the graves of loved ones. So
the Mexican Day of the Dead incorporates recognition of death as a concept
with rituals that remember the deaths of individuals.

Internationally, autumn is not the only time of year for such festivals. In
China, for instance, the care of the dead through prayers and sacrifices were
part of a spring festival of purification and regeneration. In Japan, the Bon
festival, dedicated to the spirits of ancestors, for whom special foods are prepared, occurs during the middle of the summer (one of the most important
festive periods of the year). Three days in length, it is a time when everyone

goes home (reminiscent of the American Thanksgiving). In some parts of Japan, people conduct rituals to close the three-day period, such as building a small boat to carry the spirits of the dead back to the other world and floating the boat down a river.

Throughout the Western world, 1 May, like 1 November, is a day of traditional significance. The thirtieth of April, the eve of May 1, is in areas of Germany, particularly the Harz Mountains, Walpurgisnacht, or the eve of St. Walpurgis Day. Witches are supposed to be especially active this day, as are spirits of the dead and demon creatures from the netherworld. Walpurga was a medieval nun, the daughter of King Richard the Lion-Hearted, who moved to Germany and became the abbess of the monastery of Eichstatt. After her death she was canonized and became known as the protector against magic. Her day and its traditions almost certainly are traceable to pre-Christian celebrations that took place at this time, on the first of May, just as All Saints' was an overlay on traditional first of November activities. Notice also that 1 November and 1 May are six months apart. These represent two of the four quarter days on the old Celtic calendar, the other two being 1 February and 1 August. All four were marked with feasts.

Walpurgisnacht is in many ways similar to Halloween. Witches, ghosts, and devils are said to run rampant on this day. Again, because it exists within a Christian context, its revelries are said to represent evil, but there is an undeniable attraction to the festivity of large-scale costuming, and to the licentiousness, the freedom from restraint, and the spontaneity that results. In Johann Wolfgang von Goethe's classic work *Faust,* Walpurgisnacht is a major element. In one scene, the Devil, who is tempting the professor, points out, as they overlook the witch's activities, "All in a row a hundred fires blaze; People dance, converse, concoct, imbibe, make love: Just tell me where there's anything to beat this!"[6] Our festivals of death also celebrate life, the life forces, the unquenchable urge to procreate, to live to the fullest in the face of death, and to celebrate.

I decided to study Halloween in a scholarly way after I began to notice a resurgence of adult Halloween activities in the late 1970s. This led to the development of this collection of essays. In this way, this book is itself a product of the increasing popularity and growing influence of Halloween in the United States today. The chapters deal with Halloween both historically and in the present. I have grouped the contents in three sections: Customs, Communities, and Material Culture. The categories overlap, of course, but they should suggest a few ways of approaching this widely manifested and enormously complex event. The diversity of approaches and the variety of perspectives represented are intended to suggest the richness of the subject. Everyone knows about Halloween. Yet even the most preliminary investigation will reveal the variety of customs, the many different ways in which people celebrate it, and the many interpretations of those customs.

Included are examinations of two other, related festivals: Catherine Schwoeffermann's study of Bonfire Night in Newfoundland (a variation of the English Guy Fawkes Night celebration) and Pat Jasper and Kay Turner's analysis of the Mexican American Día de los Muertos. Most chapters are concerned with Halloween in the United States or Canada, and one is a close reading of Halloween and its symbolic relations to other year's-end festivals in Northern Ireland.

The use of Guy Fawkes Night as a means of establishing differential identity is absent in (formerly British) Newfoundland, where the fifth of November is most frequently referred to as Bonfire Night and Guys are not made or displayed. Schwoeffermann's chapter is a rich, descriptive account of the central custom of the festival, the building and burning of bonfires. Basing her analysis on extensive fieldwork, she persuasively outlines potential meanings of the custom in Newfoundland today, among the people who practice it.

Historically, then, Guy Fawkes Night is related to Halloween due to an adaptation of customs from one date (31 October) to commemorate a more recent event on a nearby date. Newfoundland's Bonfire Night is a clear descendant of, or even a version of, the English Guy Fawkes Night. Notably, however, Halloween, rather than Guy Fawkes Night, is by far the more widely celebrated occasion in Scotland, which, although both Protestant and a part of Great Britain, is, like Ireland, Celtic in terms of history and national identity. Northern Ireland, the six counties of the province of Ulster that are aligned politically with Great Britain (not without controversy), is only twenty-seven miles across the Irish Sea from southwest Scotland. The two countries are easily visible to each other on clear days. As a result of this proximity, there has been constant interaction between the countries over the centuries, evident in shared family names, vocabulary, and customary behavior. Philip Robinson presents a very detailed description of Halloween customs as practiced in Northern Ireland and relates these to other calendrical festivals and to some relevant Scottish traditions. He documents contemporary Halloween traditions in a society whose history, although complex, is at least in part Celtic. The result is a chapter that not only reflects the presumed Irish and Celtic beginnings of many contemporary Halloween traditions but also serves as a corrective to the many uninformed generalizations that deal with Irish folklife as a single, homogeneous body of material.

Robinson's study places Halloween customs in Northern Ireland within a larger seasonal cycle of celebration that includes Christmas and Hogmanay (Scottish New Year's Day). Ireland is often viewed as a wellspring of Halloween traditions because of the ancient festival of Samhain, but little attention has been paid to the real complexities of Ireland, including both the Republic of Ireland and Northern Ireland. There is a historical connection between the Halloween of Ireland and that of the United States, in that many Halloween traditions were brought to America by people escaping starvation in Ireland during the mid-nineteenth century. Those fleeing the potato famine, however, were preceded by the Ulster Protestants—frequently referred to as the Scots-Irish—who left due to discrimination and poor economic conditions. In fact it was most likely through the emigrants from Ulster that the United States enjoyed its first input of Irish Halloween traditions. Today, Halloween is very important in all of Ireland and is celebrated in some ways that appear similar to those in the United States but that, in fact, differ significantly in meaning and purpose. Robinson has detailed many of the finer shades of meaning and connotation of contemporary Halloween customs and practices in Northern Ireland and contributes a chapter that not only sheds light on the interrelationships among festivals of the year's end but also provides important data concerning the celebration in the country in which it is thought by many to have begun. Further, I would like to suggest that the kinds of interrelationships Robinson discusses are also present in American calendrical festivals.

Jasper and Turner examine the very different tradition of the Texas-Mexican Day of the Dead on 2 November. Not surprisingly, given the proximity of Mexico and the United States and the pervasive quality of contemporary electronic media, there has been some conflation of Halloween with el Día de los Muertos in both Mexico and the United States. Importantly, the Texas-Mexican materials represent an additional kind of historical syncretism: along with the Western European and Christian elements of Halloween, el Día de los Muertos reflects New World, Native American ideas and concepts of death and the afterlife. Although this book remains focused specifically on Halloween and festivals related to it, Jasper and Turner's chapter reminds us that not all manifestations of the Eve of All Hallows or of All Souls' Day are Northern European. El Día de los Muertos is southern European and Mediterranean in its Spanish aspects as well as Native American. Finally, and most importantly with regard to this chapter, the materials are from the United States; these are ethnic American traditions.

Carl Holmberg contributes a chapter on Halloween noisemakers and reflects on the use of noise as a component of ritual. In his experience, noise was used to announce one's approach to people in their homes, and also, more subtly, to create an environment that actually defined the domain of Halloween activities. Although noise (as opposed to music) has been recognized as an important component of festival,[7] it is still too often overlooked or simply unnoticed in the scholarly literature. Holmberg contributes an important discussion of this aspect of the festival of Halloween.

Michael Taft examines adult costuming practices in Canada that seem to be derived from or modeled on traditional mumming formerly practiced at Christmastime. Steve Siporin reveals the ways pranking is viewed in rural Utah as a bothersome but ultimately much more respectable, and convenient, activity than trick-or-treating, which is looked down upon by many as begging. Despite the fact that the attitude described by Siporin is frequently reported, many feel the primary Halloween activity is trick-or-treating. Tad Tuleja traces the Halloween begging activity specifically known as trick-or-treating to the 1930s and concludes that the custom was intended to control and displace communally disruptive pranking activities. Ironically, today trick-or-treating itself is viewed as dangerous and in need of institutional control. Chapters by Belk and Ellis attest to different aspects of this perception of danger. Ellis looks at the effects of rumors concerning potentially deadly Halloween treats (poisoned candy, razor blades in apples, needles hidden in treats, etc.) on the activities of the evening and finds that rather than being destroyed, the festivity has emerged in some unlikely places, such as in the special hospital unit set up to X-ray Halloween treats for concealed dangers. Belk looks at corporate attempts to co-opt and control the essential subversive elements of Halloween. Interestingly, he finds that the most successful attempts appear to be those in which the festive activities were accommodated, and in which the workers themselves exhibited a good amount of control over how that would be accomplished. In these cases it is questionable whether Halloween has been co-opted and controlled or merely recognized and given its due.

In reflections on his conversations with his friend and informant Frank Briggs, A. W. Sadler finds reminders of the old idea of Halloween as the year's divider, as the point of summer's end and winter's onset, on at least a practical level. Alternatively, Jack Kugelmass documents urban Halloween festivity and spectacle in New York. Sadler hears quiet echoes of ancient times in rural Vermont; Kugelmass sees the many ways Halloween is a product of urban space and gay identity in Greenwich Village. These two chapters reveal different ends of the same spectrum. Halloween is many things to many people; we do not celebrate the day in any one way. What one does on or around Halloween varies, depending on factors such as age, place of residence (rural, urban, or suburban), region of the country, ethnicity, and associational group. Halloween is used in a variety of ways by different groups of people as a vehicle for expressing identity.

For instance, in 1990 in Bowling Green, Ohio, the town in which I live, Halloween was celebrated, or at least noted, by different church groups, the sizable Mexican American community, and a women's group associated with the university at which I work. Along with a harvest festival in October, which featured the sale of many Halloween craft items, the local Catholic church had a special Day of the Dead observance on 2 November for the sizable Hispanic community in the area. Many of the Mexican American celebrants told me that they specifically linked their Day of the Dead observances with the Anglo-American Halloween; that is, they recognized the connection, through the church calendar, of their observance of All Souls' and the popular observance of the eve of All Saints'. At the same time, a university feminist group sponsored a ritual gathering to celebrate Samhain as a pagan festival of nature. Participants were asked to bring a gift of some sort, preferably a natural or organic item, to a spot in a nearby wooded area. The announcement describing this event reads as follows:

We will be celebrating the beginning of winter and the end of the growing season. Samhain (pronounced sow' in, the "ow" rhyming with cow) is the Celtic New Year as well as the New Year for all Wiccans [witches]. It is also a time for connecting with ancestors and friends who have passed over before us. The rabblerousers who call Hallows a devil's night are merely connecting their own fear of death to a pagan holiday. Death to the pagan folk was and is merely another ritual of passage. To the pagan there is nothing to fear about dying since the Summerland is open to all and there is no bogeyman's condo for the bad. Samhain is also traditionally the time when the God takes the lead as the Lady goes to her rest. In Wicca the Lady is in rule from Beltane to Hallows or the half of the year when everything is growing and glowing.

But Women for Women is not a Wiccan group nor is it a pagan group. It is a feminist group so what are we doing in a celebration of this nature? Women for Women has always been involved in bringing so-called women's spirituality out in the open so that we can all learn other ways. This celebration will be an eclectic ritual utilizing ideas from many paths in the pagan world. We hope that it will be a learning experience for all involved. Please come with open minds and comfortable clothes. We are asking everyone to bring a small stone or shell or feather or twig that has some meaning for them. We will be exchanging these with each other so please do not bring something that is important to your heart. Blessed Be!

Two weeks prior to 31 October, the local Assembly of God church publicly denounced Halloween because it celebrated Satan, demons, and witchcraft. Meanwhile the Presbyterian church sponsored a party in which children dressed as saints, on the basis that if Halloween must be recognized at all, it may as well be done with sacred rather than profane imagery. The city of Bowling Green had its annual children's parade and Halloween party at the junior high school, and city government proclaimed the hours of 6:00 to 8:00 P.M. as the officially condoned time for trick-or-treating. In 1990, trick-or-treat night, as it is called, was on 31 October, but this is not always the case. And while some people publicly condemned Halloween as a festival honoring the devil, contemporary witches and pagans argued that Halloween was for them a holy day, the most sacred of the year. Whereas some letters to the local newspaper attempted to explain paganism and contemporary witchcraft, others expressed contempt for a holiday that celebrated the devil.

In each of these cases, personal and group identity were being expressed through the medium of holiday celebration. A neo-pagan, essentially New Age Samhain ritual held outdoors is radically different from a church-sponsored harvest festival bazaar, which in turn is very different from a Christian party offered as an alternative by a church that condemns Halloween as Satanist. All of these are different from the city-sponsored parade and officially sanctioned hours of trick-or-treating, although certainly some of the events' participants overlap. Meanwhile, the relatively large population of Mexican Americans expressed their ethnic heritage through traditional and revitalized customs that syncretized both Halloween and their own Día de los Muertos. Furthermore, in Detroit, only seventy-five miles north of Bowling Green and an urban presence felt locally in a variety of ways (many Bowling Green residents use the Detroit airport, attend baseball games and other sporting events there, watch Detroit television stations and read Detroit newspapers, for example), 30 October is Devil's Night. On the night before Halloween, the symbolism of the fires of Hell and the demons who live there join the traditions of pranking and the period of license that allows, even demands, behavior not otherwise tolerated. The combination results in widespread arson. Whole areas of the city are set ablaze. The extent to which these attacks involve political and social unrest and are related to the urban riots of the 1960s is unclear, but we see in Detroit's Devil's Night yet another variation in the way people engage and actualize the customs and symbols of Halloween, and how these ideas can be used to establish identity, to incorporate one within a group, or to express rage.

If Halloween activities vary according to one's personal and social identity, so also do they vary according to one's age. Ervin Beck has suggested that Halloween activities can act as rites of passage for children.[8] I would extend the idea to apply to the entire life cycle. Although the same is true for other holidays, the relation of age-specific customs to rites of passage is particularly relevant to Halloween. As I review my own life, for instance, I see the following: As a young child, I was escorted on my trick-or-treating adventures by members of my immediate family, either a parent or an older sister. As I got a little older, perhaps about ten years of age, I began to trick-or-treat with a group of friends from my street. When I reached early adolescence, about the age of twelve or thirteen, I continued to go out with a group of friends on Halloween, but the friends were from school, the territory we walked was larger, and we no longer rang doorbells to ask for (or demand) treats. Instead, we made mischief, soaping the occasional car window or throwing the occasional egg.

Halloween activities waned somewhat through high school, but in college, Halloween meant a masquerade party. I went to college during the latter part of the 1960s, and the costume parties were very much sixties-style events: the costumes were weird, elaborate, and psychedelic. One year, at a masquerade party held by a friend of mine who lived in an inner-city neighborhood, the annual parade of outrageously costumed, cross-dressed gay people happened by the front door. The host of the party invited them in, and they came. Soon they were followed by a local motorcycle gang who styled themselves on the Hell's Angels. No one knows who invited them, nor what it was, exactly, that they added to the punch, but the party was, to say the least, memorable.

Masquerades and costume parties continued to be my major Halloween activities through graduate school. When I moved to Washington, D.C., to begin work at the Smithsonian Institution, I began to notice the growth in urban Halloween parades. No longer were they exclusively gay. In cities all over the country, and in college towns as well, Halloween had become a night of dressing up and partying in the streets for adults of all ages.[9] In Washington, D.C., Georgetown is the scene of the street festivities. Perhaps the most famous such parades and parties are in San Francisco and in New York's Greenwich Village. In addition to the public processions, I also noticed a rise in the number of homes that were decorated, often elaborately, for Halloween, to an extent that rivaled even Christmas. Whole families were now involving themselves in this late-year festival.[10]

I now have three children. My involvement in Halloween has changed again. I teach my children how to carve jack-o'-lanterns, as I fondly remember my father teaching me. Now my wife and I provide the treats instead of begging for them. Times have changed, however. Unlike when I was a child, many parents today don costumes themselves to accompany their children on their rounds; many people handing out the treats also wear costumes and wait to receive the children at their doors. Although some folks turn their homes into haunted houses and invite the children inside to see the spooky sights and to have a doughnut and a spot of cider before they go on to the next house, Halloween is very much celebrated outdoors. Much of the fun of the evening is sensual: being surrounded by flickering candlelight on a street full of colorful, costumed creatures, tasting the treats, with a soundtrack provided by the crispy autumn leaves crunching underfoot.

The point of all this reminiscing is that the customs of Halloween vary according to age. We all do different Halloween-things at different times of life. To an extent, these different activities mark stages of life. Trick-or-treating with one's peers rather than a family guardian was, I personally felt, a sign of growing up. So was the time at which I ceased to trick-or-treat and began to simply indulge in pranks. Certainly, approaching Halloween as a parent was a major transition for me. Folklorist Margaret Yocom once told me that her college students, in a class she teaches concerning Halloween, always express nostalgia and regret over being too old to participate in Halloween in the ways they did as children. My sense of this is that these sets of activities are associated with particular age groups. Leaving aside one set of Halloween activities and embracing another reflects a movement from one stage of life to another and is an informal rite of passage. This explains the sense of loss as well as gain, because to move to a new stage of life brings to mind the awareness that one does not go back.[11]

Halloween, then, despite the fact that it is observed nationally and is highly commercialized, varies from person to person and group to group; regionally, ethnically, religiously, and, as Russell Belk demonstrates in this volume, occupationally. The traditional activities also change throughout one's life. We can describe these variations as both horizontal and vertical: traditions vary horizontally across space and vertically through time, including one's lifetime.

Autumnal celebrations of death and life are found variously among ethnic groups, age groups, regional groups, and self-identified groups such as contemporary witches; they are sponsored variously by churches, commercial establishments, corporations, and civic groups; they are realized by adults, and, of course, by children. Halloween is manifested throughout all aspects of our society. As society has changed, so has the celebration, but predictions of its demise a few decades ago have proven wrong. With this volume we have only begun to explore the richness and depth of this popular celebration that, rooted in centuries, even millennia, past, is vitally meaningful today. From the early Christian missionaries to contemporary naysayers, Halloween is no stranger to persecution. It nevertheless continues to be celebrated, not as a marginal survivor of an otherwise dead tradition, but as a thriving, contemporary, postindustrial festival. Its symbolism is powerful and its customs are elastic enough to appeal broadly to groups of different ages, national origins, sexual orientations, and regional backgrounds. Despite the economic commercialization of the customary activities of costuming and dispensing treats, it is an unofficial celebration. No day off is given for Halloween, no federal decree is proclaimed establishing it as a national holiday. People simply do it. We hope the chapters contained in this volume will contribute to the knowledge and understanding of Halloween and stimulate further research. Perhaps our work will even add to the readers' enjoyment of this exciting and complex celebration. Halloween has become one of the most important and widely celebrated festivals on the contemporary American calendar, and it is not even officially a holiday. Interesting, isn't it?

Notes

1.   Richard Huntington and Peter Metcalf, *Celebrations of Death* (Cambridge, England: Cambridge Univ. Press, 1979).

2.   Thomas Vennum, Jr., "The Ojibwa Begging Dance," in *Music and Context: Essays for John M. Ward*, ed. Anne Dhu Shapiro (Cambridge, Mass.: Harvard Univ. Dept. of Music, 1985).

3.   Roger D. Abrahams, "The Language of Festivals: Celebrating the Economy," in *Celebration: Studies in Festivity and Ritual*, ed. Victor Turner (Washington, D.C.: Smithsonian Institution Press), 163; Henry Glassie, *All Silver and No Brass* (Philadelphia: Univ. of Pennsylvania Press, 1975), 103.

4.   See the *New Catholic Encyclopedia* (New York: McGraw-Hill, 1967), 1: 318–19.

5.   Elizabeth Carmichael and Chloë Sayer, *The Skeleton at the Feast: The Day of the Dead in Mexico* (London: British Museum Press, 1991).

6.   Johann Wolfgang von Goethe, *Faust*, trans. Stuart Atkins (Cambridge, Mass.: Suhrkamp/Insel Publishers Boston, 1984), 104.

7.   Richard Dorson, "The Components of Festivals," in *Celebration: Studies in Festivity and Ritual*, ed. Victor Turner (Washington, D.C.: Smithsonian Institution Press), 1982.

8. Ervin Beck, "Trickster on the Threshold: An Interpretation of Children's Autumn Traditions," *Folklore* 96, no. 1 (1985): 26.

9. See, for instance, Keith Waldon, "Respectable Hooligans: Male Toronto College Students Celebrate Hallowe'en, 1884–1910," *Canadian Historical Review* 68, no. 1 (1987): 1–35.

10. Jack Santino, "The Folk Assemblage of Autumn," in *Folk Art and Art Worlds,* ed. John Vlach and Simon Bronner, 151–69 (Logan: Utah State Univ. Press), 1992.

11. Margaret Yocum, personal conversation, June 1991.

References

Bujak, Adam, and Marjorie B. Young. 1976. *Paths to Glory.* New York: Harper & Row.

Damon, Frederick H., and Roy Wagner. 1989. *Death Rituals and Life in the Societies of the Kula Ring.* De Kalb: Northern Illinois Univ. Press.

Danforth, Loring M., and Alexander Tsiaras. 1982. *The Death Rituals of Rural Greece.* Princeton, N.J.: Princeton Univ. Press.

Hatch, Jane. 1978. *The American Book of Days.* 3d ed. New York: H. W. Wilson.

Huntington, Richard, and Peter Metcalf. 1979. *Celebrations of Death.* Cambridge, England: Cambridge Univ. Press.

Turner, Victor, ed. 1982. *Celebration: Studies in Festivities and Ritual.* Washington, D.C.: Smithsonian Institution Press.

Russ, Jennifer M. 1982. *German Festivals and Customs.* London: Oswald Wolff.

Warner, William L. 1959. *The Living and the Dead: A Study of the Symbolic Life of Americans.* New Haven: Yale Univ. Press.

PART I

Customs

1. Harvest, Halloween, and Hogmanay: Acculturation in Some Calendar Customs of the Ulster Scots

PHILIP ROBINSON

Calendar customs have been studied in Ireland either as individual anniversaries or as a collective manifestation of the nation's folk culture. In considering the interdependence of certain calendar customs (such as those pertaining to harvest and midwinter), however, it is important to view cyclical rhythm at close range: the harmony that existed between related traditions, such as those surrounding the last sheaf of harvest and the straw wisps of New Year, can only be examined at the local level, for the cultural landscape of Ireland is far from homogeneous. Perhaps no region of Ireland is less characteristic of the received perception of Irish tradition than east Ulster, and even this small area within Northern Ireland is not internally consistent. It is clear from this study that certain calendar customs were seasonally related and that processes of innovation or obsolescence affecting any single custom could have a significant impact on the whole equilibrium of the seasonal cycle. The evidence considered is almost entirely based on oral tradition, so that unless the present or more distant past is particularly mentioned, I am concerned with a loose notion of the "recent past," that is, the century between 1850 and 1950.

People and traditions have been exchanged across the narrow sea channel between northeast Ireland and southwest Scotland for thousands of years. In the modern historic period, the descendants of seventeenth-century Scottish settlers in northeast Ireland (particularly in counties Antrim and Down) have become known in Ireland as Ulster Scots. These are essentially the same people as those involved in large-scale migrations from Ulster to America during the eighteenth century, often referred to as the Scotch-Irish. I have identified the extent of the area dominated by this group within Ulster or Northern Ireland elsewhere on the basis of dialect, surnames, religion, and politico-cultural identity.[1] Somehow, their culture falls between what is perceived externally to be "Scottish" and "Irish," and so the vague concept of the Scotch-Irish has become a hopeless muddle for the American folklorist. But Ulster Scots traditions are not simply a mélange of Scots and Irish phenomena. Significant elements are exclusive to east Ulster, and perhaps most significantly, these communities appear to have generated a distinctive pattern of calendar customs with its own set of cyclical balances and relationships. The purpose of this chapter is to examine several calendar customs as they have been practiced by the descendants of Scottish settlers in east Ulster; partly to explore these same traditions in a context of cultural contact, but also to consider the interconnections between the calendar customs themselves. Only those customs associated with the time between harvest in late summer and the New Year are described: the last sheaf of harvest, harvest knots, Harvest Thanksgiving, Halloween, Christmas rhymers, Christmas Day, New Year wisps, and Hogmanay. In tracing these customs chronologically through this particular segment of the calendar, it is possible to identify the symbolic relationships among them and also their relationships to the annual calendar.[2]

Exhaustive but separate studies have already been made by Gailey of the most relevant traditions, such as the last sheaf, Christmas rhymers, and New Year wisps, as they occur throughout Ulster (and to a lesser extent in the rest of Ireland), and Buchanan has surveyed and described the totality of Irish (particularly Ulster) calendar customs.[3] Both Gailey and Buchanan compare these customs with those recorded in other parts of the British Isles and Europe, most frequently observing parallels in Scottish folklore. Buchanan observed that calendar customs are closely related to the regular rhythmic cycle of the seasons, thus providing them with "greater permanence and stability than any other branch of folk tradition."[4] In general, Irish customs find their closest parallels in Scotland (and vice versa), the chief exception for Buchanan being the observance of Hogmanay (New Year's Eve), which Buchanan found to be of "little importance in Ireland," where Halloween was traditionally regarded as the end of the year. However, as Hogmanay was indeed celebrated in parts of east Ulster, it is best to avoid applying national labels to the folk traditions of the Ulster Scots. Buchanan's view (from an Irish perspective) that Hogmanay may have replaced Halloween as the New Year festival in Scotland seems to deny the seasonality and annual fertility cycle underlying the harvest, Halloween, and Hogmanay celebrations commonly found in east Ulster. The onset of winter in late October, combined with the harvesting of the fruits of summer growth, determine a personality for the calendar customs of this season. These contrast with the "new birth and hope" customs of midwinter, designed as they are to reassure the community of the spring, seed germination, and livestock fertility to come. Although specific traditions appear with similar manifestations at different times, the ethos of each calendar phase is essentially different.

The Last Sheaf of Harvest

Before mechanization made certain harvest customs impractical, the main crop of oats (known as corn) or hay was reaped by hand using sickles. As the harvest was being completed, a handful of stalks representing the last sheaf was plaited where it stood by dividing it into three, then fastening it at the top to keep the plait in place. The men then stood at a measured distance and competed with one another by throwing their sickles at the sheaf until it was cut at the base.[5] Gailey has recorded fifteen different names for the last sheaf in Ulster, the most common being the *calliagh, hare,* or *churn.*[6] In northeast Antrim and south Down the Gaelic word *cailleach,* (hag, nun, old woman, or witch) was used, whereas in south Antrim and northwest Down the English word *granny* appears to have been preferred. *Cailleach,* usually anglicized as *calliagh,* was also used to describe the last sheaf in Highland Scotland, as in many parts of Ireland, but in north Antrim a Norse-derived word *carlin* (old woman) appears as a probable direct import into northeast Ulster from Scotland. Most commonly, however, the last sheaf was known as the *churn* (a dialect form of 'corn') throughout Antrim and Down, or as the *hare* in Antrim. (The hare is an animal with supernatural associations, often believed to be a witch or an old woman in animal form.) Both *churn* and *hare* were well known in lowland Scotland with the same meaning;[7] although there, the female allusion was often younger (as in the terms *maiden, maid, kirn baby, bride, doll,* etc.).

     Once the last sheaf had been cut, a shout was raised, and the person having made the final cut was given a special place in the ensuing celebrations. This man would place the plaited sheaf around the neck of the master, or preferably the mistress, of the house as an implied threat requiring a reward of food or drink, and would lead the dance after the harvest supper. The last sheaf was thus triumphantly borne back to the farmhouse, occasionally

Fig. 1.1. Cutting the last sheaf or calliagh, Toome, County Antrim. Courtesy of the Ulster Folk and Transport Museum.

Fig. 1.2. Bringing home the calliagh, Toome, County Antrim. Courtesy of the Ulster Folk and Transport Museum.

around the neck of the successful marksman who had "won the churn." As in southwest Scotland, the man to cut the last sheaf was made chief guest at the harvest supper, and if a bachelor, he was expected to be the first man in the company to marry. This supper was known as the churn, the same term as that given to the last sheaf. It was an important social occasion with alcoholic (grain-derived) spirits playing an acceptable part. The churn was usually followed by a dance, and sometimes this dance was regarded as part of the churn. It was a custom in some districts to end the dance by singing "Auld Lang Syne." A marginal note in a Presbyterian kirk session book from Antrim from the late seventeenth century refers to one shilling and three pence spent after the "ingathering" (harvest) for "nagins" (drinks) at the "churn."[8]

The churn followed the completion of the harvest, and the *calliagh* (last sheaf) sometimes graced the table at the supper, although it was more often placed over the hearth, door, or somewhere on the kitchen wall. If it was placed over the door (in mistletoe fashion), the first young woman to enter the house afterward could be kissed by the reapers, or perhaps she would be fated to marry the man who had placed it there. In Scotland, the mistress of the house sometimes danced with the last sheaf on her back. Thus was the harvest connected directly and symbolically to human fertility, and the agricultural life cycle identified with the social.

Because many last-sheaf traditions have been found throughout the British Isles, and more widely in Europe, they have been regarded as ceremonies naturally arising from the high spirits that follow the end of a period of heavy work (but influenced by the legacy of former fertility rituals associated with belief in a spirit of vegetation). Always, the last sheaf retained its ears of grain, and it was kept for some time hanging in the kitchen. In later years, it seems to have been kept until decayed, perhaps several accumulating over the years. Formerly, the sheaf was reused to feed livestock around the New Year, or sometimes mixed with the seeds to be sown the following spring. In either case, the symbolic reuse of the last sheaf was a gesture toward fertility and continuity of life. It was generally believed that the sheaf should be kept to bring good luck to the house, or as a charm against witchcraft. Of course the witch, old woman, or hare (always female) that was figuratively isolated and trapped in the last sheaf has been interpreted as a metaphor for a pre-Christian goddess of fertility or a more generalized corn spirit. The reluctance of some clergymen to allow corn dollies or decorated *calliaghs* as part of the church decoration for harvest thanksgiving services testifies, perhaps in a negative way, to the persistence of the folk belief. The idea that witches can transform themselves into hares is widespread outside of harvest time.

Fig. 1.3. Three "last sheaves." The more elaborate example in the center was prepared as a church harvest decoration in Belfast. Courtesy of the Ulster Folk and Transport Museum.

Recently, a museum colleague asked a farmer in north Antrim if he knew any stories about fairies. Bluntly, he was told that people there didn't believe in that sort of thing. However, when pressed if he had never heard of old women turning into hares, the farmer replied, "That's no' a fairy story but, that's true!"[9] By whatever name the last sheaf was known—the churn, hare, or *calliagh*—it undoubtedly represented to the community many of the same aspects of fertility and bonding as its smaller version—the harvest knot—represented to individuals.

Harvest Knots and Harvest Thanksgiving

Harvest knots, known throughout Ulster and Scotland, were made by twisting and overfolding two straws (or the two ends of a single straw). The thin woven straw was then bent over in two intertwined loops and fastened at the bottom to display the ears of grain. When the harvest knot was given to a lady as a love token, which it often was, it was worn in the hair with the ears of grain left on. Those made for men were worn on the lapel of a jacket, or on a cap, and had the ears trimmed off. Almost any straw could be used—oat, wheat, rye, or even grass. In County Antrim, grass was frequently used in areas where hay was being harvested and was made using a single woven straw. A double-straw type was more common in County Down, and the material used more frequently was oats. There is some evidence that, on occasion, straw pulled from the last sheaf would be used to make a harvest knot.[10]

With the increasing shift away from agriculture in east Ulster, and with the mechanization of farming, most harvest customs have declined. However, church harvest thanksgiving services, which have long been an integral part of the customs of the season, remain popular today even in urban areas. The services held during late September and October occur on different Sundays to permit congregations to visit and view one another's decorations. Elaborate straw-work pieces, including miniature corn ricks about two feet high topped with harvest knots, were fashioned specifically for church decoration, and church interiors would be crammed with flowers, fruit, vegetables and farm produce. Intense competition still surrounds the placing and selection of the "best" produce for harvest services; and in rural areas, it is this service that is still the best attended of the church calendar. Another traditional church decoration was an especially elaborate last sheaf (a "double *calliagh*" decorated with ribbons). This was made of two thick straw plaits crossed at the bottom and joined at the top underneath the ears of corn.

Fig. 1.4. Harvest church decoration at the Grey Abbey Non-Subscribing Presbyterian Church, County Down. Courtesy of the Ulster Folk and Transport Museum.

This was placed on the front of the pulpit. Some clergy have objected to the presence of these "pagan" corn dollies in church, and as a compromise they have been hung in church vestibules. In some churches, straw plaits are woven during decorating, so that fresh flowers could be woven into the plaits. Of all the harvest customs in Antrim and Down, the church Thanksgiving service is unquestionably the only genuine and widespread survival today, but it should not be considered historically as an isolated custom.

Halloween

> Haleve Nicht was a guid nicht lang ago. Piles o tay an iverythin ye'd name,
> dookin for epples in the tub, hanchin for epples hingin frae the baak,
> spaein wi turnip peelin's an pokin at nits bleezin roon the fire. That wos
> inside: ootside wos the yins sthrivin tae blaw tow-reek in at the kay-hole.
> But, man dear, there's naethin o that noo, naethin ava.[11]

This description of Halloween in County Antrim could, in content and in dialect, just as easily have been recorded in southwest Scotland. Halloween was, and still is, one of the most important festivals of the year throughout Ireland and Scotland. It was the climax of harvest and, throughout the upland areas of Ulster, it also marked the traditional date for return of the cattle and their herds from the summer pastures on the mountains. By the first of November, the booly (transhumance) parties would return knowing that the crops were reaped and that the cattle would be free to graze the stubble on the in-field strips around the permanent lowland dwellings. Just as important, 1 November was the New Year of the Celtic calendar, a preparation for winter; and as such, the most important quarter day of the Celtic year for Ulster Scots. In fact, other Irish quarter days, such as St. Brigid's Day (1 February), were studiously ignored by the Presbyterian communities of Scottish origin in east Ulster. Indeed, during the eighteenth century, some Ulster Presbyterian congregations saw the need to have their elders inquire officially about attendance at Midsummer Eve bonfires. All Hallows' Eve, or the evening before All Saints' Day (which had been designated by the Christian church as November first as early as A.D. 731) provided a Christian rationale for the celebration. Although Presbyterians did not celebrate 1 November as a feast day in the religious sense, there appears to have been no question of any sanction over the secular festivities.

Halloween traditions included lighting bonfires, children visiting houses (guising or rhyming), practical jokes, and parties with special games and foods—all with a heightened sense of the supernatural. With the onset of

winter, it is not surprising that the period is regarded as one to commemorate the dead, or, coincidentally, that Remembrance Day (for the war dead)
should fall in early November. Halloween was regarded, of course, as a night
particularly appropriate for dabbling in the occult, or at least for mild divination. It was a night of ill omen, despite the fun and frolics, when many of the
games and tricks were designed to foretell deaths as well as marriages, and
when the supernatural was believed to be most likely to influence events. To
"protect" children from fairies on that night, older people would (with
tongue in cheek) place a pile of salt on the child's forehead.[12] Attempts to
foretell a future spouse appear to have been practiced mostly by women,
according to Buchanan, who provides descriptions of more than ten different methods of divination.[13] Most of these techniques also were found in
Scotland; and some (including the best-known one of observing the behavior of
two nuts left to burn in the fire) were common throughout the British Isles.

Pranks and practical jokes at Halloween, such as removing field gates
and placing them on the roof of a neighbor's house, may be related to the
belief in supernatural activity, for these events could be light-heartedly "explained" in that way. Bonfires are still common throughout Ulster on Halloween night. For some years fireworks were also customary, but their sale
is prohibited during the present political unrest. Large crowds often gather
to sing and play around the fires, and after the blaze subdues, a core of youth
might sit around until the early hours of the morning and eat blackened potatoes baked in the embers. In Ulster only three traditional bonfire dates
survive in contemporary practice: on the eve of 15 August, on 11 July, and at
Halloween. As the first two dates are political celebrations, enjoyed by Hi-
bernians (Catholics) and Orangemen (Protestants) respectively, the Halloween bonfires remain the only widespread manifestation of the bonfire tradition that is not generally perceived to be sectarian.

Halloween's connection to the harvest is evident in the special foods,
all vegetarian, prepared for the festival. Indoor traditional games were
played after or before a meal based on fruit, cereal, and potatoes. Apparently, no other day in Ireland was celebrated with so many special dishes.[14]
There were oat-based breads and traditional dishes, such as sowans and
barnbrack, and dishes with potatoes as the main ingredient: colcannon, potato pudding, potato apple dumplings, potato apple cake, boxty bread, boxty
dumplings, and boxty pancakes. Fortune-telling tokens such as rings, buttons, thimbles, and coins were baked in the barnbrack or perhaps in one of
the other dishes. The games included ducking for apples in a water-filled
basin and bobbing for treacle-covered apples suspended from a string.

These are now played by children, with little recent record of the rougher, boisterous games once played by adults. The games, food, divination, pranks, and bonfires associated with Halloween night are still preceded by a week or so during which children go from house to house, disguised with blackened or false faces and fancy dress, carrying turnip lanterns to beg for money, fruit, or nuts. In urban areas of east Ulster, this practice is called "Halloween rhyming," although part of the familiar Christmas rhyme is chanted in chorus:

> Halloween is comin'
> The geese are gettin' fat
> Please put a penny in the oul' man's hat.
> If ye hinnae got a penny
> a haep'ny will do
> If ye hinnae got a haep'ny,
> then God bless you
> And your oul' man too.

Perhaps a child will simply say, "Help the Halloween rhymers," but sometimes a gift is only offered after the rhymers are given a fright by the householder or when a requested popular song is sung. Practical jokes, such as knocking at the door again and running away, are frequently played should no gift be offered. In the past, adults also went from door to door performing much of the Christmas rhyme play, although this properly belongs to the Christmas/New Year season.

Christmas Rhymers

In midwinter the personality of calendar customs changes dramatically. Now reassurance that days will lengthen, spring and summer return, and the life cycle of crops and livestock will begin again seems necessary. The theme of most customs at Christmas and the New Year season relates to birth and rebirth, the continuity of fertility and the handing over from old to young. Such, of course, is also the theme of the folk drama of the Christmas rhymers, with its combat, mock death, and magical revival symbolizing the death of life in winter and its resurrection in the spring.[15] Numerous variants of the play have been collated and analyzed by Gailey.[16] Apart from some rather different versions around Dublin and Wexford, it appears that performance of the play was virtually restricted (in Ireland) to Ulster and was particularly widespread in Counties Antrim, Down, Donegal, and Fermanagh. Gailey, by analyzing the content and characters in different versions of the play, and by comparing them with English and Scottish versions, has shown conclusively that the east Ulster versions relate more closely to those from north England than to those from Scotland. He notes, however, that the play is particularly rooted in the Scots-settled areas where some influence of Scots dialect and begging rhymes can be detected. These intrusive elements occur most obviously in a group of southeast Antrim plays. In one version there are thirteen players, in order of appearance (including the presenter): Room Room, Prince George, the Turkey Champion, Old Woman (played by a man), Doctor Brown, Saint Patrick, Oliver Cromwell, Beelzebub, Bellick Ned, the Devil, Jack Stree (Straw), the Darkie, and Johnny Funny. Most characters are found in at least some other Ulster versions (and are peculiar to Ireland), but Bellick Ned, otherwise Big Bellied Ned or Uncle Ned, is only found in the east Antrim versions. His lines are:

> Here comes I, big Bellick Ned
> If you don't give us money, give us plenty of bread
> Get up ould wives and shake your feathers
> And give me nae mair of your imperent blethers
> For we're the boys that'll show you fun
> If you give us share of your Christmas bun,
> A cup o' tay and a slice o' cheese
> And rub ma belly if you please.
> And if you don't believe what I say
> Call in the Devil and he'll clear the way.[17]

Significantly, it is the early lines of Bellick Ned's part that reveal the only content (other than dialect) known to be of specifically Scottish origin, although in Scotland these begging lines are associated with Halloween or Hogmanay rather than Christmas.

In east Ulster, the rhymers traveled from house to house during the two weeks before Christmas. In rural areas, they performed inside the kitchen, entering in turn to speak their part. Their approach was noisy, sometimes sounding horns, and they wore appropriate costumes with blackened faces. Jack Straw wore straw leggings and belt with a straw hood over his face. Gailey observed that Jack Straw may represent an "ancient folk dramatic feature, much older than the rhymers' texts themselves." In west and south Ulster, the characters nearly all wore the straw costume of the *straw boys,* who also appeared at weddings. Here, too, the rhymers appeared after Christmas and were called the *Hogmanay men.*

Fig. 1.5. Christmas rhymers arriving at a Balleyboley farmhouse for a performance,
County Antrim. Photograph by Mr. John Clugston, Dundonald. Courtesy of the
Ulster Folk and Transport Museum.

Christmas Day

The religious celebration of Christmas is a modern innovation among most
Presbyterians in east Ulster. Until recently, no special church services were
held, and local stories abound of how "good" Presbyterians made a public
display of working as normal on Christmas Day (unless of course it happened
to fall on the Sabbath). As at Halloween, however, the secular observance of
the season was less restrained. A special dinner, including meat (as opposed
to the vegetable- and grain-based Halloween food), was customary following
a morning of sport. In Scotland, shinty (closely related to the Irish Gaelic
sport of hurling) was played on Christmas Day, and in the Highlands at New
Year. The outdoor activities of Christmas morning in east Ulster generally
involved competitive shooting with guns at whites (paper targets) or wild
fowl, or a no-holds-barred game of shinty. In Belfast, the most prestigious
soccer cup final involving secondary and junior clubs (the Steel and Sons
Cup) has always been held on Christmas morning and attracts much larger
crowds than normally expected of junior club matches. Of course, the Western European "traditional" Christmas with Christmas presents, decorations,
trees, cards and Santa Claus is now universal, and most Presbyterian
churches now hold a special service on Christmas morning.

Hogmanay and the New Year

New Year's Day was an important day everywhere in the British Isles, but in Scotland it was said to be "the most popular day among the people generally."[18] On Rathlin Island off the County Antrim coast in northeast Ulster, the "great shinty match" was played on New Year's Day rather than at Christmas, and shinty sticks were used in the *coullin* ritual also practiced at New Year's on the island. The Hogmanay drama of the *coullin* is a characteristic of Highland Scotland, and (unlike the Christmas rhyme) was performed in Gaelic. Its occurrence on Rathlin is probably not indicative of a more widespread distribution in east Ulster in earlier times, other than perhaps in the Glens area in the northeast of County Antrim. The theme of the ritual is more closely related to an upland pastoral economy than the lowland- and arable-related straw wisp custom discussed below.

In the Scottish Highlands, Hogmanay lads moved around the district with the leader wearing an animal hide. When they arrived at a house they would circle it, or circle the fire inside the house three times. The lads beat the hide on the leader's back with sticks, and a "blessing of the house-floor" was pronounced by way of a Hogmanay verse in Gaelic. Hogmanay gifts of food were gathered in an alms bag made of animal skin. On Rathlin, an obviously related custom was first described in 1851:

> There is another ancient custom still kept up here, and which appears very similar to one observed in some parts of the Highlands of Scotland. On the last day of the year about seven o'clock in the evening two parties of young men numbering between twenty and thirty each and sometimes many more, set out to pay a visit to every house except those of the poor they intend to assist, one party taking the upper or western, and the other the lower end of the Island. Their approach is indicated by the blowing of a horn that the inmates may be prepared with whatever offering they may choose to give. The first who enters the house has a dried sheep skin fastened on his shoulders, which is struck with a stock by the one immediately following, keeping time to a rhyme in Irish which as many as can find room in the house repeat, walking round a chair placed in the center of the kitchen. The works which they make use of may be translated thus, "Get up good woman and give us a scon [*sic*], and let it be well buttered, and if you refuse crows will come from the back of Knocklade and do much harm to your poultry," after this they wait to receive the offering which consists of money, wool or meal, which they afterwards distribute among the poor. When the charity is bestowed, they cut a small piece off the sheep skin which they give to the mistress of the house as an acknowledgement of the bounty, and an earnest of good fortune for the ensuing year. Then they invoke a blessing on the house and its inmates, and take their departure. Coullin is the name given to this ceremony.[19]

A translation of the Rathlin rhyme used in the *coullin* ritual runs as follows:

War, war under a bottle of straw,
May God bless the house in it,
Between back and hearth and bar (of door)
Many years' health may you have, man,
Get up woman of the house,
Take down a scone "bruckle" and soft,
With plenty of butter on it.
If you don't do that
May the crow come from the back of Knocklayd,
And do this and that on you.

A fly and a beetle went to the king's house,
And the fly fell into the fire.
And the beetle was lamenting,
 Chairs were crackling,
Stools were rattling.
The woman of the house was going mad,
The man of the house was going after her
with a red hot iron.[20]

One feature of the Rathlin custom not known in Scotland is the sounding of horns on the approach of the Hogmanay men. This appears to be an intrusive element from the Christmas rhymers. Other possible cross-borrowings between the rhymers and the Rathlin *coullin* rite have been observed, and of course in parts of south Ulster, the Christmas rhyme was performed at New Year by Hogmanay men.[21] Ship horns were sounded after midnight on New Year's Eve at Newry and Warrenpoint in south Down, and at Belfast. General revelry involving making as much noise as possible frequently followed the opening of the New Year, although sometimes in Belfast sectarian confrontation resulted. In the Ards Peninsula of County Down, midnight church services were attended by local bands, and after the New Year had been "seen in" at church, the bandsmen enjoyed themselves by making as much noise as possible. In County Antrim, similar "Watch Night services" were held, and in an Islandmagee diary of 1909 the diarist wrote: "The Band [Shaw's True Blues Flute Band] was out round the Island tonight to play the Old Year out and the New One in. . . ."[22] The first Sunday in January (now often a Communion date for Presbyterian churches with more than one or two such services each year) was also the date of a special "Sailors Service" in Islandmagee. On other occasions, only Lambeg drums were played in the towns and villages; and it is tempting to parallel this with the beating of the animal's hide with stocks during the *coullin* rite.

New Year Wisps

The use of a plaited straw "wisp" as a gift at New Year's symbolically bridged the midwinter threshold between the previous year's harvest and the next year's seed time. Most of the traditions surrounding the New Year center on a belief that what happens on that day will affect the events of the coming year. The luck-bringing visits of "firstfooters," Hogmanay men, and even Christmas rhymers were most important at this turning point of winter, marking the start of a new year. In Scotland and in east Ulster, the home had to be completely cleaned and all jobs completed before New Year's Day. Nothing could be loaned on New Year's Day, and nothing could be taken out of the house before noon, particularly ashes from the fire or even dirty dishwater. In recent times, in County Down, the relatively inferior status of Christmas was emphasized by the insistence that Christmas trees, cards, and decorations must also be removed before New Year's Eve (rather than on the twelfth day of Christmas as elsewhere). The first visitor to the house was an important omen of the future year's luck. To ensure that this visitor was a male, and dark-haired, an appropriate neighbor would firstfoot and bring gifts of fuel (coal or peat) or bread. In County Down, the firstfooting gifts might include a straw wisp, or might consist only of the wisp. This wisp distribution was more often performed by groups of youths on the morning of New Year's Day, and it is particularly relevant to the present study because it is localized in southeast Ulster and apparently unknown elsewhere in Ireland or Scotland.[23] The wisp could be made of straw or hay, and might consist of nothing more than some straws twisted around each other, bent, and their ends tied. Usually, however, the wisp was a plait of straw, virtually identical to the *calliagh* but without any ears of grain. One recorded instance in south Antrim involved the specific reuse of the straw of the last sheaf of harvest.[24]

Where the custom survives, it is generally a "hanselling" or begging custom involving groups of children who demand if the householder wants "to buy a wisp." Gifts were required in return, something characteristic of all rituals associated with firstfooting, but with older wisp distributors, food or drink rather than money would be offered. Although other variants have been recorded, the begging rhyme generally used by wisp distributors in County Down was:

We wish you and yours a Happy New Year
wi' your pockets full o'money
an a barrel full o' beer.[25]

The wisp in parts of south Antrim, made from the last sheaf of harvest, was
used to chase the "lucky black cat" three times around the kitchen to the rhyme:

> Pussy cat, pussy cat why do you fear
> a wisp from the Harvest, the corns ripened ear.
> In full and in plenty we made this year din
> and now we will welcome another year in.
> Now out you must go, then return to the house
> and sit in the nook there awaiting a mouse.
> While we fasten the latch to shut out the cold
> And greet the new year that replaces the old.[26]

Here a direct connection with the last sheaf suggests that the wisp may have
been a symbol of continuing last year's fertility into the next, as with the suggestion in the *coullin* rite of beating the cow's hide and making its wearer
run around the house. The black cat, popularly associated with Halloween,
is perhaps a more recent metaphor for the *calliagh* than the hare, but the
requirement that it should sit in the nook is reminiscent of the Highland
Scottish *coullin* ritual rhyme:

> Hug man a!
> Yellow bag,
> Beat the skin;
> Carlin in neuk,
> Carlin in kirk,
> Carlin ben at the fire;
> Spit in her two eyes,
> Spit in her stomach,
> Hug man a![27]

Carlin (old woman) is a name given in Scotland and north Antrim for the
last sheaf, as is, of course, *calliagh,* which in Irish can also mean "bed
outshot." The bed outshot, a bed recess in the back corner of the kitchen,
was certainly one "neuk" in the home identified with human fertility.

Although the wisp tradition of southeast Ulster is not known in Scotland, it is from there that its inspiration seems to have been drawn. In various parts of Scotland, a sheaf of oats was a common firstfooting present, and
on some occasions this was the last sheaf of harvest.[28] In other parts of Scotland and Ulster, the last sheaf (including the grain) was mixed with the seeds
for next year's planting or was fed to farm animals as a cure or charm, perhaps to ensure the animal's fertility. The title of one of Robert Burns's poems

suggests a knowledge of the custom in Ayreshire during the eighteenth century: "The Auld Farmer's New-Year Morning Salutation to his Auld Mare Maggie, on giving her the Accustomed Ripp of Corn to Hansel in the New-Year."[29]

Conclusion

When the calendar customs of a fairly homogeneous but localized community such as the Ulster Scots are studied for the winter period (from late summer to early spring), it is clear that the different customs harmonize with the seasonal rhythm. Some information about the relative importance of the various festivals to "ordinary" people in east Ulster can be gleaned from perusing the diary of a young Islandmagee girl.[30] Miss Florence Dick was the daughter of an east Antrim farmer-fisherman, and her diary for 1909, 1911, and 1912 provides a casual record of the years' activities, reinforcing the dominant role played by religion and church in shaping "traditional" behavior.

Each year, October entries record a succession of church harvest festivals. Typical entries (remembering the Dicks were Presbyterians) include one for Monday, 28 October 1911: "Harvest Festival in Methodist Church, very fine night indeed and good entertainment and fine tea," and for Sunday, 31 October 1909: "Halloween. Some good nuts. Harvest Festival in the Methodist Church. Singing was very good and the Anthem was splendid. There was a very good attendance." When Halloween did not fall on a Sunday, the entry reads (as for Tuesday, 31 October 1912), "This being Halloween, Mr. Semple came in and helped to crack the nuts. Mr. William Mawhinney called tonight. We had a great time burning nuts and they were all a fraud" (their attempts to divine future lovers unconvincing). By way of contrast, a typical entry for Christmas is brief: "Very dull day and raining hard." That was in 1911, although the following year's Christmas seems to have been a bit livelier: "Social held in Temperance Hall." Christmas rhymers called before Christmas Day, and on Tuesday, 12 December 1912 we find, "Churned today and lit a fire in the Cottage. Xmas rhymers paid a visit. Mother was very frightened." The New Year was a time for special "Watch Night Services," and in "Mr. Steen's Church" the first Sunday in January always recorded a special "Sailors Service." On New Year's Eve the local flute band "paraded round the Island . . . to play the Old Year out and the new one in, they called round this way, came down around the end of the house, paraded up the causeway and stopped at Mr. Hugh Dick's door and there gave us a few selections. Lillie, Jean and Minnie marched to the Orange Hall with them." New Year's Day, or on one occasion the second of January, seemed to be the only time Florence noted her father out shooting "scarts" (cormorants).

The entries in this diary seem to support my view that the calendar customs typifying Ulster Scots communities in east Ulster included a few significant elements that were exclusive to them, but, perhaps most important, the relationships and balances between their calendar customs generated a distinctive pattern. If certain elements of the pattern were exclusive, the underlying themes certainly were not. The horn blowing, drum beating, and shotgun firing of the Hogmanay celebrations seem to mark a rite of passage for this part of the annual cycle. It is not surprising, then, that weddings in southwest Ulster were often visited by boisterous groups of men in the same "straw-boy" costumes used for Christmas rhyming, or that in east Ulster nervous couples tried to marry in secret to avoid the somewhat unwelcome appearance of shotgun-shooting and horn-blowing neighbors. Of course, it could be argued that the occurrence of these shooting and horn-blowing activities at weddings and at New Year's was suggestive of a fertility ritual.

Midwinter festivities occur when reassurance is most needed. This period looks backwards and ahead, as the old is replaced by the new: the old, bearded Father Christmas and Father Time come and go, and the New Year's baby is born. Just as flowers represent the continuity of life in different ways at funerals, weddings, and birthdays, so the symbolism of these calendar customs can be modified by the season during which they are manifest. The typical theme of the Christmas rhyme is a mock struggle, the death of a hero and his resurrection amid much hocus-pocus and commotion. Midwinter customs reflect the nature of the season as a threshold between death and life in the plant cycle, when assurance is required of the essential continuity of the grain crop. Taking any individual custom in isolation, the nuances of fertility and life-cycle symbolism may appear secondary. However, when the customs are viewed collectively, the symbolic relationship between the seasonal cycle, the agricultural cycle, and the human life cycle becomes clearly focused. In the short period of the year considered above, harvest and Halloween customs cannot be divorced from ideas of death, darkness, and preparation for unknown hardship ahead. But even death is necessary to provide a harvest store of seeds and hope of rebirth in the following spring.

Notes

1.   Philip S. Robinson, *The Plantation of Ulster: British Settlement in an Irish Landscape, 1610–1670* (Dublin: Gill and Macmillan), 1984.

2.   I wish to acknowledge the contribution made by Dr. Jack Santino, Department of Popular Culture, Bowling Green State University, in inspiring and encouraging the broad theme of this paper.

3.   Alan Gailey, "The Last Sheaf in the North of Ireland," *Ulster Folklife* 18 (1972): 1–33; Alan Gailey, "The Folk Play in Ireland," *Studia Hibernica* 6 (1966): 113 -54; Alan Gailey, "The Rhymers of South-East Antrim," *Ulster Folklife* 13 (1967): 18–28; Alan Gailey, *Irish Folk Drama* (Cork: Mercier Press), 1969; Alan Gailey, "A New Year Custom in South-East Ulster," *Schweizerische Archiv fur Volkskunde* 68 (1972): 126–36, 754; R. H. Buchanan, "Calendar Customs," *Ulster Folklife* 8 (1962): 15–34, 9 (1963): 61–79.

4.   Buchanan, "Calendar Customs," 9 (1963): 75.

5.   H. W. Lett, "Winning the Churn (Ulster)," *Folklore* 6 (1905): 185–86; J. M'Kean, "Notes on local survivals of ancient harvest customs," *Proceedings of the Belfast National History and Philosophical Society* 32–33 (1901–2); H. McN. McCormick, "Harvest rites in Ireland," *Folklore* 25 (1914): 379–80.

6.   Gailey, "A New Year Custom," 1–33.

7.   G. Brendan Adams, "The Chirn," *Ulster Folklife* 8 (1962): 10–14.

8.   W. S. Smith, "Early Register of the Old Presbyterian Congregation of Antrim," *Ulster Journal of Archaeology* 5 (1899): 180–90.

9.   Personal communication from Dr. A. D. Buckley, curator of anthropology, Ulster Folk and Transport Museum, 26 Sept. 1987.

10.   Ulster Folk and Transport Museum (hereafter cited as UFTM) Archive Nos. 631024, 631053, 631074, 631093, 631149. Responses to questionnaire on calendar customs conducted by the museum among members of the Ulster Folklife Society (1963).

11.   W. Grant, ed., *The Scottish National Dictionary* (Edinburgh: Scottish National Dictionary Association, 1951), vol. 1.

12.   A. J. Pollock, "Hallowe'en Customs in Lecale, County Down," *Ulster Folklife* 6 (1960): 62–64; T. Porter, "A County Down School Collection," *Ulster Folklife* 10 (1964): 82–86; UFTM Archive Nos. G4-2-22, G4-6-3. MS information on calendar customs provided by the Committee on Ulster Folklife and Traditions (later the Ulster Folklife Society) (1953–57), Ulster Folklife Museum.

13.   Buchanan, "Calendar Customs," 8: 15–34, 9: 61–79.

14.   Florence Irwin, *Irish Country Recipes* (Belfast: Northern Whig), n.d. [c. 1940].

15.   E. R. R. Green, "Christmas Rhymers and Mummers," *Ulster Journal of Archaeology* 9 (1946): 3–21.

16.   Gailey, "The Folk Play in Ireland," 113–54; Gailey, *Irish Folk Drama.*

17. Gailey, "The Rhymers of South-East Antrim," 18–28; Alan Gailey, "'Mummers' and Christmas Rhymers' Plays in Ireland: The problem of Distribution," *Ulster Folklife* 24 (1978): 59–68.

18. M. Macleod Banks, *British Calendar Customs: Scotland* 2, *The Seasons* (London: William Glaisher, 1939).

19. Mary Campbell, *Sea Wrack or Long-ago Tales of Rathlin Island* (Ballycastle: J. S. Scarlett & Son), 1951.

20. John Braidwood, "The Rathlin Rite of the 'Coullin,'" *Ulster Folklife* 14 (1968): 44–50.

21. Ibid.

22. UFTM Archive No. G4-2-16/18. Diaries of Miss Florence Dick, Islandmagee, 1909, 1911, 1912.

23. Gailey, "A New Year Custom," 126–36, 754.

24. UFTM Archive Nos. 662080, 662086. Questionnaire responses on Calendar Customs (1966).

25. This verse and other related information was provided directly to me by neighbors in the Grey Abbey area of County Down.

26. UFTM Archive No. 631074. Questionnaire responses on calendar customs (1963).

27. Braidwood, "The Rathlin rite," 44–50.

28. Andrew Cheviot, *Proverbs, Proverbial Expressions and Popular Rhymes of Scotland* (Paisley and London: Alexander Gardner), 1896.

29. Robert Burns, *Poems, chiefly in the Scottish Dialect* (Belfast: W. Magee), 1793.

30. UFTM Archive No. G4-2-16/18. Diaries of Miss Florence Dick.

References

Adams, G. Brendan. 1962. "The Chirn." *Ulster Folklife* 8: 10–14.

Banks, M. Macleod. 1939. *British Calendar Customs: Scotland* 2, *The Seasons*. London: William Glaisher.

Braidwood, John. 1968. "The Rathlin Rite of the 'Coullin.'" *Ulster Folklife* 14: 44–50.

Buchanan, R. H. 1962. "Calendar Customs, Pt. 1." *Ulster Folklife* 8: 15–34.

———. 1963. "Calendar Customs, Pt. 2." *Ulster Folklife* 9: 61–79.

Burns, Robert. 1793. *Poems, Chiefly in the Scottish Dialect.* Belfast: W. Magee.

Campbell, Mary. 1951. *Sea Wrack or Long-ago Tales of Rathlin Island.* Ballycastle, Northern Ireland: J. S. Scarlett & Son.

Cheviot, Andrew. 1896. *Proverbs, Proverbial Expressions and Popular Rhymes of Scotland.* Paisley, Scotland, and London: Alexander Gardner.

Gailey, Alan. 1966. "The Folk Play in Ireland." *Studia Hibernica* 6: 113–54.

———. 1967. "The Rhymers of South-East Antrim." *Ulster Folklife* 13: 18–28.

———. 1968. "Edward L. Sloan's 'The Year's Holidays.'" *Ulster Folklife* 14: 51–59.

————. 1969. *Irish Folk Drama.* Cork, Ireland: Mercier Press.

————. 1972a. "The Last Sheaf in the North of Ireland." *Ulster Folklife* 18: 1–33.

————. 1972b. "A New Year Custom in South-East Ulster." *Schweizerische Archiv fur Volkskunde* 68: 126–36, 754.

————. 1978. "Mummers' and Christmas Rhymers' Plays in Ireland: The Problem of Distribution." *Ulster Folklife* 24: 59–68.

Grant, W., ed. 1951. *The Scottish National Dictionary* 1. Edinburgh: Scottish National Dictionary Association.

Green, E. R. R. 1946. Christmas Rhymers and Mummers. *Ulster Journal of Archeology* 9: 3–21.

Irwin, Florence. N.d. *Irish Country Recipes.* Belfast: Northern Whig.

Lett, H. W. 1905. "Winning the Churn (Ulster)." *Folklore* 6: 185–86.

McCormick, H. McN. 1914. "Harvest Rites in Ireland." *Folklore* 25: 379–80.

M'Kean, J. 1901–2. "Notes on Local Survivals of Ancient Harvest Customs." Proceedings of the Belfast National History and Philosophical Society. 32–33.

Pollock, A. J. 1960. "Hallowe'en Customs in Lecale, County Down." *Ulster Folklife* 6: 62–64.

Porter, T. 1964. "A County Down School Collection." *Ulster Folklife* 10: 82–86.

Robinson, Philip S. 1984. *The Plantation of Ulster: British Settlement in an Irish Landscape, 1610–1670.* Dublin: Gill and Macmillan.

Sloan, Edward L. 1854. *The Bard's Offering: A Collection of Miscellaneous Poems.* Belfast: Northern Whig.

Smith, W. S. 1899. "Early Register of the Old Presbyterian Congregation of Antrim." *Ulster Journal of Archeology* 5: 180–90.

Ulster Folk and Transport Museum (UFTM) Archive No. G4-2-16/18. Diaries of Miss Florence Dick, Islandmagee, 1909/1911/1912.

UFTM Archive. 1953–57. Nos. G4-2-22, G4-6-3. MS information on Calendar Customs provided by the Committee on Ulster Folklife and Traditions.

UFTM Archive. 1963. Nos. 631024, 631053, 631074, 631093, 631149. Questionnaire responses on Calendar Customs.

UFTM Archive. 1966. Nos. 662080, 662086. Questionnaire responses on Calendar Customs.

2. *"Safe" Spooks*
New Halloween Traditions in Response to Sadism Legends

BILL ELLIS

"As many parents are aware," a flyer brought home by my first-grade daughter instructed me, "Halloween can be the scariest of all nights for both parents and children combined."[1] This reaction has since the mid-1960s become the normal American reaction to a holiday previously seen as an opportunity for child play and adolescent pranks. As several folklorists have noted, legends about anonymous sadists who poison candy began to affect the practice of trick-or-treating as early as the 1970s. In the 1980s, these legends were augmented by panics caused by fear of "satanic cults" that planned to kidnap and murder young children.

Some commentators have suggested that the legends are "killing" Halloween, at least as a spontaneous child's holiday.[2] Ongoing Halloween festivities in the Hazleton, Pennsylvania, area suggest that this is an overstatement. Nevertheless, parents and public officials have placed greater restrictions on children's activities, many of which are directly or indirectly occasioned by sadism legends. One effect of these restrictions is to institutionalize the holiday, a process already noted in other American festivals. Another effect is to take the holiday out of children's hands and put it into grown-ups', claiming that those who rebel against adult-enforced Halloween "rules" now risk death.

The Classic Sadism Legends

The original festival of Samhain, as Santino notes, was fundamentally a pagan holiday, focusing on the passage of the recent dead from this world to the next.[3] As Christianity replaced older religions, these spirits were transmuted from neutral or good beings to evil ones, and the season became a rich one for the telling of supernatural legends. To some extent, as Dégh has found, this storytelling tradition remains very strong in rural America, though it now incorporates nonsupernatural horror stories and anti-legends in which frightening events are exposed as hoaxes or misperceptions of mundane objects.[4]

The season's marginality has recently brought forth two complexes of legends and beliefs in which deranged or sadistic adults of this world, not supernatural spirits, endanger children. These complexes include real-life "ostensive" actions, in which people act out (or seem to act out) such narrative scenarios. The earlier of these is "The Razor Blades in the Apple," involving children who receive poisonous or booby-trapped trick-or-treat goodies from strangers; it appeared during the mid-1960s. The later complex, "The Satanic Child Sacrifice," described cults who planned to abduct and murder a young child on Halloween as part of a ritual ceremony; this showed up sporadically in the mid-1970s before becoming a nationwide panic in 1987–88.

The precise origin of the razor blades legend is unclear, though it was given impetus by three nationally publicized cases in which poisoned treats were actually found. The earliest of these cases occurred on Halloween 1964 in Greenlawn, New York, a Long Island community, where a housewife, Helen Pfeil, was arrested for giving trick-or-treaters arsenic-laced ant-poison buttons. The truth of the matter, however, was that Pfeil had given out the buttons as part of a self-evident Halloween joke. Annoyed that too many of the trick-or-treaters were too old to be asking for free candy, she made up packages of inedible "treats" to give to teenagers. The packages contained dog biscuits, steel-wool pads, and the ant buttons, clearly marked "Poison" with a skull and crossbones.

Also, she was hardly the traditional anonymous sadist of legend: youths identified Pfeil with no trouble as the source of the poison, and she did not deny her actions, adding that she had told teens that the packages were a joke when she distributed them. Her husband, noting that she had given out candy freely to the younger children, called her use of the ant buttons "thoughtless" but not "malicious." Pfeil pleaded guilty to endangering children and eventually received a suspended sentence.[5]

This incident may have been an isolated case of poor judgment, with no connection to legendary sadism. But Pfeil likewise may have been enacting, in a prankish fashion, existing traditions about dangerous "treats." Best and Horiuchi note isolated news reports of pranks involving some physical injury dating back to 1950, when children allegedly were given pennies heated in a skillet. This motif was also recalled by Grider as a rumor current in her neighborhood in the late 1940s.[6] And the same issue of the *New York Times* that detailed the Pfeil case also noted an incident in Philadelphia in which a six year old had been given a can of ant poison and another in a Detroit suburb in which two children had been burned by chewing gum laced with lye.[7] Perhaps Pfeil was motivated by an existing tradition of tampered treats. Or perhaps she was simply inverting the belief at the core of traditional treats: in this case, a "trick" for asking for an "treat" one was too old to deserve.

Beginning in 1967 the focus of the legend shifted dramatically from poison to razors and sharp objects hidden in apples.[8] The emergence of the razor-blade motif remains to be studied, but it apparently spread rapidly in several areas of the Eastern Seaboard and Canada: the *New York Times* reported thirteen cases from isolated communities in New Jersey and noted "several" others in Ottawa and Toronto.[9] Outrage was so strong in New Jersey that the state legislature passed a law shortly before Halloween 1968 mandating prison terms for those caught booby-trapping apples. This did not forestall the discovery of thirteen *more* apples with razor blades that year in five New Jersey counties.

In many cases, the *Times* story simply noted that "children were cut," but the more detailed accounts include suspicious details. In one case a boy came to his parents with an apple containing a razor blade. He had bit into an apple, he said, but not quite deeply enough to contact the blade. In another, the child said he found the blade while cutting out a rotten spot; in a third case, the razor was found when a child turned an apple over to his father for peeling.[10] In all these detailed cases, the child was not injured, and because he was the immediate source of the apple, it seems possible that he was also the source of the blade. As Best and Horiuchi note, more than 75 percent of reported cases involved no injury, and detailed follow-ups in 1972 and 1982 concluded that virtually all the reports were hoaxes concocted by the children or parents.[11] Thus this legend type seems to have grown out of a tradition of ostensive hoaxes relying on an understood oral tradition, rather than on any core of authenticated incidents.[12]

Nevertheless, the news stories themselves did influence the course of future events. By 1970, reports of booby-trapped treats had grown so frequent that Dr. Hollis S. Ingraham, New York state health commissioner, warned in his annual Halloween safety bulletin that "children should not eat any of their collected goodies until they have been carefully examined by an adult." Psychiatrists described the sadists as "frustrated and filled with resentment against the world in general," "paranoid," and suffering from "a really deprived childhood." The answer, according to the *Times:* "Go trick-or-treating only to the homes of people that the family knows."[13]

This widespread warning apparently influenced the two actual cases in which children allegedly died of poisoned treats, though not as directly as some folklorists suggest. On 2 November 1970, Kevin Toston, five, returned from his uncle's home in a Detroit neighborhood and soon after fell into a coma. He died four days later of a heroin overdose, and analysis of some of his Halloween candy showed that it had been sprinkled with heroin.[14] The case was widely reported as a real-life example of Halloween sadism, and some later discussions included it as "proof" that the murderer had acted out the legend literally, in a deadly act of "ostensive action," as Dégh and Vázsonyi termed it.[15] What was not so widely circulated was the fact, established by police, that Toston had been poisoned by a drug stash that he found in his uncle's house, and that the family themselves had sprinkled the heroin on the candy as a smoke screen.[16]

Similarly, when Timothy Mark O'Bryan, age eight, died of cyanide poisoning after eating some candy on Halloween 1974, police work established that it was his own father, Ronald Clark O'Bryan, who committed the murder to collect on an insurance policy.[17] In both cases, family members apparently used the legend to deflect suspicion from themselves onto shadowy bogeymen elsewhere in the community. Nevertheless, these incidents perpetuated the legend and reinforced the moral of having parents examine treats—ironically, because in both cases family members were responsible for the children's deaths!

The satanic cult legend's emergence is better documented: it came to widespread public attention in 1973–1974 as part of a fast-moving rumor-panic focusing on "cattle mutilations"—mysterious animal deaths that led police to suspect occult rituals.[18] Concern over these livestock deaths first crystallized in the upper Midwest; then, as they spread into the northern Rockies, they were attached to rumors about a murderous satanic cult. After a five year old and the wife of a Baptist preacher were murdered in the spring of 1974 in Missoula, Montana, an intense panic broke out, many people speculating that a cult was looking for a third victim. Among the many rumors that the panic sparked were stories that devil worshippers met on Halloween to carry out a human sacrifice.[19] By Halloween 1975 officials in Driggs, Idaho, were warning parents to keep younger children inside after dark, after rumors circulated about people in hooded black robes gathering in areas affected by cattle mutilations.[20]

Speculation about cults spread widely among law enforcement agents, and public service warnings provided another conduit for the spread of the

child abduction legend. In fall 1978, in south-central Missouri, a deputy sher-
iff identified several cattle deaths as the work of a satanic cult. He warned
that the group would attempt a human sacrifice soon, probably near Halloween, the victim being "a thirteen-year-old unbaptized girl." When school officials in Dixon, Missouri, sent this warning home with students, a panic occurred.[21] Similar localized panics continued to occur in rural communities
across the country during the early 1980s, most notably in Arkansas, where
on Halloween 1984 a "blonde-haired, blue-eyed girl" emerged as the potential victim.[22] This same motif popped up in several locations in 1987 and then
recurred in at least nine states on Halloween 1988.[23] In the following two
years, panics continued to pop up; in 1990, Bloomington, Indiana, police
were inundated with calls about a story that a local cult was trying to round
up "as many as 100 blond, blue-eyed children."[24] The physical characteristics of the intended victim, several researchers have noted, contrast distinc-
tively "Aryan" physical features with "animallike, darker, aggressive" assail-
ants and so are paralleled by legends describing blonde-haired women of
European descent being propositioned by Native Americans, Arabs, and
other non-Western types.[25] Best has shown that widespread claims of child-
snatching cults are actually based on unreliable statistics; in fact, the FBI
has never confirmed any murder in the United States as a "cult sacrifice,"
pure and simple.[26] Still, rumors of child abductions continue to be one of
the most common motifs in press releases describing rumor-panics.[27]

Community Reactions

In the wake of these panics, several Florida, Texas, and Maryland communities in 1989 banned Halloween celebrations altogether, replacing them with
"harvest festivals" or "pumpkin fun days" that reduced or eliminated the traditional occult symbols.[28] In Newtown, Connecticut, angry citizens and
clergy forced the cancellation of a Halloween living history program for ten
to twelve-year-olds because a librarian, dressed as a historical figure, planned
to appear in response to a "mock seance." A local police officer warned, "If
you dabble in drugs, you're going to be a drug addict. It's the same if you
dabble in the occult."[29] Many other communities continued to observe the
season, but in a more constrained manner than usual.

   Do such changes mark the "death" of the holiday? Santino suggests that
this attitude neglects Halloween's deeper function as a symbolic way to ad-
dress "the dread of the unknown and the uncontrollable." Traditional images of ghosts and witches are simply augmented by images of contemporary

fears: Tylenol packages, ax murderers, and so on.[30] It is nonetheless true that legends have changed the way in which Halloween is observed in many communities. We should ask whether new practices have become nascent customs, incorporating or replacing older traditions and creating new forms for traditional functions. Also, we should ask how these new customs reflect changes in the *meaning* of Halloween for communities.

In the wake of research conducted on satanic cult legends, I closely observed two seasons of Halloween practices in my home area of Hazleton, Pennsylvania, and collected a clipping file on local celebrations. Hazleton is composed of several ethnic communities, mainly Italian and Slovak, descended from immigrants attracted to the area's anthracite coal industry. Since the decline of this economy, Hazleton, like many other coal-belt towns, now relies on a variety of light industries. Holidays, both American and ethnic, tend to be celebrated openly and with gusto, so that it makes a useful contrast with those who were willing to replace the whole holiday with a "harvest festival." Even though the Catholic church sponsored public meetings on the dangers of satanic cults in both 1988 and 1989,[31] I did not observe any efforts to abolish Halloween, even at Monsignor Molino, my seven-year-old daughter's Catholic-sponsored parochial school. After-dark trick-or-treating continued in all the local towns and boroughs, and school decorations and costume parties continued to include witches and other occult symbols. When one parent showed up at a costume party at Molino in a devil suit, carrying his newborn baby, the priest simply commented, "Please don't wear that to the baptism."

Still, I observed practices emerging in the Hazleton area that were reactions to the sadism legends. "Safety lists" setting sharp limits on children's celebration of Halloween were published and widely distributed in papers, schools, and malls. New forms of celebration were devised, particularly officially sponsored "Halloween parties." Hospitals even turned candy X-raying into a kind of festive event. On the face of it, none of these practices would seem to be folk related, but close examination shows that they continue to be shaped by the legend process.

Halloween Do's and Don't's

The publication and distribution of lists of "warnings" have become one of the first signs of the Halloween season, coincident with the display of commercial candy in stores and of holiday symbols on private homes. In some cases, these took the form of paid advertisements in the local paper; others took the form of editorial cartoons (fig. 2.1), flyers, or printed plastic trick-or-treat bags given out in local malls. Seven lists (one received twice) were collected, ranging from brief (three tips) to exhaustive (as many as thirty-seven "rules"). Many of these warnings had nothing directly to do with Halloween customs, but incorporated commonsense advice on crossing roads or walking on the left facing traffic.

But a large number of these warnings did acknowledge the presence of the sadism legends and incorporated other "horror stories" in telegraphed form. The lists, in short, comprised a series of legend metonyms, or allusions to more complete story lines that the reader was expected to fill in.[32] The most relevant were those touching on costumes, trick-or-treat practices, and how to handle candy.

The first of these categories was the most consistent and self-evidently "sensible": lists included suggestions such as placing reflective tape on costumes and wearing comfortable footwear. But a significant number of items implied "horror stories" suggesting that costumes alone could bring death or serious injury if not carefully supervised. Some cautioned that homemade outfits could be firetraps: parents were instructed to buy commercially made, fire-retardant costumes (five) and to "avoid wigs (they can burst into flames)" (one). A national PTA list added, "Avoid toy weapons that could be mistaken for the real thing," an allusion to horror stories in which police killed children carrying realistic toy guns.

These rules are, on the face of it, good advice, but they rely on a common pattern, stressing the worst possible consequence from a relatively trivial act. This pattern was underscored by the public comment of a local police chief, who commenting on the rules of costuming, told parents to make sure that the costume is warm enough for their children. "They try to rush a little too much when they're chilled," he added, "and it might cause problems. . . . They might dash across the street because they are cold and just forget for that one little second."[33] The chief's tactful silence over what happens next underscores the message: on Halloween, it takes only one trivial act of carelessness and "that one little second" to cause a child's death.

More directly legend related are the rules concerning the "do's and don't's" of trick-or-treating. All seven lists included, in some form, the advice that parents and children should agree ahead of time where to visit: the route, their companions, and their time for return. Younger children should be accompanied by a parent or adult (five); older children should travel in groups (four). Another common rule was that children should not go inside the front door of a house to accept a treat (four); likewise, adults treating

Fig. 2.1. Editorial cartoon listing Halloween "rules." *Hazleton Standard-Speaker,* 29 Oct. 1990. Used by permission of the newspaper and the artist, Bob Correll.

children should not invite them in (two). Children were warned to visit only well-lit houses (three), stay away from dark streets or areas (two), avoid strangers' houses, and remain in one's own neighborhood (one each). One list even suggested that children should try to complete their rounds while it is still light outside, a difficult task in the Hazleton area, where night falls soon after 5 P.M. at Halloween.

Implicit are fears that children who act unwisely around strangers' homes or in dark areas may be abducted and killed. To serve as added protection, the local Army National Guard unit set up a booth in a local mall the weekend before Halloween and offered free fingerprinting of children.[34] Although no reason was given for this service, previous fingerprinting campaigns were explicitly linked to the missing children "problem."

Finally, rules governing children's handling of treats reflected fears about widespread tampering. All lists stressed that children should not sample candy before parents had inspected it for tampering, a point underscored in 1990 by the death of Ariel Katz, a seven-year-old girl in Santa Monica, California, who collapsed while trick-or-treating. Local police, believing she had eaten candy from her bag, "conducted an intense door-to-door search" in the girl's neighborhood, blocking off streets, confiscating candy, and interviewing residents. Later reports conceded that Katz had died of congenital heart failure, not poison or drugs, but the nationwide publication of the initial fears obviously confirmed this "rule" in many parents' minds.[35]

Rules stressed the need to watch for sharp objects or poison: parents were told to discard unwrapped or loosely wrapped treats (two) and cut fruit into small pieces (two). (One list added that *candy* should be diced up as well.) To lessen the danger, children should be given a snack before leaving so they wouldn't be tempted to have "that one little treat" that could kill. One list conceded that some families may still want to offer homemade treats, but these should then be wrapped and the treater's name and phone number attached "so parents will know where [these treats] came from." Other lists suggested that treaters could eliminate even the implication of danger by giving out only manufacturer-wrapped candy (one) or by eliminating edibles altogether: "Consider passing out stickers, favors, and other non-candy treats. The other parents will appreciate your concern for their children's safety" (one). These rules, if followed to the letter, would place every aspect of trick-or-treat under adult care, from the design of costumes to the consumption of candy. Obviously, not every Hazleton-area family followed them (though I did convince my daughter to let me test her Caramellos for razors), but many took the warnings against dark neighborhoods seriously. On my street, which is rural and poorly lit, no more than a dozen parties of trick-or-treaters appeared, but in the upper-class, better patrolled Hazleton Heights district, residents reported up to two hundred visits. Evidently families in lower-class neighborhoods felt their children were safer in a strange but better lit part of town.

"Safe" Halloween Celebrations

To some extent, adult-sponsored activities are nothing new for Halloween. Even before the sadism scares, schools held costume parades and churches and scout troops organized parties involving traditional games such as bobbing for apples or pinning tails on ghosts. These activities continue in the Hazleton area as before. What is unusual, however, is the *timing* of these festivities. For the most part, these parties have always fallen before trick-or-treat night (and mainly still do), marking preparation for the holiday. The newer festivities fall on Halloween itself and thus serve as a *replacement* for trick-or-treat.

The Schuylkill Mall, a major shopping center twenty miles south of Hazleton, has regularly presented a Halloween "parade" on the Saturday before the holiday, including costume judging, free candy, and inexpensive photographs. Hazleton's own Laurel Mall did the same until 1989, when it chose to sponsor its own event, a "safe trick-or-treat night" on Halloween itself. As organizers planned it, parents could drop off their children inside a lighted, enclosed mall. The trick-or-treaters then could circulate around the stores inside, collect candy, and return to be picked up. "This night is basically for parents' peace of mind," a promotional flyer said. "There is no charge for the candy and the children will be safe."

Ironically, the flyer had to stress that security would be "on call" and a paging system available to locate lost children. A few years before, the *Hazleton Standard-Speaker* had published a version of "The Attempted Abduction" in which a girl is snatched from her mother in a mall by white slavers: she is barely saved by security guards' quick action.[36] But this legend shows the plot foiled when security closed all doors leading out of the mall. Thus Halloween child abductors would also have trouble spiriting children out of the building. The mall is a marginal spot, but it is enclosed, free of dark corners, and the merchants are not really strangers, only the source of manufacturer-wrapped "safe" candy.

At any rate, the initial "safe trick-or-treat night" was successful enough to be repeated in 1990, when a number of merchants added special promotions for waiting parents. One chiropractor suggested that visitors "get their skeletons out of the closet" by having a free spinal screening as they wait. And the idea of alternative parties was imitated by other agencies. In nearby Freeland, merchants organized a daylight celebration, in which children (accompanied by an adult) were encouraged to stop in at stores for free treats.[37] At McAdoo, another local village, the town hall was decorated and volunteers distributed candy as police helped check treats already collected.[38]

Most notably, the youth advisory committee of Hazleton City organized a special party for children up to the third grade, featuring the usual costume competition plus games and free candy and pizza. More than five hundred children showed up in the city council's chambers for "one-stop trick-or-treating" (fig. 2.2). This crowd caused some organizational problems: pizza soon ran out and had to be supplemented by doughnuts, and judges simply could not see all the children's costumes until they were lined up in the halls. Still, the event was popular with adults, because, as its organizers reminded people, the Hazleton Police headquarters was located in the basement of the same building.[39] Some parents still took their children trick-or-treating either before or afterward. But the strong turnout the parties received showed that parents agreed that they gave children "a place to enjoy the holiday without worrying about traffic, tainted candy, and other terrors that can accompany Halloween."[40] Perhaps the most interesting innovation in the area was local hospitals' candy X-raying as a last stop for children's trick-or-treat rounds. The idea, established by many hospitals nationwide during the 1970s, has come under fire in recent years. In 1987, the American Association of Poison Control commented that X-rays detected foreign bodies in food only 14 percent of the time and could not spot poisons or drugs at all. Citing fears of liability suits if children were harmed by X-rayed candy, the AAPC advised hospitals to stop the practice. Some did; others, like the Logan General Hospital in Logan, West Virginia, refused, a source saying, "At least we're giving the child a chance."[41]

Hospitals in the Hazleton area took a similar attitude; both major hospitals, St. Joseph's and Hazleton General, publicized their service before Halloween. Margaret Gorski, manager of Hazleton General's X-ray department, conceded that nothing had ever been found in children's treats, but she defended the service as "invaluable despite any costs." In addition to protecting children and calming fears, she added, "it also gives children a different view of the hospital. They get to see the candy being X-rayed and, therefore, see the hospital as not intimidating or frightening."[42] Given the death-ridden atmosphere of Halloween, hospital workers welcome the chance to relieve

Fig. 2.2. The Hazleton "safe Halloween" party at city hall.

the tensions of their work by stressing that X-rays and hospital treatments can mean life as well as death.

So what might have been a rather intimidating, sterile procedure in fact took on something of a party atmosphere. In 1989, the X-ray technicians at Hazleton General dressed as witches. In 1990, St. Joseph's Hospital created a party atmosphere for guests under twelve: "safe treats" were given to the first one hundred children. "The nurses developed the idea," a source said, "to promote a safe and enjoyable Halloween."[43] At Hazleton General, all hospital workers were instructed to wear costumes for Halloween (even surgeons?). In the X-ray department, technicians met visitors wearing pumpkin orange and black robes topped with battery-operated blinking deely-boppers. Halls were decorated with paper cutout "ghosts," and commercial posters of jolly ghosts, witches, black cats, and other traditional symbols filled available spaces around ultrasound and mammography offices.

To be sure, parents were handed an official-sounding disclaimer, warning that glass, plastic, or wood items would not be detected, nor would "chemicals," so parents should inspect treats and discard "questionable" items. But children were encouraged to help spread out their candy on the

X-ray table, then shown the resulting negative. Nurses put coins on the plates with the candy to show children what a metal object would look like if it did appear. Otherwise, the plates showed ghostly images of the children's treats, sometimes accompanied by staples in bagged candy, but no needles or razor blades (fig. 2.3). Children were obviously fascinated by the results and delighted when the nurses said they could keep the X-ray plates as a souvenir of the visit—in effect a final "treat" (fig. 2.4).

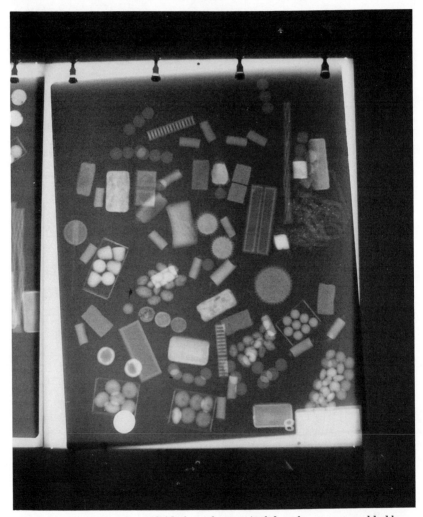

Fig. 2.3. X-ray image of one child's bag of treats. (Solid circles are coins added by nurses for comparison.)

Fig. 2.4. One family of trick-or-treaters ready to take their X-rays home.

New Customs, New Meanings

The new Halloween customs represent an attempt by well-meaning adults to appropriate the holiday, taking control not only of its customs but also of its economic aspects. Nominally, the customs keep children "safe" by making them proxy consumers of commercial products and by eliminating individual choice in matters from costumes to treats. The overall message is quite clear: individuals are dangerous or foolhardy; institutions and corporations are "safe."

There is nothing new about adults wishing to sanitize this holiday; in fact, the 1920s saw a nationwide effort to solve "the Halloween problem." Civic and religious organizations in many communities argued that the good-natured pranks always associated with the season had become too anarchic. Youthful energy was channeled into organized parties and charitable drives to collect food or clean up neighborhoods. Ironically, this early effort to tame Halloween also saw the first widespread practice of trick-or-treating, previously a rare custom among Irish-based communities and as likely to be attached to Thanksgiving or Christmas as to Halloween.[44] The traditional Halloween inversion of status thus became a reciprocal relationship: adults give a treat; children refrain from the trick.

Some of the new customs are motivated by official desire to limit the "trick" side of Halloween further by stressing the "treats." As early as 1969, some police were offering children free candy, using the motto, "Don't trick, we'll treat."[45] Nevertheless, the vandalistic aspect of Halloween was in decline as early as the 1950s, when Gregory P. Stone noted that children were mainly unaware of the "trick" implied by the request for treats and saw the holiday as simply an occasion to receive candy.[46] Yet in areas like Hazleton, where vandalism has been suppressed for years, the idea of reciprocity seems stubbornly present, as many children insist on telling a joke or riddle before accepting the treat.

Many other calendar holidays (Christmas, Easter, Valentine's Day) and rites of passage (birthdays, loss of teeth) have shown a similar transformation, during which American children now can expect to receive gifts and sweets for no particular reason other than custom. This process also gives such holidays the status of institutions, taking them out of the hands of individuals and giving them to commercial and civic establishments. So the sadism legends probably hastened an existing evolutionary process working to make Halloween conform to other institutionalized holidays.

Nevertheless, it is significant that this crusade, like that of the 1920s, corresponds to a national trend toward prohibition as a ready answer for what is perceived as adults' loss of control over the next generation. The two popular sadism legends are obvious reversals of traditional Halloween themes. In "The Razor Blades," the treat that originally forestalled the child's trick becomes itself a cruel adult trick on the child. In "The Child Sacrifice," the custom of normal children impersonating agents of death becomes the image of murderous adults putting on the mask of normal-seeming neighbors. Neither reversal is new, though: the one can be recognized in the poisoned apple given Snow White; the other in the gingerbread treats that tempt Hansel and Gretel to enter the cannibal-witch's house.

But these narratives are *Märchen,* symbolic frights that psychiatrists such as Bruno Bettelheim argue are healthy ways of externalizing and expressing childhood anxieties.[47] Some authorities have criticized charities for setting up "haunted houses" filled with realistic-looking sights of death and dismemberment, saying that they teach children that it is fun to kill people and chop them up.[48] Even Dégh and Vázsonyi suggest that through such displays "adults seem to grab the opportunity to frighten as a means necessary to exorcise authority from their usurping children."[49]

But Sabina Magliocco has observed that the "haunted houses" oppose life and death in an imaginative way that results in *engrossment,* not literal fear. She argues that, in fact, "the haunted house makes fear enjoyable by localizing it and confining it to a limited area." The adolescents who visit it are well aware that the horrors they see are fictitious; in fact, she argues, "the illusory quality of the performance is intrinsic to its entertainment value."[50] In similar "mock-ordeals" at summer camps, I noted, children of the ten-to-twelve age group were able to enjoy allegedly "real" attacks by monsters when counselors provided enough implicit hints that what they were seeing were elaborate fictions. But when these hints that mark off play from reality were not provided, or when adults gave mixed signals by feigning fear, children often became extremely anxious.[51]

Perhaps we should consider whether the new customs are driven by real concern for children's well-being, or whether they are, in fact, preemptive narrative acts of aggression against the younger generation. A traditional part of the season has been "status reversal," children's and adolescents' license to demand treats from adults. This custom allows youngsters to impersonate threatening forces who will attack homes and property if not appeased by a special ritual act, parallel to the leaving of a bowl of milk outside for fairies or bogies. In so doing, the younger generation is temporarily allowed political and economic privileges normally controlled by adults.[52] These very customs are the ones that authority now find the most objectionable. Put bluntly, the new customs don't keep children "safe"; they save *adults* from the fears children provoke.

The message of Halloween does seem to have changed. Before, the holiday relied on imaginative reversal of roles: youngsters could play at being scared and master their anxieties by impersonating the entities they feared. At the same time they could temporarily flout adult authority and play at being irrational, antisocial forces. These dynamics are now preempted by a social threat—presented as genuine, not imaginative—that cannot be left behind in a narrow space of time but instead remains with youngsters as part of an irrational, unpredictable adult world. Whether this is psychologically "safer" for youngsters than the original folk holiday remains to be seen. The core of Halloween remains on some level unchanged: the seasons still slip from life to death. Hence this holiday, more than any other, will continue to generate legends about the fear of death. And if the new customs reveal an intense generational conflict over who should own this holiday, the last word will always belong to the child:

"Are you a clown?" a reporter asked one child at the Hazleton City Hall's "Safe Halloween" party.

"A killer clown," the eight-year-old replied.[53]

Notes

Material for this chapter was contributed by Jeffrey A. Victor, Kevin D. Quitt, Richard Tyce, and my daughter Elizabeth. I also appreciate Jack Santino's suggestions on an early draft.

1.   This flyer, beginning "Dear Educator," was sent by Kellie Guzzardo, public relations director of the Laurel Mall, Hazleton, Pennsylvania, to principals of local elementary schools shortly before Halloween 1989. It invited them to photocopy it for children to take home to parents. The flyer promoted Laurel Mall's "Safe Trick or Treat Night."

2.   Linda Dégh and Andrew Vázsonyi, "Does the Word 'Dog' Bite? Ostensive Action: A Means of Legend-Telling," *Journal of Folklore Research* 20 (1983): 13; Sylvia Grider, "Razor Blades in the Apples: The Proto-Legend That Is Changing Halloween in America" (Paper presented at the annual meeting of the American Folklore Society, Cincinnati, Oct. 1985); Michael Goss, "The Lessons of Folklore," *Magonia* 38 (Jan. 1991): 12.

3.   Jack Santino, "Halloween in America: Contemporary Customs and Performances," *Western Folklore* 42 (1983): 6–8.

4.   Linda Dégh, "The Living Dead and the Living Legend in the Eyes of Bloomington Schoolchildren," *Indiana Folklore and Oral History* 15 (1986): 127–52.

5.   *New York Times* (hereafter cited as *NYT*), 2 Nov. 1964, p. 21; *NYT*, 22 Apr. 1965, p. 6.

6.   Joel Best and Gerald T. Horiuchi, "The Razor Blade in the Apple: The Social Construction of Urban Legends," *Social Problems* 32 (1985): 492; Sylvia Grider, "The Razor Blades in the Apples Syndrome," in *Perspectives on Contemporary Legend*, ed. P. Smith, 133–34.

7.   *NYT*, 2 Nov. 1964, p. 21.

8.   Best and Horiuchi, "The Razor Blade," 493.

9.   *NYT*, 3 Nov. 1967, p. 51.

10. *NYT,* 1 Nov. 1969, p. 24.

11. Best and Horiuchi, "The Razor Blade," 491.

12. More detailed research into the many unexamined local reports seems called for. Celie Benton, in "The Curious Case of the Needle in the Banana," conducted a case study of one such incident—a needle found in a store-bought banana shortly before Halloween 1982 in Bloomington, Indiana—and she found irreconcilable differences between what the victim said happened and official police, health service, television, and wire service accounts of the same incident. Here an implicit legend predisposed reporters to treat cases of apparently tampered treats in terms of the legend, so that media accounts alone may not be our best guide to the exact nature of such events.

13. *NYT,* 28 Oct. 1970, p. 56.

14. *NYT,* 7 Nov. 1970, 33.

15. Dégh and Vázsonyi, "Does the Word 'Dog' Bite?" 12.

16. Best and Horiuchi, "The Razor Blade," 490.

17. Grider, "The Razor Blades in the Apples Syndrome," 134–35.

18. Bill Ellis, "Cattle Mutilation: Contemporary Legends and Contemporary Mythologies," *Contemporary Legend* 1 (1992): 53–57.

19. Robert W. Balch and Margaret Gilliam, "Devil Worship in Western Montana: A Case Study in Rumor Construction," in *The Satanism Scare,* ed. Richardson et al., 249, 257.

20. Michael D. Albers, *The Terror* (New York: Manor Books, 1979), 86–87.

21. Ibid., 74–75.

22. Nancy H. Owen, "Preliminary Analysis of the Impact of Livestock Mutilations on Rural Arkansas Communities" (Report prepared for the Arkansas Endowment for the Humanities, Little Rock, Ark., Jan. 1980); Martha Long, "Is Satan Alive and Well in Northeast Arkansas?" *Mid-America Folklore* 13, no. 2 (1985): 18–26.

23. See Jeffrey S. Victor's "A Rumor-Panic About a Dangerous Satanic Cult in Western New York," *New York Folklore* 15 (1989): 23–49 and "Satanic Cult Legends as Contemporary Legend," *Western Folklore* 49 (1990): 51–81 for overviews of these panics. Fall 1988 panics occurred in north-central Montana, northeast Indiana, north-central Wisconsin, and eastern Kentucky/adjacent West Virginia, as well as in the areas around Kansas City, Missouri/Kansas; Chicago, Illinois; Richmond, Virginia; and Juneau, Alaska. A Halloween 1982 panic in southeast Ohio, occasioned by a real-life murder blamed on Satanists, is described in Ellis, "Death by Folklore." Probably a more detailed survey of rural areas would turn up additional panics not documented by folklorists or in major newspapers.

24. *Bloomington Herald-Times,* 20 Oct. 1990, p. A1.

25. Barre Toelken, *The Dynamics of Folklore* (Boston: Houghton Mifflin, 1979), 272–73; Jan Harold Brunvand, *The Choking Doberman and Other "New" Urban Legends* (New York: Norton, 1984), 92; Victor, "Rumor-Panic," 39.

26. Joel Best, "Rhetoric in Claims-Making: Constructing the Missing Children

Problem," *Social Problems* 34 (1987): 101–21; Kenneth V. Lanning, "Satanic, Occult, Ritualistic Crime: A Law Enforcement Perspective," *Police Chief* 61, no. 10 (Oct. 1989): 62.

27. Victor, "Satanic Cult Legends," 74.

28. AP release, 30 Oct. 1989.

29. *Newsletter on Intellectual Freedom* (Jan. 1991): 11.

30. Santino, "Halloween in America," 18.

31. See Bill Ellis, "The Devil-Worshippers at the Prom: Rumor-Panic as Therapeutic Magic," *Western Folklore* 49 (1990): 27–49.

32. See Bill Ellis, "When Is a Legend? An Essay in Legend Morphology," in Bennett and Smith, *The Questing Beast,* 40.

33. *Hazleton Standard-Speaker* (hereafter cited as *HSS*), 30 Oct. 1990, p. 17.

34. *HSS,* 23 Oct. 1990, p. 28; *HSS,* 1 Nov. 1990, p. 20.

35. *Los Angeles Times,* 2 Nov. 1990, p. A21.

36. Jan Harold Brunvand, *The Mexican Pet: More "New" Urban Legends and Some Old Favorites* (New York: Norton, 1986), 79–81.

37. *HSS,* 27 Oct. 1990, p. 13.

38. *HSS,* 30 Oct. 1990, p. 17.

39. *HSS,* 1 Nov. 1990, p. 21.

40. *HSS,* 30 Oct. 1990, p. 17.

41. David Wilkison, "X-rays don't detect tampered Halloween treats," AP press release, 31 Oct. 1989.

42. *HSS,* 1 Nov. 1989, p. 5.

43. *HSS,* 25 Oct. 1990, p. 8; *HSS,* 30 Oct. 1990, p. 17.

44. Lesley Pratt Bannatyne, *Halloween: An American Holiday, An American History.* (New York: Facts on File, 1990), 124–26, 142.

45. Dégh and Vázsonyi, "Does the Word 'Dog' Bite?" 12.

46. Gregory P. Stone, "Halloween and the Mass Child," *American Quarterly* 11 (1959): 372–79.

47. Bruno Bettelheim, *The Uses of Enchantment: The Meaning and Importance of Fairy Tales* (New York: Knopf, 1976).

48. See Bill Ellis, "Death by Folklore: Ostension, Contemporary Legend, and Murder," *Western Folklore* 48 (1989): 201.

49. Dégh and Vázsonyi, "Does the Word 'Dog' Bite?" 16.

50. Sabina Magliocco, "The Bloomington Jaycees' Haunted House," *Indiana Folklore and Oral History* 14 (1985): 25.

51. Bill Ellis, "The Camp Mock-Ordeal: Theater as Life," *Journal of American Folklore* 94 (1981): 486–503; Bill Ellis, "'Ralph and Rudy': The Audience's Role in Recreating a Camp Legend," *Western Folklore* 41 (1982): 189.

52. Dégh and Vázsonyi, "Does the Word 'Dog' Bite?" 10.

53. *HSS,* 1 Nov. 1990, p. 21.

References

Albers, Michael D. 1979. *The Terror.* New York: Manor Books.

Balch, Robert W., and Margaret Gilliam. 1991. "Devil Worship in Western Montana: A Case Study in Rumor Construction." In *The Satanism Scare,* ed. Richardson et al., 249–62.

Bannatyne, Lesley Pratt. 1990. *Halloween: An American Holiday, An American History.* New York: Facts on File.

Bennett, Gillian, and Paul Smith, eds. 1989. *The Questing Beast.* Sheffield: Sheffield Academic Press.

Benton, Celie. 1983. "The Curious Case of the Needle in the Banana." Paper presented at the Annual Meeting of the American Folklore Society, Nashville, Tenn., Oct.

Best, Joel. 1987. "Rhetoric in Claims-Making: Constructing the Missing Children Problem." *Social Problems* 34: 101–21.

Best, Joel, and Gerald T. Horiuchi. 1985. "The Razor Blade in the Apple: The Social Construction of Urban Legends." *Social Problems* 32: 488–99.

Bettelheim, Bruno. 1976. *The Uses of Enchantment: The Meaning and Importance of Fairy Tales.* New York: Knopf.

Brunvand, Jan Harold. 1984. *The Choking Doberman and Other "New" Urban Legends.* New York: Norton.

———. 1986. *The Mexican Pet: More "New" Urban Legends and Some Old Favorites.* New York: Norton.

Dégh, Linda. 1986. "The Living Dead and the Living Legend in the Eyes of Bloomington Schoolchildren." *Indiana Folklore and Oral History* 15: 127–52.

Dégh, Linda, and Andrew Vázsonyi. 1983. "Does the Word 'Dog' Bite? Ostensive Action: A Means of Legend-Telling." *Journal of Folklore Research* 20: 5–34.

Ellis, Bill. 1981. "The Camp Mock-Ordeal: Theater as Life." *Journal of American Folklore* 94: 486–503.

———. 1992. "Cattle Mutilation: Contemporary Legends and Contemporary Mythologies." *Contemporary Legend* 1: 39–80.

———. 1989. "Death by Folklore: Ostension, Contemporary Legend, and Murder." *Western Folklore* 48: 201–20.

———. 1990. "The Devil-Worshippers at the Prom: Rumor-Panic as Therapeutic Magic." *Western Folklore* 49: 27–49.

———. 1982. "'Ralph and Rudy': The Audience's Role in Recreating a Camp Legend." *Western Folklore* 41: 169–91.

———. 1989. "When Is a Legend? An Essay in Legend Morphology." In Bennett and Smith, *The Questing Beast.* 31–53.

Goss, Michael. 1991. "The Lessons of Folklore." *Magonia* 38 (Jan.): 10–14.

Grider, Sylvia. 1984. "The Razor Blades in the Apples Syndrome." In *Perspectives on Contemporary Legend,* ed. P. Smith, 128–40.

————. 1985. "Razor Blades in the Apples: The Proto-Legend That Is Changing Halloween in America." Paper presented at the annual meeting of the American Folklore Society, Cincinnati, Oct.

Lanning, Kenneth V. 1989. "Satanic, Occult, Ritualistic Crime: A Law Enforcement Perspective." *Police Chief* 61, no. 10 (Oct.): 62.

Long, Martha. 1985. "Is Satan Alive and Well in Northeast Arkansas?" *Mid-America Folklore* 13, no. 2: 18–26.

Magliocco, Sabina. 1985. "The Bloomington Jaycees' Haunted House." *Indiana Folklore and Oral History* 14: 19–28.

McDowell, John H. 1985. "Halloween Costuming among Young Adults in Bloomington, Indiana: A Local Exotic." *Indiana Folklore and Oral History* 14: 1–18.

Owen, Nancy H. 1980. "Preliminary Analysis of the Impact of Livestock Mutilations on Rural Arkansas Communities." Report prepared for the Arkansas Endowment for the Humanities, Little Rock, Ark., Jan.

Richardson, James T., Joel Best, and David G. Bromley, eds. 1991. *The Satanism Scare.* New York: Aldine.

Santino, Jack. 1983. "Halloween in America: Contemporary Customs and Performances." *Western Folklore* 42: 1–20.

Paul Smith, ed. 1984. *Perspectives on Contemporary Legend.* Sheffield: CECTAL.

Stone, Gregory P. 1959. "Halloween and the Mass Child." *American Quarterly* 11: 372–79.

Toelken, Barre. 1979. *The Dynamics of Folklore.* Boston: Houghton Mifflin.

Victor, Jeffrey S. 1989. "A Rumor-Panic About a Dangerous Satanic Cult in Western New York." *New York Folklore* 15: 23–49.

————. 1990. "Satanic Cult Legends as Contemporary Legend." *Western Folklore* 49: 51–81.

Wilkison, David. 1989. "X-rays don't detect tampered Halloween treats." AP press release (31 Oct.).

3.   Halloween Pranks
"Just a Little Inconvenience"

STEVE SIPORIN

The first hint I had that Halloween was not the same holiday for all Americans came from my wife. In our household, I was always the one who bought the candy (too much of it). I was the one who answered the trick-or-treaters at the door. I was the first to take each of our children trick-or-treating as they reached what I thought was the appropriate age, and I accompanied them over a larger territory than my wife considered reasonable. One year she finally told me. "Halloween embarrasses me," she said. "We never went trick-or-treating."

Ona grew up on a farm in Iowa—where modesty and reserve are highly valued, sometimes to a fault. It took Ona fifteen years, for example, to tell me that she did not like Halloween. But I still did not know if this unfamiliarity with the fun of Halloween as I knew it was her idiosyncrasy or something familial, ethnic, regional, or rural.

I began to ask others with rural childhoods about their celebration of Halloween and discovered that many of them had feelings and experiences similar to Ona's. My conversations included informants from widespread parts of North America, including Alberta, Canada, as well as Arizona, Idaho, Iowa, Massachusetts, and Utah.

In this chapter I will explain what I learned from them about the differences between Halloween in the city and Halloween in the country. Specifically, I found that although urban/suburban Halloween can be characterized by trick-or-treating, costumes, and yard displays or *assemblages* (Santino

1983, 1986), many rural North Americans traditionally assign these customs a minor role and instead celebrate a Halloween characterized by pranks. I will describe the specific "types" of Halloween pranks and their traditional nature. And last, I will offer a functional explanation for Halloween pranks, suggesting that in rural areas, youthful aggression was, and is, given license on this night because it serves useful social ends.

One person who grew up in rural southern Arizona—from a high school graduating class of twenty ("the largest in years")—said his father would not let him go trick-or-treating because he considered it to be "begging" (Summers 1986, 1987). I have found this idea—that trick-or-treating is equivalent to begging—expressed in many papers from students with rural backgrounds. Some rural Iowans even call Halloween "Beggar's Night" (T.W.), which is one of the traditional names for the festival (Gregory 124). Other people who grew up in rural areas also used the term "embarrassed" when discussing Halloween. They said they did not like the holiday even today and felt uncomfortable accompanying their children from house to house because trick-or-treating was not something they had done as children growing up on farms (Keating 1986). Others saw trick-or-treating as "undignified," but recalled that some families had driven their children into town to trick-or-treat from house to house. A few rural children might come by rural homes, driven by their parents, especially after travel by car became common, but such a habit seems to have been regarded as inappropriate, tasteless city behavior. My wife explained the reason:

> The direct approach, the blunt request involved in trick-or-treating would be uncomfortable and unusual behavior for everyone I knew. People who "appear suddenly" were usually magazine salesmen or the likes . . . and they usually wanted something. (Siporin)

It is not accurate, however, to claim that trick-or-treating and wearing costumes were never traditional in rural North American communities. But where rural trick-or-treating took place, the problem of "begging" had to be accommodated, as Darryl M. Hunter makes clear in his article on Halloween in the small town of Pinehill in southeastern Saskatchewan. Describing the types of costumes and their significance, Hunter (44) writes:

> The preponderance of roles which involve lower socio-economic classes or minority groups is significant. This costuming reinforced their appeals for handouts when visiting households for treats. By hiding behind disguises and masks, the participants were allowed to leave behind normal standards of ethics which might prevent them from demanding "welfare,"

soliciting "handouts," or "creating mischief." The mask is a passport for entry into an imaginary world where this behavior is socially acceptable.

Michael Taft describes costumed adults going from house to house in Ponteix, a small town in Saskatchewan, uttering the formula "trick or drink." He says that these adults "make the rounds of selected houses in the town where they have friends or where they know there is a Hallowe'en party" (1983, 9). I would argue that this custom resembles urban/suburban Halloween only superficially: in urban/suburban settings, the socializing associated with trick-or-treating is minimal. Children go to the houses of strangers, often trying to "get" as many houses as possible in the course of the evening. In rural areas, socializing with friends is the point of the trek.

The same individuals who denigrated trick-or-treating also described an alternative Halloween tradition that did, and to some extent still does, flourish in rural America—the trick or prank side of the "trick-or-treat" formula.[1] Urban and suburban trick-or-treaters also play tricks such as soaping windows, throwing eggs on cars and mailboxes, and covering houses and trees with toilet paper (known as "teepeeing"). In fact, it is my impression that most participants understand the phrase "trick or treat" to mean "give me a treat or I'll play a trick on you."[2] The *Oxford English Dictionary* identifies the phrase as mainly American and defines it as "a traditional formula used at Hallowe'en by children who call on houses threatening to play a trick unless given a treat or present." The oldest citation in print dates only to 1939. Logically, then, we should be saying "treat or trick," rather than "trick or treat," but poetry wins out. Nevertheless, some urban and suburban children say "trick *and* treat" and have tricks—such as handstands and riddles—ready to perform if they are asked what their trick is. But the elaborate pranks of country youth indicate a much stronger tradition of tricks.

In fact, one can identify specific "types" of the Halloween prank, related to one another in their meaning and symbolism, as well as in their intent to create mischief. One prank type is the moving of a large piece of equipment to an unlikely place. Usually, this means disassembling a piece of farming machinery or a vehicle and reassembling it on top of a building. Here is an example from Iowa:

We had one neighbor . . . who was always joking with the boys. So the evening of Halloween . . . the boys . . . stole one of his wagons . . . and took it all apart and carried it up on the roof of the Farrar school. And then put it all back together again. [Laughter] So the wagon was setting on the roof . . . all complete, and the process had to be repeated the next day by B.R. himself. (J.H.W.)

Elsewhere in this volume, Michael Taft writes that in Brome-Missisquoi, Quebec, the most common prank was putting a farmer's cart on the roof of his barn. This tradition precedes the age of mechanized farming, but it continues today with modern machinery, sometimes at the less dramatic level of moving combines and tractors into the streets around town (T.W.). The biographer of an artist who grew up in western Wyoming writes that as a youth, the artist "looked forward to the pranks of Halloween. . . . Once he took a neighbor's buggy completely to pieces and reassembled it on the roof of the blacksmith's shop" (James 93). As the examples illustrate, an important part of carrying out this type of prank is to place the reassembled item in plain public view, preferably in town.

It is worth bearing in mind that, as Alan Dundes (103) puts it, "some actual pranks become the subjects of traditional narratives [and] it may be difficult to determine whether the pranks described in prank narratives ever actually occurred [sic]."[3] Dundes reports the same prank/narrative in a different ritual context:

> During a vacation period, a student's car is completely disassembled and
> then put back together inside his dormitory room. When the student returns
> from vacation, he is astonished to find his automobile parked in his room. (103)

A second prank type is moving outhouses. Like the first type, this one sometimes involves moving a large object to an inappropriate, surprising place; but outhouses have unique possibilities (and symbolism),[4] and more stories appear to be told about outhouse pranks than any other kind.[5]

Sometimes the outhouse was simply tipped over. One person recalled that on Halloween "we had the privilege of dumping over outhouses and taking anything that was loose and scattering it along the road" (J.H.W.). Other times, the outhouse was moved slightly backward so that the person approaching it in the dark would stumble into the open hole over which the outhouse had stood earlier in the day:

> There was an older oriental man who lived in town. Perhaps due to race
> or other factors unstated this man had been singled out to receive a large
> portion of the attention of the boys of the neighborhood. It was, for ex-
> ample, tradition that his outhouse be tipped year after year on Halloween
> eve—to trick is better than to treat. This Hallows Eve my father and two
> of his friends had taken it upon themselves to do this dirty deed and were
> gliding like shadows across the darkened field that guarded the approach
> to their target. Caution was essential and every nerve was taut, for a shot-
> gun with a load of rock-salt oft awaited the unwary trickster.

As the skirmish line of three closed the last yards to the outhouse the taste of victory was already on the tongue. Then my father's friend, to his left and middle in the line, vanished. Moments later followed a throaty, muted cry for help. The tables had been turned, the outhouse moved in anticipation leaving waiting the gaping hole, and this year the old man had won. (Rampton)

A more elaborate variation was to trap someone inside the outhouse. Another student from Utah reports that her grandfather would "pull over outhouses and sometimes put them on the roof of the barn" (Trimble). An Iowa informant says that an ideal prank (combining elements of the first prank type with the second) would be to trap someone inside an outhouse and move it to the top of a building (Siporin). Did that ever happen? Here is a detailed narrative example from New York:

It was Halloween night in the town of Newark Valley, New York (population, several hundred) back in about 1920. Most of the outhouses in town had been torn down and people had been using indoor plumbing for some time, but the town drunk, who lived in a kind of shack at the edge of town, never had the money or inclination to make the switch. He was the type who would pass out anywhere and just sleep until he came to.

The older teens in the village, my grandfather chief among them, decided to play a trick on him and knock over his outhouse while he was in it. They waited for nature to call the man in, and then pushed the outhouse over. What they didn't know was that this particular outhouse had a floor in it, so instead of leaving the man sitting on the throne, exposed to the elements, the drunk went over with the house. However, he didn't come storming out of the shack; in fact, he made no noise at all and they wondered if he was dead. One of them peeked into the crescent moon cut in the door and saw that the drunk was breathing but had passed out and didn't even know what had happened.

This was not as much fun as they thought it would be, so they decided to try something else. They dragged the outhouse over to the town square and used some ropes to haul it up to the top of a small gazebo where bands used to play. They tied it up good and left it there.

The next morning the town fathers saw the outhouse, brought it down, laughed a bit, and took it back and set it up at the man's house, not knowing that he was still inside. The drunk wandered out later and never knew what had happened. However, he told people later that day that he was going to get indoor plumbing put in because "that little house out back just isn't as comfortable as it used to be." (Boyes)

A third traditional prank type, besides moving machinery and re-moving outhouses, is making noise near a house to irritate those inside and to get them
to come outside—at which point a second trick may be sprung. Here are
some examples:

> You'd always take a . . . paper bag and put manure in it and light it on fire
> and put it on somebody's doorstep and knock on the door. They'd come
> out and stomp on it. Try to put the fire out. (J.W.)

> That was probably as bad as it got—other than taking pieces of lath, maybe,
> and sticking them up in the top of the door . . . in the house. And then bal-
> ancing a watermelon up there. And knocking on the door and running
> around the corner. They opened the door and everything falls down. . .
> explodes. (J.W.)

A variation involves creating a thunderous noise, usually on the window of
someone's house:

> On another Halloween we rigged up a string on a big quart tomato can.
> We cut a hole in the bottom (one end was cut out) and we put a hole right
> in the middle of the other end. We'd run this string through this hole and
> tie a nail on it. Then we'd stretch the string out and one guy would hold
> the can against the window and we'd run rosin up and down that string.
> I'll tell you, that makes a racket; it sounds like its gonna' break every win-
> dow in the house, sounds like thunder. (Hazleton 17–18)

Folklorist Michael Taft describes a similar prank in Quebec Province elsewhere in this volume. Other traditional means of creating noises were vi-
brating a notched spool on a window surface or simply throwing corn kernels
at a window (J.H.W.; Pitcher). The noise prank, with its sometime auxiliary
trick, may be one of the most traditional of Halloween pranks. William
Shepard Walsh, writing about Scotland in 1887, says:

> Mischievous boys push the pith from the [cabbage] stalk, fill the cavity
> with tow which they set on fire, and then through the keyholes of houses
> of folk who have given them offence blow darts of flame a yard in length.
> If on Halloween a farmer's or crofter's kailyard still contains ungathered
> cabbages, the boys and girls of the neighborhood descend upon it *en
> masse*, and the entire crop is harvested in five minutes' time and thumped
> against the owner's doors, which rattle as though pounded by a thunder-
> ous tempest. (Walsh 509–10).[6]

Boisterous noise in rites of passage has been noted and interpreted by Lévi-
Strauss (288) and Dundes (105–6), among others. The charivari tradition—

known as *chivaree, shivaree,* or *rough music* in many English-speaking areas—provides a striking parallel to rural Halloween pranks in its use of noise.[7]

The North American shivaree is a community hazing of a newlywed couple. Typically, the couple is "surprised" by a boisterous group of visitors on the wedding night or some night soon after the couple has returned from the honeymoon. The visitors will not leave until they are given refreshments. While the refreshments are being served and the couple is distracted, the visitors play pranks: they sew bedclothes shut, attach noisemaking devices to the bed, or short-sheet the bed—all to stymie the couple's lovemaking. The shivaree, like rural Halloween, involves pranks, takes place in the dark, and marks a rite of passage (though in the life cycle, as contrasted to the seasonal cycle, marked by Halloween pranks). The point here is that both activities, shivarees and Halloween pranks, often occur in the same communities—and it should not be surprising for parallel symbols and actions to have parallel meanings within a community's ritual repertoire. Indeed, a classic shivaree prank is to attach bells to the newlywed's bedsprings.

Unstoppable noise is a Halloween prank, too. One year a group of boys in Maxwell, Iowa (population seven hundred), played an innovative (yet traditional) prank on the whole town:

> There'd usually be groups of ten or fifteen of us and we'd go out and we'd locate up and down the street. Find different cars that were unlocked . . . and everybody kind of had their watches set at about the same time. And everybody'd have a roll of athletic tape. And . . . at a certain time everybody'd get in the cars and tape people's car horns down. And then lock their car doors . . . and take off. All these car horns were goin' off all over town. And people'd come runnin' out with their pajamas on and what not and can't get into their cars. (J. W.)

Many pranks were, and are, spontaneously improvised. They share much that is traditional with the older pranks: the Halloween setting, the manifest purposes of the prank (to embarrass and to create work for someone else), and the shared understanding among the pranksters of the acceptable limits to damage. Boys in Tremonton, Utah, for instance, once dumped out truckloads of sugar beets that were to be loaded onto railroad cars the next day. The farmers had to reload the beets the morning after the prank (Jensen; Keating 1987–88).

There are practical considerations that partially explain the custom of rural pranking on Halloween. For one thing, to be successful and to allow the perpetrators escape and anonymity, most pranks must be played under the cover of darkness. By late October, darkness comes early enough that there is time for pranks. Then why not play pranks all winter long? From a practical standpoint, the snow and cold, which begins soon after Halloween in many localities, would make it difficult. It is significant that the other day of pranks, April Fools' Day (which has a different set of traditional pranks), comes at the opposite end of the same season.[8]

One reason pranks may be more popular in the country—including small country towns, the commercial, religious, and educational centers for local people—has to do with the internal logic of pranks. Think of the reassembled piece of farm machinery on top of the post office. Part of the fun of the prank is that the whole community sees the results and knows who the prank caught unawares (adding to his embarrassment or delight). The "victim" has a good idea of the identity of the perpetrators and he knows that he is probably in contact with them, but he does not know for certain who they are, or how to find out, *or* how to prove guilt. The perpetrators witness this uneasiness, adding to their pleasure and solidarity in the prank— all possible because the community is small enough.[9] Elaborate tricks only make sense in a small group or a small community—where perpetrators can see the results and know that the victim may be uneasy, confused, uncertain, and suspicious—due to the fact that he does not know who is continuing to laugh at him. Conversely, the "victim" may appreciate the prank as much as the perpetrators; there may even be an unstated element of pleasure and solidarity between them.[10] In either case, this personal level of motivation is lacking in most large urban and suburban settings where daily contact does not take place between most members of the geographic community.

Deeper level explanations of the contrasts and comparisons between a rural Halloween characterized by tricks and an urban/suburban Halloween characterized by treats come readily to mind.[11] Jack Santino (1983, 1986) describes assemblages that bring the country to the city, transforming nature into culture, through pumpkins, corn shocks, and other harvest symbols. My own fieldwork suggests that these displays are not as common in the countryside—which makes perfect sense: the country is already there. As Santino writes, "The pumpkins and the corn represent a nostalgic and romanticized idea of the harvest and of rural life styles" (1983, 14). One would not expect a farmer to romanticize his own life-style, but it would be a perfectly likely expression to encounter in a suburb or a city.

Assemblages and traditional pranks, like the reassembled machinery or the outhouse on the roof, do share at least one major communicative characteristic: they are both public statements about the nature of the seasonal change in late October. But the statements are different. Assemblages do not trespass on others' property, are not secretive, and are not directed at anyone in particular; pranks are aimed at specific individuals as well as at the community, are produced in secret, and trespass against the boundaries of private property.

What about the prevalence of trick-or-treating in cities and its absence, or at least different nature, in rural settings? Rural informants explain that the low population density makes trick-or-treating impractical and unrewarding. The density of urban and suburban neighborhoods offers instant and plentiful gratification for city kids.

But at a deeper level, does the exchange of food and the right of anyone to go to anyone else's home symbolize a fictive reciprocity in the suburbs, where there is little real, direct reciprocation between neighbors on an ongoing basis? Would trick-or-treating then be a submerging of the hierarchical structure of daily life in favor of *communitas,* to use Victor Turner's term, a brief, annual setting aside of convention in order to announce and remember a deeper, but not always livable, truth? Did the experience of daily reciprocity in traditional farm communities—particularly in the regular exchange of labor and food—render trick-or-treating ritually unnecessary and redundant? If reciprocity were a lived reality, then there would be no need for the compensation of ritual. In rural communities in which trick-or-treating exists, it may carry a different meaning and structure, as I have suggested above.

These and other provocative questions cannot be answered with the limited evidence I have. But, I would like to speculate about one pivotal matter: Pranks are a central expressive genre of rural Halloween. Why?

Above, I cited practical reasons why pranks work in late fall and why they function well in small communities. Certainly, the very fact that pranks are traditional and secret, and that younger boys are initiated into the genre each year by older boys (and it seems to be only boys), contributes to their ongoing viability. The fact that Halloween pranking is mainly an adolescent/ young adult male activity (and rite of passage) indicates that it fulfills some of the same functions as the charivaris Natalie Davis writes about. She observes that charivaris and other festivals of misrule were managed by "organizations of the unmarried men in peasant communities who have reached the age of puberty" (104).[12] Although the organizations Davis describes no longer exist, there are still the dynamics of ingroup solidarity among high school males, as well as the dynamics of feuds, vendettas, and traditional rivalries. Moreover, the kinds of cooperation traditional agricultural work requires might be enhanced by the cooperation necessary for pranking, the group exercise of initiative, playful problem solving, and imagination, and the formation of male cohorts that result from the shared pranking experiences of young men of similar ages. But these are only partial answers and do not tell us what pranks *mean* on Halloween, and, perhaps most interestingly, why they are not only tolerated but expected and, perhaps, even enjoyed.

We know that the roots of Halloween lie, at least in part, in the Celtic Samhain, the New Year harvest festival (Linton; Messenger 228–29; Santino 1983; Smith 163). The season marked the end of the year's agricultural labor.[13] By this date, cattle were to be back from their summer pasture, the crops were to have been harvested, and the farm and all the animals were to have been secured against winter weather. In much of North America, Halloween still marks the boundary at the end of the agricultural year. The harvest is, hopefully, finished by this time; in the West, cattle should be down from their alpine summer pastures by this season. In other words, by Halloween, what is vulnerable should be protected; whatever is not protected is fair game for Nature. Nature's surrogate—the pranks of local youth—reinforce this essential information and remind everyone that the wintry season, *still* the season of the devil, is upon the world once again. This message is relevant for farmers, but not for suburbanites. Farmers' livelihoods and lives are vulnerable, and they must be prepared. Nature will not be kind to those who are unprepared, and perhaps Halloween pranks are a startling, yet comparatively safe, reminder that it is time to be on one's guard. This is the message that needs to be communicated at this season. The wonderful reversals—a vehicle on a roof, for instance—symbolize not only reversible and unpredictable weather but also elements in delicate balance that can strike at any moment, turning the world upside down. One person recalled switching horses and shifting cattle between their neighbors, another set of reversals (J.H.W.).[14] By Halloween it is time to secure your animals as well as your crops.

Another person recalled that the noise made by the spool on the window could sound like your house was collapsing (Toelken). Indeed, by this time annual house repairs should be completed if one's house is going to last through the winter without damage. Pranks involving outhouses reinvest the metaphor of "being caught with your pants down" with fresh meaning.

The idea that Halloween is time to be wary is an old one, as John Campbell wrote in *Superstitions of the Scottish Highlands:*

> The season on which their [the fairies] festivities are held are the last
> night of every quarter . . . particularly the nights before Beltane, the first
> of summer, and Hallowmas, the first of winter . . . they [the fairies] are
> given to leaving home, and taking away whomsoever of the human race
> they find *helpless,* or *unguarded* or *unwary*" (emphasis added). (18)

When the children in Scotland thump the farmer's house with unharvested cabbage, it reminds the unwary that their harvesting should be finished by Halloween time, and, if it isn't, the offending farmers are vulnerable.

Natalie Davis's comments on festivals of misrule in early modern France apply remarkably well to the pranks of Halloween in twentieth-century North America:

> License was not rebellious. It was very much in the service of the village community. . . . Total violence or disorder in the course of Misrule was a mistake, an accident (so we learn from the brawls and murder cases that ultimately found their way to the royal courts). (107)

So, in contemporary North America, rural communities give their tacit approval to pranks on Halloween as long as they do not cross the line between inconvenience and harm, between simply causing someone else work and the destruction of property or harm to farm animals.[15] Vesta Jensen, a woman from Tremonton, Utah, said that no one was ever punished. Her comment may mean that no one was ever punished so long as he stayed within unstated but understood limits (Keating 1986).[16]

One traditional response to a prank is a better prank—like the boys who planned to move an outhouse and were sometimes unpleasantly surprised to find out that the outhouse had *already* been moved and *they* were the victims (see above). This version of "the surpriser surprised" (Jansen) was sanctioned by the community because it bore the same symbol and message— that winter is laying in wait.

The rural Halloween of pranks did not try to suppress "political" and potentially antisocial impulses; it acknowledged them "with all due respect," gave them their day (actually, night), and subtly harnessed them for the good of the community—exactly what Devil's Night fails to do in Detroit.[17] In the annual agricultural struggle, near the end of the season of "wresting a living from the earth," rural North American communities chose to see death as a part of life, not life as a part of death. Through pranks, they symbolically made the forces of destruction serve creation.

In rural areas, youthful aggression was, and is, given license on this night because it serves useful social ends. Halloween pranks, like other traditional customs of misrule, are more than a social "safety valve"; they awaken the community and remind its members that the season of real danger is upon them and tasks must soon be completed. One might say that rural youths not only imitate the unpredictability of Nature, they preempt it and become Nature's surrogates. Their "preemptive strikes" were, and are, warnings that appear annually, as if they were an inevitable part of the natural cycle. The calendar triggers the custom that, in turn, triggers appropriate behavior. Halloween pranks are alarms in the seasonal clock. Like alarms, they must startle, and like alarm clocks, some pranks use noise itself to startle the would-be dreamer.

Traditional pranks are inconvenient, as opposed to malicious, but they are not harmless—they are helpful. They are playful, yet "practical" reminders (as in "practical jokes") of the winter that lies ahead. As one man recalled, "We had one night. It was wrong to do it any other night. We had the privilege of dumping over outhouses and taking anything that was loose and scattering it along the road" (J.H.W.). But there was "never really any damage," just "a little inconvenience" (C.W.).

Notes

An earlier version of this chapter was first presented at the annual meeting of the American Folklore Society in Albuquerque in 1986. I would like to thank Sydna Keating, Jack Santino, Ona Siporin, and Michael Taft for their responses and encouragement, and Ona Siporin for her fieldwork in Iowa.

    1.   Other formulas include: (1) Trick or treat, / Smell our feet, / Or have you something good to eat? (Hunter 45); (2) Trick or drink (Taft 1983, 9); and (3) Trick or treats, / Money or eats (Pitkin).

    2.   Taft remarks that in Saskatchewan "the host often demands that the masquers sing or dance in return for their traditional 'trick or drink'" (1983, 9).

    3.   For a micro-analysis of the reciprocal relationship between practical jokes and practical joke narratives in terms of aesthetic structure and content, see Bauman 33–53.

    4.   For more on the folklore of outhouses, see Thomas 221–43.

    5.   Here is an example from a Methodist college, evidently in the early twentieth century:

> Apparently, one Halloween they were going around dumping over outhouses and being particularly belligerent, and they dumped over the dean's outhouse. Unfortunately, the dean was sitting in the outhouse at the time. The dean identified them and they were about to be expelled from school and they pleaded and carried on and finally the powers that be decided that if they would buy the dean a new outhouse and put it up and build it with their own hands, then they would be reinstated in school. So they built the outhouse and they decided to have a dedication ceremony

on campus. And they made a very large deal out of it and probably half the campus was there. They had a prayer and a little speech and then they decided to sing a hymn. And the hymn that they chose was a good Methodist hymn called "I Need Thee Every Hour" and they were expelled from school! (William Hatch; Alexandria, Virginia). [Zeitlin et al. 35]

6.   This, of course, recalls—or anticipates—the burning manure on the front porch.

7.   See Alford 505–18 and Thompson 285–312, for the English chivaree.

8.   Appropriately, April Fool's Day, in the spring, marks the transition from death to life, whereas Halloween, in the fall, marks the transition from life to death (Dundes 108). As Dundes writes, "It seems unlikely to me that the occurrence of pranks on these two particular dates is only a matter of coincidence" (Dundes 108–9). In fact, Halloween and April Fools' Day (or All Fools' Day) are our only calendrical pranking days. Note also the verbal symmetry between "All Fools' Day" and "All Saints' Day" (the day that follows Halloween, the Catholic church's transformation of Samhain).

9.   This again recalls shivarees, which take place only in small, rural communities. Morrison (293) remarks on the motivation for elaborate pranks in connection with the shivaree, but her remarks apply to Halloween pranks as well and explain why narrating pranks is as essential as pranking:

Although the bedroom prank is an invasion of the privacy of the newly-weds, that privacy still frustrates one of the pranksters' aims: viewing the discomfiture of the couple. The pranksters' satisfaction must come from imagining its fulfillment. . . . They cannot see the look of astonishment and confusion on the faces of their victims. Only in the narrative can this be realized and it must be in the telling of the narrative that the pranksters get their satisfaction.

10.   What Robert McCarl writes about pranks in occupational folklore applies equally well to agricultural communities: "In the fire service, to be joked with, or 'messed with' is a sign that the other members of the trade know you well enough to kid you or play pranks on you. These jokes and pranks create and reinforce a sense of community so essential in fire fighting culture" (McCarl 78).

11.   Again, see Taft and Hunter for examples of trick-or-treating in rural communities. As I argue above, rural trick-or-treating, where it occurs, is quite different from urban/suburban trick-or-treating.

12.   These young men's societies organized the festivities but everyone participated in them, just as everyone participated in shivarees throughout North America. Halloween pranks seem to be the cultural property of adolescent males, though there are exceptions.

13. Santino (1983, 4) cites Danaher's description (206) as follows:

Samhain, 1 November, was the first day of winter and the end of the
farmer's year. All his crops, all his livestock had to be secure for the hard
season to come. Corn of all sorts, hay, potatoes, turnips, apples must by
now be harvested and stored with ricks well made and well thatched and
tied. Dry cattle and sheep were moved from distant moorland and
mountain pastures and brought to the fields near the farmstead. Milking
cows were brought into the byre for the winter and hand-feeding with
stored fodder began. In the South-east of Ireland, where this crop was
grown, winter wheat had to be in the ground by this date.

Turf and wood for the winter fires must have been gathered and
lucky was the household which had in store a pile of bog-deal, the sweet-
smelling, clean-burning roots or stems of ancient pine trees, found in
cutting turf.

14. Ted Humphrey recalls cows being placed in school classrooms.

15. Taft (1978, 51) gives an example of a prank that is recognized within the
community as going too far:

A: What about old Pat Squibb's horse there?
B: Oh yeah that. We pretty near got in trouble over that.
MT: What was that? . . .
B: . . . he kept him [the horse] in a barn over here by the . . .
Methodist Church. So the boys—he was all white, the horse was—the
boys figured they were going to fix Pat's horse up. So they striped him
with tar. And they took the hair pretty well all off the horse. Yeah, and
there was pretty well some trouble over that.

Notice that this narrative is not volunteered by the teller but has to be solicited
and that it is told without bragging, celebration, or laughter (all of which typify
prank narratives) but rather with regret. There is no savoring of discomfiture, one of
the key motivations for prank narratives.

16. And, as Michael Taft says of Halloween masquers in Saskatchewan, "It is
easy to see that they show their respect for community rules and order through this
ritual breaking of them" (1983, 12). The meaning of Halloween pranks in rural Ireland, at least in the Ballymenone area, seems to have been aggressive and personal.
Henry Glassie writes that "on Hallow Eve bachelors in straw dresses disrupted the
home, unhinging the gates, dismantling the cart, and stuffing up the chimneys of
the man whose eligible daughters had not been released to courtship or the man
against whom the straw boys' leader held personal spite" (778).

17. For a brief description of Devil's Night in Detroit in 1986, see Chafets.

References

Alford, Violet. 1959. "Rough Music or Charivari." *Folklore* 70: 505–18.
Bauman, Richard. 1986. "'We Was Always Pullin' Jokes': The Management of Point of View in Personal Experience Narratives." In *Story, Performance, and Event: Contextual Studies of Oral Narrative,* 33–53. Cambridge: Cambridge Univ. Press.
Boyes, Kate. 1988. "Human Condition Legend: The Halloween Outhouse Story." Student folklore collection. Fife Folklore Archive, Utah State Univ., Logan.
Campbell, John Gregorson. 1900. *Superstitions of the Highlands and Islands of Scotland.* Glasgow: J. MacLehose.
Chafets, Ze'ev. 1990. *Devil's Night: And Other True Tales of Detroit.* New York: Random House.
Danaher, Kevin. 1972. *The Year in Ireland.* Cork: Mercier.
Davis, Natalie Zemon. 1975. "The Reasons of Misrule." In *Society and Culture in Early Modern France.* Stanford, Calif.: Stanford Univ. Press.
Dorson, Richard M. 1972. *Folklore and Folklife: An Introduction.* Chicago: Univ. of Chicago Press.
Dundes, Alan. 1989. "April Fool and April Fish: Towards a Theory of Ritual Pranks." In *Folklore Matters,* 98–111. Knoxville: Univ. of Tennessee Press.
Glassie, Henry. 1982. *Passing the Time in Ballymenone.* Philadelphia: Univ. of Pennsylvania Press.
Gregory, Ruth W. 1975. *Anniversaries and Holidays.* 3d ed. Chicago: American Library Association.
Hazleton, Dru. 1987. "The Weaver Family Stories." Student folklore collection. Fife Folklore Archive, Utah State Univ., Logan.
Humphrey, Ted. 1991. Comments following lecture by Sylvia Grider, "The Commercialization, Institutionalization, and Gentrification of Halloween." Fife Folklore Conference lecture, Utah State Univ., Logan.
Hunter, Darryl M. 1983. "No 'Malice in Wonderland': Conservation and Change in the Three Hallowe'ens of Ann Mesko." *Culture and Tradition* 7: 37–53.
James, Rhett S. 1987. *The Painter: A Western Odyssey.* Denver: Western Profiles Publishing.
Jansen, William Hugh. 1979. "The Surpriser Surprised: A Modern Legend." In *Readings in American Folklore,* ed. Jan Brunvand, 64–90. New York: Norton.
Jensen, Vesta A. 1986. Tape-recorded interview.
Keating, Sydna. 1986. Personal communication.
———. [1987–88]. Personal correspondence.
Lévi-Strauss, Claude. 1969. *The Raw and the Cooked.* New York: Harper & Row.
Linton, Ralph, and Adelin. 1950. *Halloween Through Twenty Centuries.* New York: Henry Schuman.
McCarl, Robert S. 1986. "Occupational Folklore." In *Folk Groups and Folklore Genres: An Introduction,* ed. Elliott Oring, 71–90. Logan: Utah State Univ. Press.

Messenger, John C. 1972. "Folk Religion." In *Folklore and Folklife: An Introduction*, ed. Dorson, 217–32.

Morrison, Monica. 1974. "Wedding Night Pranks in Western New Brunswick." *Southern Folklore Quarterly* 38: 285–97.

Pitcher, Joanne Hudson. 1987. "The Pumpkin Walk: Ida Beutler's Love for Halloween Turned into a Folk Festival." Student folklore paper. Fife Folklore Archive, Utah State Univ., Logan.

Pitkin, Willis. 1991. Personal communication.

Rampton, Malan D. 1991. "Practical Joke: The Outhouse." Student folklore collection. Fife Folklore Archive, Utah State Univ., Logan.

Santino, Jack. 1983. "Halloween in America: Contemporary Customs and Performances." *Western Folklore* 42: 1–20.

———. 1986. "The Folk Assemblage of Autumn: Tradition and Creativity in Halloween Folk Art." *Folk Art and Art Worlds*, ed. Vlach and Bronner, 151–69.

Siporin, Ona White. 1987. Personal communication.

Smith, Robert J. 1972. "Festivals and Celebrations." In *Folklore and Folklife: An Introduction*, ed. Dorson, 159–72.

Summers, Reece. 1986. Personal communication.

———. 1987. Personal communication.

Taft, Michael. 1978. "A Preliminary Folkloristic Survey of Brome-Missisquoi, Quebec: A Report to the Service de Conservation du Patrimoine." Ministère des Affaires Culturelles du Québec.

———. 1983. "Unmasking Hallowe'en: A Preliminary Look at a Small Town Celebration." Paper presented at the Annual Meeting of the Folklore Studies Association of Canada. Quebec.

Thomas, Gerald. 1989. "Functions of the Newfoundland Outhouse." *Western Folklore* 48: 221–43.

Thompson, Edward P. 1972. "'Rough Music': Le Charivari Anglais." *Annales, Economies, Sociétés, Civilisations* 27: 285–312.

Toelken, Barre. 1987. Personal communication.

"Trick." A Supplement to the Oxford English Dictionary. Oxford: Oxford Univ. Press, 1986.

Trimble, Patty. 1982. "Halloween." Student folklore collection 176-1982. Fife Folklore Archive, Utah State Univ., Logan.

Turner, Victor. 1977. *The Ritual Process: Structure and Anti-Structure*. Ithaca: Cornell Univ. Press.

Vlach, John Michael, and Simon Bronner, eds. 1986. *Folk Art and Art Worlds*. Ann Arbor: UMI Research Press.

Walsh, William Shepard. 1897. *Curiosities of Popular Customs and of Rites, Ceremonies, Observances, and Miscellaneous Antiquities*. Philadelphia: J. B. Lippincott.

W., C. 1987. Tape-recorded interview by Ona White Siporin.

W., J. 1987. Tape-recorded interview by Ona White Siporin.

W., J. H. 1987. Tape-recorded interview by Ona White Siporin.

W., T. 1987. Tape-recorded interview by Ona White Siporin.

Wrigley, Krissa. 1991. "Prank: The Halloween Outhouse." Student folklore collection. Fife Folklore Archive, Utah State Univ., Logan.

Zeitlin, Steven J., Amy J. Kotkin, and Holly Cutting Baker. 1982. *A Celebration of American Family Folklore: Tales and Traditions from the Smithsonian Collection.* New York: Pantheon.

4. Bonfire Night in Brigus, Newfoundland

CATHERINE SCHWOEFFERMANN

In many parts of Newfoundland the November fifth Bonfire Night is still a vital tradition, with strong historical links to Halloween. This chapter focuses on one community's enactment of the occasion. In Brigus, Conception Bay, the bonfire celebration has maintained its popularity to the present day, in spite of the fact that modernization has altered other social occasions in the community.

The Brigus celebration can be divided into two distinct types of bonfire events, familial and neighborhood groups of adolescents. Each of these share common characteristics, including physiospatial location of the fire, sociospatial location of the fire, participation, use of a potentially dangerous natural element, means of collecting materials, and representation of everyday norms and ideals. Though all of these involve a degree of movement, the manner in which movement is expressed in the characteristics of each of the events is quite different. In the family events, the movement is inward directed and expressive of the maintenance of family unity, whereas the neighborhood-group events are outward directed and representative of a more extended exploration of the surrounding natural and social environment. These two different types of movement, in turn, display and express attitudes and meanings that exist outside of the celebration. In effect, the celebration can be looked at as a stylized rendition of idealized norms concerning two different stages of childhood in Newfoundland, early childhood and adolescence.

The Community Setting

Brigus, Newfoundland, lies at the head of a narrow and deeply curved bay, within Conception Bay proper, along the base of the northernmost arm of the Avalon Peninsula. Surrounded on the north, south, and east by a band of rugged coastal hills, the settlement sits in a bowl-shaped valley of rough and rocky ground. One of its residents described it to me as "just a hollow between two hills really. Cause you get the hills on the south side and the hills on the north side, and its just a small community in the center, set down in the valley."[1]

Brigus is a town of approximately nine hundred inhabitants, and its nearest neighbors are the towns of Cupids, four miles to the northwest, and Georgetown, six miles to the south. Across Conception Bay to the east, Bell Island can be seen nine miles away as the crow flies. Within the last thirty years two paved roads have been built, connecting Brigus to neighboring communities and to the provincial capital of St. John's, which is forty-five miles away.

From the time of its original settlement, as early as 1675, the traditional character of Brigus was determined by the organization of its fishery. From the late spring through the late fall, schools of fish swarmed into the Newfoundland waters in abundance, and this period saw fathers and sons, or teams of two or three neighbors, fishing the nearby grounds each day, with trawl lines or "jiggers." A Brigus fisherman explained, "Oh my, this was a busy time of year for us. Me brother and meself, we went down, and we used to have a man with us see. And we'd be dragging those nets just about every day."

While the women tended to the domestic responsibilities, the men were usually involved in various aspects of the fishery, even in the off season. When they were not out on the water fishing, they were busy repairing their equipment or building boats. Besides being well versed in boat construction, they also built their own homes, sheds, and barns. When they were not busy at this, they were often out in the woods cutting and hauling wood for fuel or hunting for game such as moose, rabbit, and grouse.

In the midst of this work there was a good deal of cooperation and shared effort. As well as lending a helping hand with work when it was needed, there were other occasions involving personal interaction between community members. "Regardless that there were few hours for idleness we could always find time for a bit of human contact see," an older community member explained. Probably the most informal and common of these was the "house visit," particularly in the evening when people had taken care of most of the chores and responsibilities of the day.

There were also social occasions that were peculiar to specific seasons. Everyone looked forward to these with great anticipation, for they provided the community, and adults in particular, with a short respite for a great deal of visiting and drinking. Summer usually included events such as weddings, community concerts, and church garden parties. Winter brought Bonfire Night, Christmas "times," and Mummering. Of these seasonal celebrations, the one that was of greatest interest to children, and the one in which they were most deeply involved, was Bonfire Night. "Sure it was the child's night. It was that time of year when children were the masters, and they did it all. Adults were not allowed." Although seasonal occasions such as Christmas mummering and community concerts have completely disappeared, one of the traditional seasonal occasions in Brigus that shows no evidence whatsoever of disappearing is Bonfire Night. This celebration is still reenacted with all the fervor and excitement that it had in former times.

Newfoundland's November Fifth Bonfire Celebration

With its shift to North America, and a different cultural context, the fall British fire festival of Guy Fawkes Night has become known in Newfoundland as Bonfire Night. Though this is by far the most commonly used name, some areas of the island refer to it as Bon-a-fire Night or Bonnie-fire Night. It is also called Guy Fawkes Night on occasion, but this is infrequent, and as one Newfoundlander noted, "'Guy Fawkes' is only used by old people around the community. You won't catch nobody nowadays calling it that. It's just 'Bonfire Night' to us."

Sentiments associated with this celebration are strong and deep. Evidence of this goes beyond the prevalence of the actual enactment itself, for it has frequently been the inspiration of localized songs and poetry as well. In the village of Renews, someone wrote a poem about an incident in which a resident tried to get the practice banned because she felt it was endangering her property. Responding to her unsuccessful attempt, another resident composed the following verse:

> Oh Aggie dear, don't talk like that,
> And on us do not scorn,
> There was a bonfire, made up here,
> Before ever you were born.[2]

This poem is often recited when people of the area get together, and it is especially popular on Bonfire Night. Other examples of this kind include a poem written by a man from Little Harbour, Twillingate, entitled "Uncle

Charlie's Punt," which describes an actual incident concerning the stealing and burning of an old man's boat on November fifth.[3] Another song, from Heart's Delight, Trinity Bay, also documents the burning of a boat on this night.[4]

The 1980 Bonfire Celebration

The bonfire celebration can be divided into three stages: the preparations, the lengthy and diligent collecting of materials for the bonfire; the actual event itself; and the aftermath, what occurred after the fire died that evening as well as during the next few days. My observations are based on fieldwork I conducted in 1977 and 1980.

In the early gathering stages beginning in late September, adolescent boys asked for donations by going from house to house and store to store in the community. Except in the case of the local merchants and tradespeople, the boys asked for materials only from members of their particular neighborhoods, or from those people they were most familiar with. They collected anything combustible that was no longer in use—paper, cardboard boxes, pieces of wood, discarded fences, boats, and furniture. Especially prized, and the main ingredient for most of the fires, were rubber tires. As one boy said, "We gets whatever we can now, old cartons, tires and boughs, and whatever we can get. The thing now is tires. There's lots of them on the go and they burns like the devil."

During the early part of October there was a noticeable difference in the attitude toward collecting materials for the neighborhood-group bonfires. The gathering was now being done in earnest, especially on weekends. The boys began to collect in small groups of two or three as well as individually. They also began to branch out in their collecting, going beyond their immediate neighborhoods. When I asked one of the fellows where he had gotten his recently acquired barrels, he explained, "As they were finished in the fish plant, emptying the plant, well I had my eye on them. I got there about closing and asked 'em if I could have the barrels. So's they gave 'em to me."

During this time, three distinct neighborhood groups began to form: Bunker's Hill, Cupid's Hill, and Clark's Hill. Whenever I asked one of the boys where his fire was going to be, the typical answer was such-and-such a hill. An elderly community member explained this preference: "You have it on the highest hill for two reasons; first to be noticed, and second, that you were away from the houses of the community. Brigus is all hills, in case you can see. No problem to have a bonfire." Each of the three fires was at a different edge of the community and in close proximity to the neighborhood or neighborhoods that sponsored it. The size of each group varied at any one time, but the approximate range was between twelve and thirty. Those actively participating were always male adolescents, aged ten to twenty, with the majority falling between twelve and sixteen. An older man described the age range: "Could be twelve, could be fifteen, or around eighteen there. Just when there's lots of life in you, lots on the go, nothing sloff of ya. It's mostly in the school days."

When I asked the boys why there were no females taking part in the lengthy and diligent preparations, I received answers such as "'tis more of a man's job" or "oh girls, they're too lazy." The girls, as well as the adults and young children, were passive participants. They periodically helped in an indirect way, but basically their role was that of spectator. One older resident gave the following description: "The girls sort of stayed back, they stood back. They never—you know this was a man's thing, you know it was. Very few girls. They came to the fires, and had fun and that sort of thing. But the girls didn't really get involved. Not getting boughs and tires and that sort of thing."

The participants in each group lived either in the same neighborhood or in adjacent neighborhoods. If they had formerly participated in the celebration, it was always with the same group the next year. When I asked one of the boys how they formed the different groups, he explained that they were "the ones you normally play with on Saturday and that kind of stuff. And they live mostly around your neighborhood, your area."

Each member of the group would initially collect materials on his own and store them in his family cellar, barn, or other suitable area. But gradually, as the materials began to pile up, as the storage places threatened to become filled to capacity, and as Bonfire Night drew closer, each group began to store its materials collectively, in a large space such as a barn or uninhabited house.

By late October gathering materials took priority over other activities. Once the boys had asked just about everyone in the vicinity for contributions, they began to go outside of their immediate neighborhoods and communities to collect materials. For instance, one Saturday the boys arranged their family chores and weekend hockey game around a tire-collecting expedition that took them out along the Conception Bay highway past Avondale. Junior Mercer, one of the oldest members of the Bunker's Hill crowd, had offered to drive some of the group "round the bay"[5] in his pickup truck to ask for tires from various garages, automobile dumps, and gas stations scattered along the highway.

As the time drew nearer to Bonfire Night and the materials readily available for donation became more scarce, the adolescents began to scout around the community in small groups and developed schemes to "swipe"[6] various combustible objects. One adolescent explained: "You go and ask for it and if they don't give it to you then you take it. Take whatever you can, barrels, tires, mattresses, anything." The closer the day to Bonfire Night, the more daring the gangs became in what they would steal and where they would steal it from. At first they concentrated on easy prey that was out of sight from the owners and neighbors, such as spare tires or firewood piles stored in back yards. But eventually, they graduated to breaking into barns and stores for barrels, disjoining a neighbor's gate, and taking tires off cars. Raiding another group's collection also occurred, and initiated retribution on the part of those robbed. A Bunker's Hill member said: "Many times one group will steal from another or try to. We'll raid their places where they have their barrels hid. If they raid us one night, on the night after, we'll go back and try to get back what they stole from us, plus a little more."

Adults in the community were well aware that this kind of collecting accompanies the more legitimate type. They accepted the activity and rarely sought retribution for materials taken and burned. Rather, beginning in early October, the adults became much more careful of what they left out in the yard or unlocked. If they were caught unprepared, they considered it their own fault for not having protected their property.

THE FAMILY BONFIRE

The Sunday before Bonfire Night, I observed the Wilkinson family preparations. In some respects, their family bonfire celebration can be considered atypical. Because they were British and had lived in Brigus for only five years, the manner in which they celebrated the occasion was heavily influenced by the way it is celebrated in England as Guy Fawkes Night. The Wilkinsons burnt an effigy and lighted fireworks, but before they came to Brigus no one had ever seen either of these activities on Bonfire Night.

Aside from these differences, their fire was similar to other family fires in the community in the way it was organized and enacted. Only members of the nuclear family participated in the preparations. The collecting began on the third of November, with the entire family driving down to the Frog Marsh beach to collect driftwood for their fire. In addition to this expedition, the three children gathered driftwood from around the house and yard, including two old crates and a barrel. As the material was collected, it was stored in the family barn directly behind the house.

On the afternoon of the fourth of November, the Wilkinson children, under the direct supervision of their mother, built a "Guy." His frame consisted of two pieces of wood nailed together in the form of a cross. Over this was fitted a discarded pair of long johns, into which was stuffed an old daybed's "innards," to fill the Guy out and give him substance. His head was made of a woman's nylon stocking crammed full of straw. Accessories included unmatched gloves, a pair of beaten work shoes, a knitted cap, Styrofoam eyes, ears, mouth, and a carrot for his nose. All of the children helped in the endeavor and made additions where they saw fit. When completed, the Guy was crammed into the hayloft, banned to the barn until the next evening.

The other family fire preparations in Brigus also involved the adults and the young children of the household. The children were usually ten and under, an age at which they were not yet considered independent enough to participate in the neighborhood-group fires. Together or separately, the adults and children gathered combustible materials, usually the day before or the day of the bonfire. The materials gathered included tires, wood, potato stalks, and trash. The manner in which they were accumulated always conformed to the everyday ethics of the community—that is, everything was obtained legitimately. Usually, the individual families tended to supply their own materials, gathering them from around the house and yard. Enough was gathered to fuel a small fire for an hour or two.

By about 6:30 P.M., tufts of fire could be seen rising one by one, flecking the darkness like stars. Those first visible were the family bonfires in the dwelling areas of Brigus. A little before seven, the Wilkinsons placed their Guy on the top of their bonfire teepee. Mr. Wilkinson doused it with kerosene and lit it. Immediately, the teepee was ablaze and the Guy in the spotlight. While it was burning, members of the family sat and chatted, staring into the fire, and some of the children played around it, throwing sticks and stones at the diminishing Guy. The dominating sounds were those of the fire crackling and the tide lapping up against the pebbled beach. Later in the evening, after the Banks family had joined them, Mr. Wilkinson lit three fireworks that spewed off different colors into the sky. Once the remains of the Guy had crashed down to the ground, Mrs. Wilkinson put wrapped-up fish and potatoes into the embers. At this time, the adults began to drink beer and whiskey while the children drank Cokes. This celebration ended at around eight.

The other family bonfires ran a similar course, only without the presence of a Guy or fireworks. The family fires, in general, were quite sedate, especially in comparison to the neighborhood-group bonfires. The adults managed all of the fire-related activities; the extent of the children's participation was that they acted as helpers and spectators under the supervision of an adult.

Fig. 4.1. The Wilkinson family assembling the Guy, stuffing him with an old daybed and giving him a wooden-framed backbone.

Fig. 4.2. A tire pilgrimage up to the Bunker's Hill bonfire site.

Fig. 4.3. The Wilkinson family bonfire.

THE NEIGHBORHOOD-GROUP BONFIRE

By about 7:00 P.M., a small signal fire was started at the base of Bunker's Hill and burned for about half an hour, attracting all the members of the Bunker's Hill group as well as a number of spectators. Those with torches lit them and proceeded up the hill with others trailing behind.

Though there was no obvious person in authority, in an indirect, behind-the-scenes fashion, there was one individual who acted as the organizing force behind each neighborhood-group fire. For the Bunker's Hill gang this was Junior Mercer. When I asked different members of the group how the leader was chosen, all of them shrugged their shoulders and said, "He's the oldest" or "he's the strongest." Junior determined when the fire was to be lit and also when the fire was to be fed or tended to. He was, in essence, responsible for the evening's safe development, a kind of overseer who kept the celebration under control. One of the older community members made this observation, based on the night's events: "In their own way it was well organized. It wasn't something that you just went up and lit a fire and walked away and left it. It was done, and done properly, and you watched it through and made sure that everything was under control."

Once Junior gave the word, the pyramid was doused with kerosene and one of the lit torches was hurled into it. Immediately the entire heap was ablaze. The fire cast its light onto all of those close by and threw ghoulish shadows as the prevailing northeasterly wind caused the flames to grow and recede. In fact, as the evening wore on, the winds became so strong that the fire gave the impression of burning horizontally rather than vertically. The strength of the wind, the intensity of the heat, and the size of the flames made it unsafe for anyone but those tending the fire to be near it. Watching the flames soar and change direction unpredictably, one of the bystanders commented, "You have to wonder someone isn't burned, with a big fire like that. But you know, I don't remember anybody ever got burned and they won't tonight."

The majority of the crowd situated themselves a little above the fire, sitting on and leaning against the rocks. Throughout the evening, people of all ages flowed continually up and down the hill to view the fire and take part in the celebratory activities. Even families that had had their own family fires came up afterward to watch the big one. Adolescent girls began to appear as well. Other spectators included relatives or friends of the various members of the group involved, and those who lived in the Ratley Row and Inner Harbour Pond neighborhoods.

With the gathering of spectators, and particularly the girls, the serious and hushed mood of the crowd shifted to one of playfulness. Activities included passing around Hallowe'en candy, drinking beer—even by those under legal age—playing games of chase around the fire and throwing torches into the air, socializing, passing local news and gossip, and becoming lost in reverie.

As more fuel was needed, one or two of the members of the neighborhood group hurled more materials into the fire. The pyramidlike shape had, by this time, all but disappeared. One of the boys with a long stick in hand always stayed close by the fire, occasionally poking it, and generally just being there to tend it. Junior was never far away from the center of the activity, and it was obvious that when something major was done to the fire, it was with his knowledge and approval.

At about half past nine, Junior gave the signal to the person tending the fire to fish a tire out of it. The boys speared a flaming tire and sent it plummeting down the side of the hill into the harbor. This flying comet spectacle was received with applause and animated conversation, with remarks such as "Jesus, it looks like a star falling from heaven." Tire rolling was performed periodically for the next hour, each time producing the same level of enthusiasm. But this, as well as the bonfire itself, was cut short at about half past ten by a torrential rain shower that sent everyone home in a hurry and caused the celebration to come to a premature end.

The Bunker's Hill bonfire of 1977 ran its natural course, and what happened that evening is probably what would have occurred at the 1980 celebration. At the 1977 bonfire, when the spectacular flames began to die and the hour became late, most of the spectators, especially the adults and young children, began to drift home. After the crowd had thinned out and the fire was so low that it was no longer considered dangerous, and as the last of the fuel was disappearing in the flames, some of the boys made a game of jumping over the residue. Others picked up the charred remains and chased one another, trying to blacken their faces. When only the burning embers remained, Junior and another fellow stayed at the site to quench the fire, while others left to comb the community for possible mischief making. Reminiscing, an older man described this time of night to me: "There were other things that went on after the fire, devilment sort of things. Now anything to do with badness, Bonfire Night you did it. That's when you let off all the steam and when you could stay out as late as you wanted."

Though I did not go with them, the boys told me the next day that later that night they had let the air out of the tires of some of the cars they'd passed by, unhinged a few garden gates, and stolen garden vegetables for a midnight meal. Some of the underage boys, who had been drinking beer for the first time that night, continued to do so as they traveled the lanes, and some of those who had never smoked a cigarette before indulged in that as well. This was also a popular time for courting. Several of the older boys and their girlfriends fell behind the pace of the main group and eventually disappeared to the more remote areas of the community.

Gradually, the remaining boys dispersed to their homes, covered with soot, smelling of smoke and very tired from a day full of intense, exhausting work and play.

An Analysis

From these descriptions, it is readily apparent that the Bonfire Night celebration is still a special time of year in Brigus, particularly for the adolescents. "It's the best bit of fun you get in the fall," was a remark often made to me. As well as being a "bit of fun," the celebration is obviously something more. An elderly resident was probably referring to its historical background when he said, "They're still keeping it up, and lots don't know what's on the back of this, the bonfire." But he could just as easily have been suggesting that there is a more complex reason for the celebration's retention, that it has a contemporary significance for those involved that reaches beyond its traditional meanings.

I will discuss the manner in which this particular celebration displays multiple levels of symbolic meaning for members of the community through the intensification, inversion and recoding of everyday life.

The Brigus bonfire celebration can be viewed as an enactment,[7] expressing normalized and idealized interactive encounters centering on two stages of childhood: early childhood and adolescence. The community's pervasive evaluation of these two stages are encapsulated and commented on within each of the two bonfire events, the family and the neighborhood group. Both of these, in turn, are part of a larger whole that the people of Brigus refer to as Bonfire Night.

The entire celebration is framed both in time and space. The time, extending from the beginning of the preparations through the aftermath of the fire, is specially sanctioned and conventionally set apart by the community. During this period the children are allowed to follow a certain course of action of which the entire community is aware, for everyone in Brigus knows that "come October, preparations for Bonfire Night begin." They also know that November fifth will always give witness to a number of bonfires in the area.

This celebration is also framed spatially. There are specifically designated places for the bonfires, the majority of which are located either on a high promontory, as in the case of the neighborhood-group fires, or in a space close to the home, for the family fires. The use of the space during this period, however, is vastly different for the two types of groups.

This framing takes the celebration out of the realm of everyday life, yet, paradoxically, it epitomizes the everyday. Through the creation of a play world "very much like the real world but psychologically (and often physically) removed from it in time and space," the children's activities sometimes give the impression of chaos and upendedness, yet they also display regulated and predictable behavior.[8]

In everyday life there is a distinction between the way young children and adolescents are treated and acknowledged by the community. This is expressed within the celebratory context in which the two different configurations, the family and the neighborhood-group events, display vastly different orientations of movement.

The family bonfire events are semiprivate celebrations in which the movement is within highly familiar, intimate realms and is inward directed.

They are formal and relatively self-contained, for the preparations and the burning almost always involve the immediate family to the exclusion of the rest of the community, except insofar as they can view it because it is outdoors. The behavior of the participants is regulated by adults, and there is an all-pervading sense of composure. It can be seen as an example of the maintenance of the status quo, a mirrored representation of what early childhood is like in everyday Brigus, that is, behavior controlled and directed by adults.

If the family fires exude a sense of maintenance, the neighborhood-group fires, or public displays, are an outward-directed experiential exploration of the adolescent's natural and sociocultural environment. Movement in this event is from the familiar to the less familiar, and even unfamiliar, realms of the community—a kind of spatial and cognitive reaching out. This is a time when the adolescents hold the cultural stage and the rest of the community members are compelled to acknowledge their presence. This occupancy, by its very nature, includes elements of "sense" and "nonsense."[9] These fire events display licentious behavior side by side with highly regulated and predictable behavior.

The adolescents' exploration of their environment involves testing it to its limits. This is exhibited in the "serious play" that is carried on within the celebratory context, where the activities become unreal and yet more real at the same time. Therefore, the family events intensify much of everyday life, whereas the neighborhood-group events upend as well as intensify.

SPATIAL LOCATION OF THE FIRE

The spatial location of the family fire is on level ground, and on privately owned and cultivated land. All of these characteristics reinforce basic values related to early child-rearing. The fire is almost always within the confines of the yard. The ground here is relatively level and clear of debris, so a child is less likely to stumble and fall there than on the more rocky or sloped land that is outside of the yard. Additionally, the fact that this is personally owned and cultivated land makes it familiar to child and adult, cutting down on the possibility of unpredictable occurrences.

The neighborhood-group fire is always on a high hill, where it is conspicuous to the entire community. This physical space gives a sense of expanse, both outward and upward. It is also uncultivated and publicly traversed land, connoting movement from the familiar to the unfamiliar, and from the specific to the general. The adolescents are in a period of life in which they are reaching outside the cultivated and ordered home environment toward unworked and more extensive environs.

SOCIAL LOCATION OF THE FIRE

Closely related to the physical location of the fires are the social locations. The family fire is always in the immediate vicinity of the home sponsoring it, usually in the backyard vegetable garden or another area near the house. In the larger context, this spot is within the community proper. These areas are traversed daily by the family and are cultivated with flowers and vegetables, the lawns are tended, clothes are hung on the lines, and fish are dried on platforms within the yards. These are all spaces that are culturally altered and therefore "lived-in."[10] In addition, these spaces are located within socially designated "neighborhoods"—boundaried spaces.

In comparison, the adolescents' fires are outside of the immediate community proper and the familiar cultural environment. They edge toward the unfamiliar, natural landscape. On rocky barren cliffs, these are uncultivated, "wild" territories, which people occasionally pass through on their way to pick berries, chop wood, or go hunting. They are beyond the well-traversed and named zones of the townscape, reaching into the unknown, neutral, and ambiguous areas. Though there is a name for each of the hills where these fires burn, these are not nearly so boundaried as the spaces within the community proper. They are less clearly designated by the community than the neighborhoods and the family yards.

MEANS OF COLLECTING MATERIALS

Within the family bonfire event, the means of collecting materials also points toward the familiar. It is always done legitimately in terms of everyday community norms and usually supplies are obtained from the family's personal stock or that of a nearby neighbor. If the collecting is done farther away from the home, it always includes at least one adult as well as the children. For example, when the Wilkinson family went down to the beach the parents were there to oversee the activities; the children were not allowed to go on their own.

On the other hand, the youths involved in the neighborhood-group events have two methods of collecting materials, by asking for donations—normally legitimate—and by swiping things—normally not legitimate. As the gathering progresses, it moves from the highly familiar areas of the youths' own homes and those of their immediate neighbors to the general community, to the regional businesses such as the gas stations and dumps that were scoured by the Bunker's Hill group, to the less familiar natural surroundings such as Molly's Island and the woods out past Frog Marsh where the boys cut boughs, or to the harbor in which they jigged tires from the ocean floor. In addition, there is a great deal of movement when the boys go out swiping. One night, when I took part in the thievery, the boys traversed every neighborhood in town, weaving in and out of the narrow lanes and through back yards and fields.

USE OF A POTENTIALLY DANGEROUS NATURAL ELEMENT

Fire, which is such a prominent feature of the celebration, is used in two quite different capacities in the two events. Practically speaking, the fire is a means by which the community can get rid of a good portion of its accumulated rubbish. In effect, the fire can be seen as physically purifying the town of useless accumulated materials such as discarded tires, broken fences, old boots, and garbage. More than once while I was in Brigus, I heard comments such as, "It's a darn shame that the bodies of those old car wrecks don't burn, because then they could be burned-up on Bonfire Night along with all the other rubbish."

At the family bonfire, the potentially dangerous natural element of fire is used with great reverence and care. The element is kept in its controlled cultural niche during the entire burning. It is under constant surveillance by the father. He takes full control and responsibility for lighting it, tending it, and extinguishing it, while the children sit and admire it or help out under close supervision. The children's lack of direct power is due to the fact that they are not considered old enough to responsibly look after themselves. Just as parents protect their children from everyday risks and hazards, they also shelter them from the dangers of the fire. Metaphorically these fires can be seen as outdoor hearths representing the concept of familial continuity.

At the neighborhood-group events, the boys have full reign with respect to the fire. The use of fire, and particularly the control of it, displays the boys' developing mastery over a potentially dangerous natural element. It can destroy unless placed in the confines of a cleared or protected area. By placing it thus, as well as by being careful and attentive, the adolescents exhibit competence and responsibility. Within this context, they also play with the element and test it to extremes. The boys often throw their lighted brands up into the air, pitch them over the cliff into the sea, or whirl them around in the air trying to extinguish them. They also fish flaming tires out of the blaze and guide them down the side of the hill into the sea. Rather than letting the fire burn on its own and be admired from afar, as with the family fires, much of the reason for having the larger fires is so that the boys can play with it once it is lit. They take fire out of fire, separating and dissecting it, to explore its possibilities. The tires rolling down the side of the hill can be seen as the ultimate extension of outward movement from the focal point of the fire.

"Playing with fire" can be seen as an intensification of the boys' everyday activities. It is a metaphor for adolescence generally, and for its specific part in the overall celebration. It becomes readily apparent that its physical properties are similar to many of the characteristics of adolescence, and especially those that are enacted within the celebratory context. For example, fire's capacity to destroy is analogous to adolescents' potential threat to the community. As the children get older, their personalities become more forceful, they begin to exercise a degree of independence, and they question authority. This is exhibited in the inverting of the idealized norm of honesty, when the boys swipe materials for the fire.

The ability of fire to change form and yet remain the same is analogous to the adolescent's stage of life. He is neither child nor adult, and yet he has the freedom during this stage of life to play with both roles. As the shifting of the fire on Bunker's Hill was unpredictable, so too is adolescent behavior.

Like the powerful presence of fire, this period of youth also commands attention. The adolescents are often loud in the evenings as they play throughout the lanes. They test authority in various ways, such as by gunning their cars and speeding them along the roads or taking apples from private orchards. This testing extends into the celebratory context when they swipe materials and when they cavort on Bonfire Night.

Fire is also a metaphor for sexuality, which is ever present in adolescence. It is a period of life when the young are becoming sexually aware. The opposite sex is a continual topic of conversation. A sharp division between the sexes in the work and play activities of everyday life is more prevalent at this time than in early childhood. The boys' interests often mirror the work of their fathers; their chores include cutting and hauling wood, building, and fishing. The girls are usually much more involved in the domestic realm, indoors helping their mothers with household responsibilities or baby sitting. Yet the boys and girls do get together for social activities, setting up places of rendezvous such as the local fish-and-chips drive-in or the steps of one of the confectioneries.

These roles and attitudes are enacted in the celebratory context as well. The preparatory stages involve a large degree of manual labor, and this is carried out only by the boys. Girls do not appear on the scene at all until the actual bonfire lighting, taking part initially as spectators, and later as partners in after-hours courting.

PARTICIPATION

Participation in the family fires involves small numbers of people, and primarily members of the immediate family, although occasionally there may be two households involved. When this occurs, it is with families that are close in everyday life.

The neighborhood-group fires, on the other hand, include many people whose participation is on different levels of activity. The adolescent boys are by far the most active participants. They may be from different families throughout a neighborhood, or from adjoining neighborhoods. Thus, this inclusion reaches far beyond the individual family and also through a relatively wide age group, for those actively involved range in age from ten to eighteen. Others involved, though in a much more passive way, include adults who donate materials or give a helping hand and other community members who show up at the bonfire as spectators. So, compared to the family events, the participants of the neighborhood-group fires cover a much wider spectrum of people, as well as a much larger number.

REPRESENTATION OF EVERYDAY NORMS AND IDEALS

The family bonfire events can be seen as a representation, intensification, and maintenance of everyday norms and ideals. As in their daily lives, during this time, the young children are closely supervised, protected from potential dangers, and kept close to the center of the family. Their physical and cognitive movement is limited and inward rather than outward directed.

Norms and ideals in the adolescent neighborhood-group bonfires are inverted as well as intensified. At this time, there is a simultaneous identification with the real social world and a distancing from it. The adolescents take control of the natural and social environment. Many of the behaviors exhibited and sanctioned during this time are considered inappropriate in everyday life. For instance, adolescents are allowed to stay out much later on November fifth than they normally are. However, they do not ask permission to remain out, but simply take it upon themselves to make the evening's rules and return home when they wish.

On November fifth the adults have no active hand in the neighborhood-group celebrations; they are simply passive spectators. Rather, it is the adolescents who implement and supervise all action. Adolescents, who in everyday life are in an inferior position in the social structure of the community, are transformed during this time to a position of structural superiority, whereas the normally structurally superior adults are temporarily cast down.

There is a great deal of drinking and cigarette smoking, both of which are typical everyday adult activities. There is also an overall lack of restraint during this period. The boys play with fire, stay out late, drink, and steal. In everyday life, the ideal norms state that people must have respect for one another's property, whereas in the celebratory context anything that is available is taken. But this, too, has its purposes. Not only does it minister to the immediate desire for materials, but it also serves as a means by which the boys test the community's sense of preparedness.

Bonfire Night in Brigus tells us what happens in the typical, recurring events of everyday life. In his observations of the Balinese enactment of the cockfight, Clifford Geertz says, "Its function, if you want to call it that, is interpretive; it is a Balinese reading of Balinese experience; a story they tell themselves about themselves."[11] Likewise, Bonfire Night displays the special relationships that exist between the participants, between the participants and the community at large, and between the participants and their natural environment. Within this framed context, these relationships are established, displayed, and celebrated. Much like the cockfights in Bali, Bonfire Night in Brigus can be seen as a stylized rendition of some of the fundamental motives of the community.

Notes

This article is drawn from my master's thesis, completed at Memorial University, St. John's, Newfoundland, Canada, 1981.

1. This and all subsequent uncited quotations are from fieldwork notes or tapes done from 1977 through 1980. All are in the possession of the author.
2. Memorial Univ. Newfoundland Folklore and Language Archive, MSS. 73–106, p. 29.
3. Harold Pardy, "Uncle Charlie's Punt," *Decks Awash* (August 1980): 33–34.
4. Memorial Univ. Newfoundland Folklore and Language Archive, MSS. 72–260, p. 33.
5. This colloquial term is used to refer to travel along the Conception Bay highway, which hugs the coastline of the bay and winds through or nearby all of the communities that are settled along its perimeter.
6. The term connotes that the stealing is expected and, to a degree, sanctioned by the community.
7. See Roger D. Abrahams, "Toward an Enactment-Centered Theory of Folklore," in *Frontiers in Folklore,* ed. William Bascom (Boulder, Colo.: Westview, 1978), 79–120.

8.	See Roger D. Abrahams, "Complex Relations of Simple Forms" in *Folklore Genres,* ed. Dan Ben-Amos (Austin: Univ. of Texas Press, 1976), 193–214.

9.	These terms are borrowed from Abrahams and Richard Bauman, "Sense and Nonsense in St. Vincent," *American Anthropologist* 73 (1971): 762–72, and refer to acceptable and unacceptable community behaviors.

10.	See Gerald Pocius, "Calvert: A Study of Artifacts and Spatial Usage in a Newfoundland Community" (Ph.D. diss., Univ. of Pennsylvania, 1979).

12.	See Clifford Geertz, "Deep Play: Notes on a Balinese Cockfight," in *Myth, Symbol, and Culture,* ed. Clifford Geertz (New York: W. W. Norton, 1971), 26.

References

Abrahams, Roger D. 1972. "Christmas and Carnival on St. Vincent." *Western Folklore* 31: 275–89.

Abrahams, Roger D. 1976. "Complex Relations of Simple Forms." In *Folklore Genres,* ed. Dan Ben-Amos, 193–214. Austin: Univ. of Texas.

Abrahams, Roger D. 1971. "Sense and Nonsense in St. Vincent." *American Anthropologist* 73: 763–72.

Abrahams, Roger D. "Toward an Enactment-Centered Theory of Folklore." In *Frontiers of Folklore,* ed. William Bascom, 79–120. Boulder, Colo.: Westview Press.

Bachelard, Gaston. 1964. *The Psychoanalysis of Fire,* trans. Alan C. M. Ross. London: Routledge & Kegan Paul.

Bartlett, William. 1977. "History of Brigus." Unpublished MS.

Gailey, Alan. 1977. "The Bonfire in North Irish Tradition." *Folklore* 88: 3–38.

Geertz, Clifford. 1971. "Deep Play: Notes on a Balinese Cockfight." In Geertz, *Myth, Symbol and Culture* (New York: W. W. Norton).

Halpert, Herbert, and G. M. Story, eds. 1968. *Christmas Mumming in Newfoundland.* Toronto: Univ. of Toronto Press.

Hole, Christina. 1960. "Winter Bonfires." *Folklore* 71: 217–27.

Huizinga, J. 1955. *Homo Ludens: A Study of the Play-Element in Culture.* Boston: Beacon Press.

Newall, Venetia. 1972. "Two English Fire Festivals in Relation to their Contemporary Social Setting." *Western Folklore* 31: 244–74.

Pocius, Gerald L. 1979. "Calvert: A Study of Artifacts and Spatial Usage in a Newfoundland Community." Ph.D. diss., Univ. of Pennsylvania.

Sapir, J. David, and J. Christopher Crocker, eds. 1977. *The Social Use of Metaphor: Essays on the Anthropology of Rhetoric.* Philadelphia: Univ. of Pennsylvania Press.

Turner, Victor. 1969. *The Ritual Process: Structure and Anti-Structure.* Ithaca: Cornell Univ. Press.

Wheelwright, Philip. 1954. *The Burning Fountain: A Study in the Language of Symbolism.* Bloomington: Indiana Univ. Press.

5.   Trick or Treat
Pre-Texts and Contexts

TAD TULEJA

Majority opinion on the origins of trick or treat has it as a relic of the Celtic New Year. The ancient Celts believed that at Samhain the spirits of the dead returned to visit the living. To welcome them—and to protect themselves from supernatural mischief—people unbolted their doors, kept hearth fires burning, and set out gifts of food as propitiation. Later, according to a commonly cited explanation, they dressed as spirits themselves, using mimicry as a magical defense and demanding contributions from their neighbors for communal feasts. Some suggest that these collections were made in the name of the Druidic deity Muck Olla; others that they were a form of mumming. Whatever the wrinkles, the root assumption is the same: trick or treat had its beginnings in the Celtic dawn.[1]

At first glance this neo-survivalist interpretation seems eminently reasonable. Not only do the demonstrable links between Halloween and Samhain invite comparison on a point-by-point basis, but, because Halloween only took hold in America after the arrival of Irish immigrants in the 1840s, it seems right to assume they packed their ancient customs into steerage with them and transplanted them, one by one, on New World soil. Unfortunately, there is a paucity of primary evidence to support this reading.

Irish sources do mention the tradition of food for the dead, and Jack Santino has suggested ingeniously that the saga hero Nera may be a model for our door-to-door beggars; but costumed begging does not figure in here, and propitiatory food is hardly unique to the Emerald Isle. An exhaustive

Victorian survey of Irish calendar customs mentions divination games and apple bobbing as Halloween pastimes, but says nothing about food collection or a procession of "spirits." Muck Olla enters the record only in 1902, in Wood-Martin's *Traces of the Elder Faith in Ireland.* There we find that the Druidic deity is confined to county Cork and that his agent in the masked procession wears a horse's head—making him look suspiciously like the British hodening horse or its Welsh variant, the Mari Lwyd. On the practice of masked begging at the Celtic New Year, authorities on the Druids do not say a word.[2]

A second reason to question the Samhain link is, to use art historical jargon, the discontinuity in the custom's provenance. "If the 'pre-Christian religious ceremony' theory of origin of calendar customs is correct," observes E. C. Cawte, "then ideally there would be records of them at all periods since pre-Christian times. On the whole, such records do not exist." Cawte is speaking of British animal disguise, but the comment applies well to trick or treat. As Santino sagely observes, the road from the sagas to today's masked children "is a long one, with many intersections and forks and sideroads and curves"; taking it straight is to play Procrustes with the record. Maybe nineteenth-century immigrants did bring costumed begging with them, but American sources do not make that case. Indeed, trick or treat does not become a widespread feature of the American Halloween until a century after the Great Famine. By that time, traces of the elder faith are faint, and the United States is filled with more than Irish immigrants.[3]

If Druidism provided the only model for trick or treat, one might forgive this spotty record, faute de mieux. In fact, what Thomas Vennum nicely calls "masked ritual solicitation" appears throughout the world, and the British Isles and Ireland themselves provide several examples of harvest-time begging to rival hoary Samhain's claim as single source. I begin this chapter by examining these other sources.[4]

A Cornucopia of Precedents

If Samhain provides the most popular choice for a prototypical trick or treat, it is certainly not the only one. Ethnographers cite several examples of ritual begging among native Americans, and even if we confine ourselves to Western Europe, from whose customs the American ritual might reasonably be thought to have evolved, we are not short of plausible candidates. The scholarly literature, up to now, has focused on three: the All Souls' Day tradition known as *soul caking,* the masked begging of Guy Fawkes Day, and peasant collections taken up for Saint Columba.[5]

SOUL CAKING

In medieval Europe, on All Souls' Day (2 November), beggars sought alms as payment for prayers that they promised to say for the faithful departed. In an English variant, they asked for soul cakes that had been prepared for the occasion: one tradition held that for each cake consumed, a soul would find release from the torments of Purgatory. The begging ritual, taken up by nonindigents and by children, involved the recitation of a souling rhyme, which typically requested "mercy on all Christian souls for a soul cake." Some writers have found in this custom a link between the ghostly repasts of pre-Christian days and the candy begging of the modern era. The conjecture is lent weight by a twentieth-century British survival: the traditional soulmass cake prepared for the November custom is an oatmeal and molasses treat now eaten at Halloween.[6]

"A PENNY FOR THE GUY"

In commemoration of Guy Fawkes's abortive attempt to blow up the Houses of Parliament on 5 November 1605, English children have for centuries built bonfires, dressed rag effigies (and sometimes themselves) as tatterdemalion "Guys," and begged money from strangers to purchase fireworks. Although Guy Fawkes Day itself clearly postdates Halloween, the juvenile custom of begging "a penny for the Guy" could have influenced the older holiday's ritual pattern, so that masked solicitation informs both holidays in the modern era. Their calendrical proximity supports the notion of a seasonal "fusion," and although a direct line to American trick-or-treating cannot be traced, North Americans did celebrate Guy Fawkes Day in colonial times.[7]

SAINT COLUMBA

The sixth-century missionary Columba, or Columkille, founded the monastery of Iona off the Scottish coast and was partly responsible for the conversion of the Picts. Some sources say that Irish peasants begged alms in his name ten centuries after his death, on the same day that English villagers asked for soul cakes. Masking, evidently, did not figure in here, and again the trail cannot be found after the famine migrations. Thus, however widespread the custom may have been in the seventeenth century, the link to modern trick or treat is no better than Samhain's.[8]

Lesser candidates also present themselves. The Christmas guisers of southern Poland, the traditional "false-face" beggars of the Swiss Alps, German soul cakers, the *schnorers* of Central European Jewish tradition, British mummers and hobby horse impersonators, Irish straw boys—all of these European "masked ritual solicitors" structurally resemble contemporary trick or treaters. Any one of them might have lent a brushstroke to the tableau of the Halloween ritual in North America.[9]

The same may be said of an indigenous begging custom that was observed, well into this century, in New York City. Beginning in the middle of the nineteenth century, children dressed in costume on Thanksgiving Day and asked for pennies from grown-ups on the city streets. Whether they wore fancy dress or tatters, the common term for these ritual indigents was *ragamuffins*. Because of their terminological and sartorial similarity to British guisers, Appelbaum takes them as descendants of the Guy Fawkes urchins. The more patriotic-minded Lillian Eichler sees them as reflections of the Indians at the Pilgrim Thanksgiving. Whatever their provenance, the ragamuffins enlivened New York Thanksgivings into the 1930s, and thus may stand as the most plausible "missing link" between European solicitation customs and trick or treat. It is of particular interest that the ragamuffin begging formula—"anything for Thanksgiving?"—clearly parallels the modern child's "anything for Halloween?"[10]

As Eichler's chauvinistic conjecture suggests, which begging performance you choose as a point of origin for the American custom may depend as much on nationalist bias and intellectual fashion as on an examination of the indistinct record. Phillipe Aries, for example, discusses an old French festival called the *masquerade of the cherubim,* in which young people wore festive garments at the beginning of November. All Souls' Day has pushed it from the calendar, he says, but it has survived in North America as Halloween. That such Gallocentric stretching would do credit to Gumbi seems obvious. But given the "forks and sideroads" in the record, it may be no more reasonable to opt for Samhain or souling, Guy Fawkes or New York ragamuffins, as a single source.[11]

Seeking any single source, indeed, may be fruitless. Customs are created, I would suggest, not tree fashion, but river fashion—out of constantly shifting tributaries rather than taproots. Especially in an ethnically hybrid society such as the United States, holidays conflate past and recent practices: they fuse vestiges and innovations, ancient paradigms and local variations, into "models" that are always still evolving. Hence, the modern Thanksgiving is not simply a Puritan feast. It is Puritans plus Sarah Josepha Hale and the Butterball trademark and football and (in some Italian families) lasagna as a traditional side dish. The European May Day is not merely a fertility survival. It is that plus the Haymarket bombing and Communist rallies and red carnations—all of which resonate with meaning for current participants.

The English Halloween illustrates this process with particular clarity. Many writers have remarked that in Britain, Guy Fawkes Day and Halloween have become "entangled." Bonfires and begging now characterize both celebrations; "guying" and guising" have so fused that some revelers beg "a penny for the Gueyeer"; and prank-filled Mischief Night, mysteriously transferred from 30 April in the nineteenth century, is celebrated variously on Halloween and 4 November. Ervin Beck even claims that the children involved see not two discrete holidays but "a single, more or less coherent, season of events." What has evolved, evidently, is a ritual complex that incorporates elements of older, distinct celebrations into something new. The same process very likely underlay the evolution of the North American trick or treat.[12]

Romantic agonizing aside, this process need not be seen as devolutionary. Halloween itself has often been described as "degenerate," but as lived reality, it is nothing of the kind. Trick or treat is no more a degenerate Samhain custom than the singing of the Internationale is a degenerate Maypole rite or an adult is a degenerate child. Therefore, especially in hybrid America, where customs are continually affected by immigration and ethnic "boundary negotiation," the best course of inquiry may be to acknowledge a complex origin and turn to the custom's function within its society. Such an inquiry might profitably begin with recent history, to show how the tradition has evolved within changing social contexts.

Growing a Tradition

Whatever its parallels to Samhain or Guy Fawkes Day, trick or treat, as we know it today, clearly grew out of more recent, and readily identifiable, social conditions. The custom evolved, I will suggest in this section, as a response to two forms of social tension: the boyish vandalism of the nineteenth century Halloween and the social turmoil of the Great Depression. To both disruptions, trick or treat provided a corrective, one that—perhaps ironically, perhaps predictably—ceremonialized rather than resolved the implicit tensions.

In a 1939 story in *American Home,* Doris Moss mentions the "age-old Halloween salutation Trick or Treat," but older sources do not endorse this characterization. There may of course have been isolated instances of trick or treat–type activities in the nineteenth century, but neither magazine articles, greeting-card illustrations, nor memoirs from this century's opening decades suggest that the custom was conventionally established by that time. Witches, black cats, jack-o'-lanterns, ghosts—all of these icons figure frequently as part of the "traditional" holiday decor. Costume parties are mentioned frequently, as are divination rituals, apple bobbing, nut roasting, bonfires, and boyish pranks. But neither the phrase "trick or treat" nor the ritual linkage of threat and reward becomes widely known before the 1930s. The Merriam-Webster Company's files do not show the term in use until 1941, when it was the title of a poem in the *Saturday Evening Post;* that same year, a *Life* story on Halloween traditions fails to give a nod to trick or treat; and Catherine Ainsworth did not hear the expression until 1955.[13]

To judge from frequency of citation, the most popular amusements of the nineteenth-century American Halloween were Irish imports: private divination rituals and public mayhem. Not surprisingly, participation reflected stereotyped gender roles. Girls resorted to spells and magic to get glimpses of their future husbands; boys played the devil with private property, threatening domestic order with as much vitality as their sisters spent keeping it together. Walter Prichard Eaton, reminiscing on his own midcentury boyhood, wrote that "apple bobbing and trips down cellar with a lighted candle and a mirror to see your future spouse were all very well for girls and 'dress up' parties. But they weren't the essence of Halloween. The essence was robbery, destruction, arson." To see how this "essence" was transformed by trick or treat, let's look more closely at those boyish "tricks."[14]

Victor Turner and Jack Santino have discussed Halloween usefully as an exploration of liminality, and most of the destruction visited on nineteenth-century householders by Halloween pranksters may be seen as an attack on domestic borders. The majority of popular pranks were "threshold tricks" that assaulted, if only temporarily, ordered space. Gates and fences were removed, windows were soaped or rattled with "tick tacks," bells were stuck ringing, and doors were tied shut. Buggies, which provided cohesion to far-flung rural communities, were "dysfunctionalized" by being placed on barn roofs. Even the popular custom of tipping over outhouses served metonymically as an attack on the house-as-home.[15]

Throughout the nineteenth century, such mayhem was at least tolerated, if not encouraged, by adults who had played the same game themselves, and who recalled the pleasant fiction—imported from Ireland and Scotland—that such rambunctiousness was the work of "witches" and "goblins." William Walsh, in his 1897 compilation of popular customs, bemoans the American Halloweeners' "spirit of rowdyism," but few Americans seemed to share his concern. Even those who spoke of children "utterly terrorizing" their home towns reflected that modest vandalism was an acceptable part of the domestic pattern. As Roger Abrahams and Richard

Bauman have remarked, such "inversive" behavior may even have served to intensify rather than disrupt social harmony. Ritually controlled, the Other vindicates the common order.[16]

However, as urbanism increased the opportunity for anonymous mayhem and householders became more nervous about its potential, the traditional forgiving attitude began to change. Catherine Ainsworth recalled it was in the 1930s that childish "goblins" first started to smash porch jack-o'-lanterns, and Dorothy Barclay observed that Halloween got "out of hand" about the time that the population "moved to town." Margaret Mead provides a gloss on such recollections by distinguishing between the "self-policed" pranks of rural children and the "angry destructiveness" visited by "alienated youngsters" on "strangers and the unidentified people who run things." The observation complements that of Abrahams and Bauman and may help to explain why in the 1920s and 1930s, with class distinctions and urban anomie on the rise, the high spirits of the old Halloween are seen as suspect.[17]

An early sign of a new hard line toward border ruffians appeared in the Chicago school system in 1925. Repelled by "extreme rudeness" and a growing disrespect for private property, school officials sought to encourage "citizenship" by asking pupils to pledge respect for all citizens—especially, although presumably not exclusively, the city's taxpayers. "If I promise to protect all these people," an official pledge read, "and within 24 hours of making my promise, I annoy and injure them through interference with their rights, I am a liar, I am a traitor, I am, myself, a Benedict Arnold on a small and contemptible scale." In cooperation with the police, who reported those who "forgot their citizenship on Halloween," school officials claimed good results, although the pledge concept failed to take hold nationally.[18]

More successful as a national strategy against vandalism was the adoption of small-town fairs and community carnivals. To combat what was commonly identified as "the Halloween problem," local governments and business groups in the 1930s provided entertainments that were designed, in the words of one Long Island community, to "foster a carnival spirit within bounds of decency." The magazines *Playground* and *Recreation* carried regular October features on managed fun, explaining how various communities had solved their Halloween problem and urging readers to follow their salvific leads. With the fervor and predictability of conversion testimonials, the articles described the excesses of undirected energy, presented cures (games, contests, costume parties), and held up the happy results: "Everyone has a glorious time and there is a complete absence of rowdyism." In the spirit of enlightened self-interest, merchant groups cheerfully sponsored these affairs, secure in the knowledge that a teenager competing in a tug-of-war was a teenager, at least for the moment, not soaping windows.[19]

The sublimating process I am describing—a sanitization of the anarchic—has continued throughout the century, as the spiritual nature of All Hallows has given way to purely secular entertainments, as the holiday has become simultaneously commercialized and infantilized, and as rowdyism has found more sociopathic outlets that the occasional displaced gate or broken window. A more recent manifestation of the sanitizing process, for example, occurred just after the end of World War II, when merchants offered their windows as "art" surfaces to prevent them from being defiled with wax or soap. The "civilized" witches-on-glass of today's American cities testify to the ongoing effectiveness of such cooptation.[20]

Less well recognized is the fact that trick or treat, which seems so much a "child-directed" phenomenon, displays evidence of this same rationalizing impulse. Those who observed the custom in its infancy often drew attention to this fact. Recalling her Depression childhood, Lois Hudson remarked ruefully that in 1935, nobody in Cleveland, North Dakota, had ever heard of trick or treat. Calling it an "apologetic form of annoying neighbors," she twits children of the 1950s for having "sold their rights to rebellion for some sugar in expensive wrappings." Doris Moss, writing in 1939, recommends inviting potential window-soapers in for cider and doughnuts, quite consciously as a way of redirecting their energies. It seems clear that this quintessentially "child-directed" pursuit, no less than window painting or Halloween festivals, serves the adult need to harness, and thus control, the Other.[21]

That this should have occurred in the 1930s will surprise no one who recalls the disruptions of that period. A custom that successfully transmutes "anarchy" (the term is Lois Hudson's) into an appreciation of confectionery consolations does more than merely rewrite the rules of a game. It transforms the destructive "essence" of the holiday into disciplined "fun." It disguises public disorder by making it a semiprivate ritual—by making it, after the standard formula of American holidays, commercial in intent and infantile in appearance. At the same time, it teaches good capitalist values—specifically, the value of consumption—at a historical moment when the urge to accumulate is in jeopardy. By offering to "buy off" potential tricksters with candy treats, homemakers like Doris Moss succeeded in delegitimizing mischief, commodifying the exotic, and—not least of all—marginalizing social "anarchy" as beyond the rules.[22]

The "point of origin" here is admittedly imprecise. Like most holidays, Halloween combines hieratic, or "top-down," elements with demonic, or "bottom-up" ones, and the former are always easier to trace that the latter. We can say confidently that Pope Gregory III established the November date of All Saints' Day in the eighth century and that Labor Day was an 1894 invention of the United States Congress. We cannot confidently say "Doris Moss invented trick or treat in October of 1939." What we can say is that she and other 1930s homemakers offered treats to costumed children at Halloween, that they saw this custom as a defense against violence, and that trick or treat has gradually replaced buggy stealing as the "appropriate" way for children to enjoy the holiday. That some young atavists persist, even today, in soaping windows means only that the sanitizing process here, as elsewhere, is incomplete.

Perhaps not coincidentally, New York's ragamuffins disappeared at about the same time that trick or treat became established. Noting that the Thanksgiving custom had long been denounced by reformers who objected to children being "taught to beg," Appelbaum suggests that it succumbed, in the 1930s, to "hard times." Perhaps it reemerged—trailing clouds of Guy Fawkes, Druids, and St. Columba—at a festival with a contrary festive impulse. If begging was deemed inappropriate at a national holiday celebrating plenty, it might be seen as perfectly suited for Halloween, which had always provided an arena for controlled resentment. In the 1930s, that resentment was highly visible. Trick or treat, by shifting and reformalizing its ludic focus, may have served the social function of sapping its strength. Certainly, by the postwar period, its strength was sapped: the children in Gregory Stone's 1950 sample of trick-or-treaters had no idea what "tricks" they were supposed to perform; the promise of candy had made the threat a distant memory.[23]

Contexts, 1940–1990

Trick or treat arises in urbanizing, polyethnic America in the period between the two world wars. I have suggested that the "Other" that the custom originally mediated was related to the social tensions of that period. But the custom has not sat still; it has continued to evolve in the past fifty years, and it is to be expected that its permutations in this period would also have responded to changing social conditions. A look at the normative ritual from about 1940 to the present shows this to be true.

Consider the children's costumes. According to defenders of the survivalist thesis, "ancestral" trick-or-treaters dressed as ghosts, witches, goblins, and other figures meant to dramatize the hidden fears and unresolved tensions of medieval culture. Dressing as these religious outlaws was still popular in the 1930s, and indeed has remained a mainstay of Halloween costuming into the present. But nonreligious fright figures—purely social outlaws—have also long been elements in the ritual iconography.

In the late 1940s, when I first rang New Jersey doorbells in search of candy, supernaturals shared sidewalk space with a cadre of quite natural, and yet no less threatening, social outcasts. Boys "dressed down" in the blackface of the burglar, the rags and satchel of the hobo, the feathers and paint of the "wild" Indian, or the eyepatch and cutlass of the pirate. The cowboys had no interest in cows: the iconographic center of their "good guy" outfits was the deadly six gun. Girls, who had not yet read Betty Friedan, were more conservative in their self-presentations, with witches vying most frequently with fairy princesses. Stereotypical gypsy garments, however, attested to some girls' fascination with a fashionable underclass, and both genders copied the clown— that modern fool who, like his medieval counterpart, mediates rebellion.[24]

The social point is obvious. When the children of Depression parents played at trick or treat, most of them disguised themselves (or, to be more accurate in many cases, *had* themselves disguised) as social and economic outcasts. In the 1940s and 1950s, such costumes would have reminded householders of the troubles they had only recently escaped, and which they might avoid in the future by a combination of apotropaic mimicry and appropriate bribes. Parents who dressed their children as bums were doubtless unaware of such sympathetic magical vibrations. Yet willy-nilly their particular "threshold tricksters," their social "Others," reflected the times.

So too, with formulaic precision, did the ritual visit. Women's magazines, counseling homemakers on how to deal with masked visitors, stipulated inviting the children inside, and rewarding them with home-baked goods after guessing their names. Site and liturgy were strictly defined. Masked representatives of the Other sought admittance to domestic space; feigning terror, the householder complied; after some obligatory guessing of names, the maskers were revealed as not goblins or tramps after all, but Bonnie and Tim from down the street. They were then treated to cider and doughnuts and sent on their way. The normative ritual was one of "incorporation," where what Brian Sutton-Smith says about the children actors also applied, no less comfortingly, to the indulgent adults: "Despite all the evil things and fears you may harbor, they are really nice people. The world may appear nasty, but it is really nice," filled with folks who would give you a meal if you needed one.[25]

A Pennsylvania researcher found in 1966 that this pattern still hung on in some areas: homemade goods were giving way to store-bought ones, but the unmasking and the living room snack were still at least a regional norm. At the same time, however, suburbanization was helping to create a more diffuse social environment, and the trick-or-treat visit was gradually evolving into "hit and run." In the 1970s, stories of kidnappings and razor-embedded apples transformed the symbolic seasonal fears into real ones, further intensifying the holiday's drift toward impersonal contact. By the 1980s, the normative ritual had changed significantly.[26]

Ritual costuming, to begin with the obvious, became more varied—and far more linked than in previous decades to "celebrity status." Black cats, ghosts, and sundry monsters still made their way through the dark, but the focus on celluloid heroes that had begun in the 1950s with Disney's Tinker Bell and Davy Crockett had by the 1980s reached exotic proportions. A 1988 poll found that the most popular purchased disguise was Freddy Krueger, the villain of a string of "slasher" movies. Following Freddy in the top ten were the Madison Avenue creatures Spuds McKenzie and the California Raisins; the television "witch" Elvira; Freddy's box-office rival Jason; and the extraterrestrial prime-time star Alf. The only actual persons figuring in the top ten—various political characters and Jim and Tammy Bakker—might also be seen as electronic creations. The image of the Other, by the 1980s, was thus doubly "mediated."[27]

The begging ritual itself also changed. Rather than being invited in for homemade treats, costumed children now typically waited on the porch or doorstep, stuck in liminal space, while the host or hostess brought their goodies to the door. It was one thing to have Bonnie and Tim in for doughnuts, quite another to open one's door to a gaggle of strangers—the typical tricksters of a mobile society and sprawling exurbias. Thus, the guessing game was largely dropped, and the masks stayed on. A sociological assessment that would have seemed outrageous in 1950 sounds quite accurate today: with the quick distribution of individual treats—"something that could never be part of a meal"—the ritual reflects isolation and anonymity.[28]

In comparing the 1940s and 1980s versions of trick or treat, three elements stand out as most significant. First, although costumes still advertise the Other, it is an Other transmuted by, and in many cases subdued by, "personal expression." John McDowell found, in a 1984 study of college students, that originality and cleverness were highly prized in the selection of disguises because "costuming, a representation of the other, was clearly perceived as an extension, even a revelation, of the self." Hence, those who presented themselves as "positive" characters tended to choose not types (like the old "pirate" or "clown") but specific, recognizable individuals: Marilyn Monroe, the Blues Brothers, Ronald Reagan. Those who "dressed down" sought idiosyncratic, self-consciously shocking expressions of the "outlawed": fraternities and sororities hosted "Whores and Pimps" parties, and the more daring revelers outfitted themselves as Tylenol capsules, douches, sperm cells, bongs, tampons, and bathroom walls. Although young children, predictably, do not achieve this level of adolescent lubricity, their play acting also embodies "self" expression to a greater degree than in previous generations. Recent Halloween visitors to my door have included rock stars, cartoon superheroes, and a Rubik's Cube.[29]

Second, the presentation of the self is heavily influenced, even dictated, by media fashions. To be sure, this is not a recent development; it was well under way in the 1950s, thanks to Walt Disney. But the difference in the range of choices is, I think, remarkable. Ironically, today's media saturation obviates even as it inspires individual creativity, leading to Halloweens that resemble back lots of B-film studios. Given the alacrity with which costume companies follow the studios' lead, the child may now appear as Princess Leia or Darth Vader, a Gummi Bear or a Mutant Ninja Turtle, within months of the character's screen debut. Jay Mechling, in writing about the theatrical games of a Boy Scout summer camp, has observed the recent incorporation of television ensembles (the Gilligan's Island shipwrecks, the crew of Star Trek) into camper "scripts." A similar mediation has topicalized Halloween.[30]

Third, the masked solicitation ritual, which in the 1940s led to snacks with the neighbors, has become so transformed by the art of manufacture that it now generally endorses mass production and commodity fetishism. Not only are the treats and the costumes both store bought, but the exchange relation that the ritual's actors model has itself become commodified, like the "let's get on with it" formality of fast-food purchasing.

Gregory Stone noted thirty years ago that trick-or-treaters canvassed their neighborhoods as model consumers—docile, unreflective, and happily aggrandizing. They are not rewarded, he claimed, for producing. He was, I think, half right. Certainly, consumption is the root "lesson" of trick or treat. But the consumers *do* work for their "purchases." As McDowell's study showed, they work feverishly to outdo their peers, and in fact their very presentations of themselves, neatly packaged, may be seen as "production." Trick-or-treaters are their own best products, and like other products, they must bid for consumers' attention.[31]

The direction of this attention, it should be noted, is not toward the general enhancement of community harmony. In a fine analysis, Thomas Vennum shows the Ojibwa begging dance, in which young men mimic the begging of dogs to elicit gifts of food from their neighbors, to be a ritual of redistribution, celebrating sharing as essential to community health and providing sanctions for those who refuse to endorse this value. Modern America's trick or treat ritual, in spite of UNICEF's modestly successful efforts to communalize it, typically endorses a contrary economic ethos. Packaging themselves *in* and *as* manufactured products, children offer themselves, door to door, as both market options and competitors for householders' scarce resources. At the same time, the ritual's capture by the candy and costume industries ensures that the children's image vending will help grow the economy. Far from encouraging communalism or redistribution, the ritual certifies, and even models, competitive vigor: the successful trick-or-treater is a budding entrepreneur, whose packaging and legwork have provided personal income. Ervin Beck is on the mark when he describes the ritual as a symbolic exercise in "making a living."[32]

Two recent developments underline this point. One is the frequent appearance, in all media, of trick-or-treating guidelines. Responding to parental anxieties about razor-studded or cyanide-poisoned apples, Halloween "experts" urge costumed children to exercise caution. They must travel in groups, visit only people they know, and eat no treat that has not been wrapped. Best and Horiuchi call such caution "an annual reminder of the fragility of the social bond." But an economic lesson is also being conveyed. In accepting only "wrapped" treats, children are doing more than protecting themselves; they are implicitly confirming the message that "reliable" products are packaged by "established" companies, such as Hershey and Mars. As reasonable as such finickiness may appear, it also exacerbates, rather than ameliorates, social "dis-bonding," by delegitimizing homemade treats such as cookies and fruit and requiring that merchants profit from the custom. The Mars Company has recently ratcheted this commodification process one notch higher, by offering a coupon for M&M's in Hallmark greeting cards.[33]

The second development, also a Hallmark contribution, is the production of trick or treat cards with slots for coins—to be filled by the costumed accumulators as they make their rounds. A typical card shows a grinning jack-o'-lantern, its eyes and teeth ready to receive dimes. Here we find the ultimate rationalized depersonalization of a bonding custom—and further evidence that evolving traditions reflect their milieu. In a society where eternal damnation is the ultimate Other, ritual begging takes the form of cakes and prayer. Where inequality is a social evil, solicitation exalts the generous and demeans the hoarder. Where value is monetary and commodities rule, the games of children model capitalist designs. Thus, trick or treat, no less than soul caking or the Ojibwa begging dance, reveals a truth that unites functionalist and symbolic perspectives: Each culture begets the customs it requires.

Notes

1. For tracings of trick or treat to Samhain see, for example, Ralph and Adelin Linton, *Halloween through Twenty Centuries* (New York: Henry Schuman, 1950), 102–3; Joseph D. Clark, "All Saints' Day and Halloween," *North Carolina Folklore* 20 (Aug. 1972): 133; John W. Howe, "What Is Happy About Halloween?" *Christianity Today* 22 (21 Oct. 1977): 16; Jane Hatch, ed., *The American Book of Days*, 3d ed. (New York: H. W. Wilson, 1978), 968–71; Jack Santino, "Halloween in America: Contemporary Customs and Performances," *Western Folklore* 42 (1983): 5; and "Night of the Wandering Souls," *Natural History* 92 (Oct. 1983): 47. The Lintons and Hatch both mention Muck Olla, who appears originally in W. G. Wood-Martin, *Traces of the Elder Faiths of Ireland* (London: Longmans, Green, 1902), vol. 2: 268.

2. For the Irish tradition of food left for the dead, see James Mooney, "Holiday Customs of Ireland," *Proceedings of the American Philosophical Society* 26 (1889): 411; Seán Ó'Súilleabháin, *A Handbook of Irish Folklore* (1942; rpt. Detroit: Singing Tree Press, 1970), 345; E. Estyn Evans, *Irish Folk Ways* (New York: Devin-Adair, 1957), 277; Alwyn and Brinley Rees, *Celtic Heritage: Ancient Tradition in Ireland and Wales* (London: Thames & Hudson, 1961), 90. Cf. the Breton tradition of leaving a pancake supper for the "souls," cited in Ruth Edna Kelley, *The Book of Halloween* (Boston: Lothrop, Lee, & Shepard, 1919), 116. Santino's Nera connection appears in "Halloween in America," 5. Wood-Martin, *Traces of the Elder Faiths of Ireland* 2: 268 Celtic sources notably silent on masked begging include Mooney, "Holiday Customs"; Marie Sjoestedt-Jonval, *Dieux et heros des celtes* (Paris: Lerous, 1940); Anne Ross, *Pagan Celtic Britain* (London: Routledge & Kegan Paul, 1967); Stuart Piggott, *The Druids* (New York: Praeger, 1968); and Proinsias MacCana, *Celtic Mythology* (New York: Peter Bedrick, 1985).

3. E. C. Cawte, *Ritual Animal Disguise: A Historical and Geographical Study of Animal Disguise in the British Isles* (Totowa, N.J.: Rowman & Littlefield for the Folklore Society, 1978), 215. Santino, "Halloween in America," 5.

4. Thomas Vennum, Jr., "The Ojibwa Begging Dance," in *Music and Context: Essays for John M. Ward*, ed. Anne Dhu Shapiro (Cambridge, Mass.: Harvard Univ. Dept. of Music, 1985), 54.

5. For Native American begging rituals, see Elsie Clews Parson and Ralph Beals, "The Sacred Clowns of the Pueblo and May-Yacqui Indians" *American Anthropologist* 36, n.s. (Oct.–Dec. 1934): 491–514; Harold Blau, "Function and the False Faces," *Journal of American Folklore* 79 (Oct.–Dec. 1966): 564-80; Vennum, "The Ojibwa Begging Dance," 54; and William N. Fenton, *The False Faces of the Iroquois* (Norman: Univ. of Oklahoma Press, 1987), 447–48.

6. Soul cakes and souling at Hallowtide were described two centuries ago by the English antiquarian John Brand, who recalls Shakespeare's Speed, in *Two Gentlemen of Vernoa*, likening Valentine to "a beggar at Hallowmas." See the ex-

panded edition of his *Popular Antiquities of Great Britain,* ed. W. Carew Hazlitt (London: John Russell Smith, 1870), 216–20. See also Christina Hole, *English Custom and Usage* (New York: Scribner's, 1942), 10–12; Peter and Iona Opie, *The Language and Lore of Schoolchildren* (Oxford: Clarendon Press, 1959), 275–76; and Maggie Black, "Saints and Soul-Caking," *History Today* 31 (Nov. 1981): 60. For modern survivals of soul caking, see Homer Sykes, *Once a Year: Some Traditional British Customs* (London: Gordon Fraser, 1977), 130 and 144.

7.   Virtually every writer on Halloween notes the holiday's similarity to Guy Fawkes Day. For the pair's entanglement, see note 12.

8.   Hazlitt, *Popular Antiquities,* 219–20; and Mooney, "Holiday Customs," 407. Interestingly, one of the earliest published records of American trick or treat mentions the Columba connection. See George William Douglas, *The American Book of Days* (New York: H. W. Wilson, 1937).

9.   For Polish guisers, see B. Bazielichowna and S. Deptuszewski, "The Guisers of Koniakow," *Folk-Lore* 68 (Dec. 1957): 497; and B. Bazielichowna, "Further Notes on the Polish Guisers," *Folk-Lore* 69 (Dec. 1958): 254–61. Swiss Alpine beggars are described in Fenton, *False Faces,* 496, and in C. Hansmann, *Masken Schemen Larven: Volksmasken der Alpenlander* (Munich: F. Bruckmann, 1959). I am indebted to one of the University of Tennessee Press's anonymous readers for noting that *schnoring* was practiced in New York in the 1920s; see also Leo Rosten, "The Schnorrer: A Study in Piety and Paradox," in *Next Year in Jerusalem,* ed. Douglas Villiers (New York: Viking, 1976). An excellent source for the hobby horse phenomenon is Cawte, *Ritual Animal Disguise.* The literature on mumming is vast, but see particularly E. K. Chambers, *The English Folk-Play* (Oxford: Clarendon, 1933); Herbert Halpert and G. M. Story, eds., *Christmas Mumming in Newfoundland* (Toronto: Univ. of Toronto Press, 1968); Richard Bauman, "Belsnickling in a Nova Scotia Island Community," *Western Folklore* 31, no. 4 (Oct. 1972); and, for Irish variants including the "straw boy" custom, Henry Glassie, *All Silver and No Brass: An Irish Christmas Mumming* (Bloomington: Indiana Univ. Press, 1975). For structurally related British "collection performances," see Sykes, *Once a Year.*

10.   Diana Karter Appelbaum, *Thanksgiving: An American Holiday, An American History* (New York: Facts on File, 1984), 186–93; Lillian Eichler, *The Customs of Mankind* (Garden City, N.J.: Doubleday, Doran & Company, 1924), 445.

11.   Phillippe Aries, *Centuries of Childhood: A Social History of Family Life* (New York: Knopf, 1962), 78.

12.   For the fusion of the two holidays, see Peter and Iona Opie, *Language and Lore,* 269–83; Christina Hole, *British Folk Customs* (London: Hutchinson, 1976), 91; Maggie Black, "Saints and Soul-Caking," 60; and especially Ervin Beck, "Trickster on the Threshold: An Interpretation of Children's Autumn Traditions," *Folk-Lore* 96, no. 1 (1985): 24–28.

13.   The "age-old" salutation is mentioned in Doris Hudson Moss, "A Victim of the Window-Soaping Brigade," *American Home* 22 (Nov. 1939): 48. For traditional

Halloween entertainments, see William Sharp, "Halloween: A Threefold Chronicle," *Harper's Magazine* 73 (Nov. 1886): 842–56; Helen Philbrook Patten, *The Year's Festivals* (Boston: Dana Estes, 1903); Isabel Gordon Curtis, "A Child's Celebration of Halloween," *St. Nicholas* 32 (Oct. 1905): 1124–27; Catherine Heath, "Hallowe'en Tricks and Fortunes," *Delineator* 78 (Oct. 1911): 312; "Quaint Halloween Customs," *Harper's Bazaar* 46 (Nov. 1912): 578; Ruth Edna Kelley, *The Book of Halloween* (Boston: Lothrop, Lee, & Shepard, 1919); and these memoirs of nineteenth-century childhoods: Walter O'Meara, *We Made It Through the Winter* (St. Paul: Minnesota Historical Society, 1974) and Alvin Schwartz, ed., *When I Grew Up Long Ago* (Philadelphia: Lippincott, 1978), 127–30. None of these sources mentions trick-or-treating, nor is it depicted on any of the turn-of-the-century Halloween greeting cards shown in Roy Nuhn, "Portfolio: Ellen Clapsaddle," *American History Illustrated* 17 (Oct. 1982): 30–33. The Merriam-Webster file date was supplied by their research department; the poem is Ethel Jacobson, "Trick or Treat," *Saturday Evening Post*, 1 Nov. 1941, 75. The *Life* article is "Halloween: Pranks and Pumpkins Are Traditional," 3 Nov. 1941, 69–70. Catherine Ainsworth, "Hallowe'en," *New York Folklore Quarterly* 39, no. 3 (Sept. 1973): 164.

    14. For the Irish background to Halloween divination and mischief, see Mooney, "Holiday Customs," 407–9; Rees and Rees, *Celtic Heritage,* 92; Ó'Súilleabháin, *Handbook,* 345; Evans, *Irish Folk Ways,* 277; Jeanne Cooper Foster, *Ulster Folklore* (Belfast: H. R. Carter, 1951), 27–28; and Helen Sewell Johnson, "November Eve Beliefs and Customs in Irish Life and Literature," *Journal of American Folklore* 81, no. 320 (1968): 134–35. Walter Prichard Eaton, "Pungkins," *Outing* 61 (Oct. 1912): 33.

    15. Victor Turner, *The Ritual Process* (Chicago: Aldine, 1969), 95–96, 172–83; Santino, "Halloween in America." On "border disruption" pranks, see Kelley, *Halloween;* Bellamy Partridge and Otto Bettmann, *As We Were: Family Life in America 1850–1900* (New York: McGraw-Hill, 1946), 24; O'Meara, *We Made It Through;* Stephen Sears, Murray Belsky, and Douglas Tunstell, *Hometown U.S.A.* (New York: American Heritage, 1975); and Schwartz, *When I Grew Up,* 127–30.

    16. William Walsh, *Curiosities of Popular Customs* (1897; rpt. Philadelphia: Lippincott, 1925), 511. Roger Abrahams and Richard Bauman, "Ranges of Festival Behavior," in *The Reversible World,* ed. Barbara Babcock (Ithaca: Cornell Univ. Press, 1978), 206–7.

    17. Ainsworth, "Hallowe'en," 165. Dorothy Barclay, "Halloween Fun Without Deviltry," *New York Times Magazine,* 15 Oct. 1950, 40. Margaret Mead, "Halloween: Where Has All the Mischief Gone?" *Redbook* 145 (Oct. 1975): 31–34.

    18. "The Teaching of Citizenship and Halloween Pranks in Chicago," *School and Society* 22 (7 Nov. 1925): 585–86.

    19. The "bounds of decency" directive is described in Rex Cate, "Halloween in Manhasset," *Recreation* 33 (Oct. 1939): 409–10. See also, for example, Era Betzner, "A Ghostly Gambol for Halloween," *Playground* 21 (Sept. 1927): 334–37;

"When the Goblins Are About," *Playground* 24 (Oct. 1930): 395–98; "A National Occasion for Merrymaking," *American City* (Oct. 1930), rpt. in *Hallowe'en,* ed. Robert Haven Schauffler (New York: Dodd, Mead, 1933), 8; Virginia Settle, "An Effective Substitute for Hallowe'en Deviltry," *School and Society* 44 (24 Oct. 1936): 541–43; "Prescriptions for Halloween Hoodlums," *Recreation* 32 (Oct. 1938): 385–87; "Hallowe'en Damage Disappears with City Celebrations," *American City* 56 (Oct. 1941): 99. For similar civic "rationalizations" of carnival-like behavior, see Charles E. Welch, Jr., "Some Early Phases of the Philadelphia Mummers' Parade, *Pennsylvania Folklife* 9 (Winter 1957–58): 25–26; and Keith Walden, "Respectable Hooligans: Male Toronto Students Celebrate Hallowe'en, 1884–1910," *Canadian Historical Review* 68, no. 1 (1987): 25–27.

20.   Barre, Vermont, was among the first, if not the first, municipality in which downtown merchants encouraged window painting as a substitute for soaping: Joseph Brislin, "Solving a Halloween Problem," *Recreation* 42 (Oct. 1948): 302. Sparked by Lions, Rotarians, and other business professionals, countless towns followed Barre's lead. See "Windows Bloom on Globlin Night," *Recreation* 44 (Oct. 1950): 261; "Here's Halloween," *Women's Home Companion* 77 (Oct. 1950): 161–66; Barclay, "Halloween Fun without Deviltry," 40; and "Jersey Says No Soap to Halloween," *Life,* 27 Oct. 1952, 64.

21.   The term "child-directed" is in Ainsworth, "Hallowe'en," 163. Lois Phillips Hudson, "The Buggy on the Roof," *Atlantic* 210 (Nov. 1962): 98. Doris Hudson Moss, "A Victim," 48.

22.   Hudson, "The Buggy on the Roof," 98.

23.   Appelbaum, *Thanksgiving,* 193. Gregory Stone, "Halloween and the Mass Child," *American Quarterly* 11, no. 3 (Fall 1959): 372–79. I do not suggest that the sanitizing process Stone describes was absolute. In the 1950s, trick or treat frequently became trick *and* treat, as a designated "Mischief Night" preceded Halloween by one day. Subsequent decades provide other examples of the "returned repressed."

24.   For the clown as a mediator of disorder, see William Willeford, *The Fool and His Scepter* (Evanston, Ill.: Northwestern Univ. Press, 1969).

25.   For guidelines on hosting Halloween visitors, see Priscilla Gardner, "Goblins Are Gormands," *Better Homes and Garden* (Oct. 1937): 150; and Louise Bell and Stella McKay, "Trick or Treat—and Happy Looting," *American Home* 38 (Oct. 1947): 150. Brian Sutton-Smith, "What Happened to Halloween?" *Parents* (Oct. 1983): 64.

26.   For the Pennsylvania study, see M. Mook, "Halloween in Central Pennsylvania," *Keystone Folklore Quarterly* 14 (1969): 124–29. For the "razor in the apple" motif, a 1970s urban legend, see Joel Best and Gerald T. Horiuchi, "The Razor Blade in the Apple: The Social Construction of Urban Legends," *Social Problems* 32, no. 5 (June 1985): 488–99.

27.   "Halloween at the Polls," *U.S. News & World Report* 105 (31 Oct. 1988): 82. As of 1988, movies featuring Freddy Krueger (*Nightmare on Elm Street*), Jason

(*Friday the 13th*), Michael Myers (*Halloween*), and Leatherface (*The Texas Chainsaw Massacre*), had grossed a total of more than $500 million. "Horrors," *People* 30 (7 Nov. 1988): 189.

28. The "sociological assessment" is Theodore Caplow, Howard Bahr, Bruce Chadwick, Reubin Hill, and Margaret Holmes Williamson, *Middletown Families* (Minneapolis: Univ. of Minnesota Press, 1982), 232.

29. John McDowell, "Halloween Costuming among Young Adults in Bloomington, Indiana: A Local Exotic," *Indiana Folklore and Oral History* 14, no. 1 (1985): 1–18.

30. Jay Mechling, "Mass Media and Traditional Play at a Boy Scout Camp" (n.p.). Cf. Blau, "Function and the False Faces," 569–70, citing an "acculturative rite" among the Onondaga in which children parody false faces with Disney costumes.

31. Gregory Stone, "Halloween and the Mass Child," 372–79. McDowell, "Halloween Costuming," 2–9.

32. Vennum, "Ojibwa Begging Dance," 77–78. Beck, "Trickster on the Threshold," 26.

33. Best and Horiuchi, "Razor Blade in the Apple," 497.

References

Abrahams, Roger, and Richard Bauman. 1978. "Ranges of Festival Behavior." In *The Reversible World*, ed. Barbara Babcock. Ithaca: Cornell, 1978.

Ainsworth, Catherine. 1973. "Hallowe'en." *New York Folklore Quarterly* 29, no. 3 (Sept.): 163–93.

Appelbaum, Diana Karter. 1984. *Thanksgiving: An American Holiday, An American History.* New York: Facts on File.

Aries, Phillippe. 1962. *Centuries of Childhood: A Social History of Family Life.* New York: Knopf.

Barclay, Dorothy. 1950. "Halloween Fun Without Deviltry." *New York Times Magazine* (15 Oct.).

Bauman, Richard. 1972. "Belsnickling in a Nova Scotia Island Community." *Western Folklore* 31, no. 4 (Oct.): 229–43.

Bazielichowna, B. 1958. "Further Notes on the Polish Guisers." *Folk-Lore* 69 (Dec.).
———, and S. Deptuszewski. 1957. "The Guisers of Koniakow." *Folk-Lore* 68 (Dec.): 497.

Beck, Ervin. 1985. "Trickster on the Threshold: An Interpretation of Children's Autumn Traditions." *Folk-Lore* 96, no. 1: 24–28.

Bell, Louise, and Stella McKay. 1947. "Trick or Treat—and Happy Looting." *American Home* 38 (Oct.).

Best, Joel, and Gerald T. Horiuchi. 1985. "The Razor Blade in the Apple: The Social Construction of Urban Legends." *Social Problems* 32, no. 5 (June): 488–99.

Betzner, Era. 1927. "A Ghostly Gambol for Halloween." *Playground* 21 (Sept.): 334–37.

Black, Maggie. 1981. "Saints and Soul-Caking." *History Today* 31 (Nov.): 60.

Blau, Harold. 1966. "Function and the False Faces." *Journal of American Folklore* 79 (Oct.–Dec.): 564–80.

Brislin, Joseph. 1948. "Solving a Halloween Problem." *Recreation* 42 (Oct.).

Caplow, Theodore, Howard Bahr, Bruce Chadwick, Reuben Hill, and Margaret Holmes Williamson. 1982. *Middletown Families.* Minneapolis: Univ. of Minnesota.

Cate, Rex. 1933. "Halloween in Manhasset." *Recreation* 33 (Oct.).

Cawte, E. C. 1978. *Ritual Animal Disguise: A Historical and Geographical Study of Animal Disguise in the British Isles.* Totowa, N.J.: Rowman & Littlefield for the Folklore Society.

Chambers, E. K. 1933. *The English Folk-Play.* Oxford: Clarendon.

Clark, Joseph. 1972. "All Saints' Day and Halloween." *North Carolina Folklore* 20 (Aug.): 131–36.

Curtis, Isabel Gordon. 1905. "A Child's Celebration of Halloween." *St. Nicholas* 32 (Oct.): 1124–27.

Douglas, George William. 1937. *The American Book of Days.* New York: H. W. Wilson.

Eaton, Walter Prichard. 1912. "Pungkins." *Outing* 61 (Oct.).

Eichler, Lillian. 1924. *The Customs of Mankind.* Garden City, N.J.: Doubleday, Doran & Company.

Evans, E. Estyn. 1957. *Irish Folk Ways.* New York: Devin-Adair.

Fenton, William N. 1987. *The False Faces of the Iroquois.* Norman: Univ. of Oklahoma.

Foster, Jeanne Cooper. 1951. *Ulster Folklore.* Belfast: H. R. Carter.

Gardner, Priscilla. 1937. "Goblins Are Gormands." *Better Homes and Gardens* (Oct.).

Glassie, Henry. 1975. *All Silver and No Brass: An Irish Christmas Mumming.* Bloomington: Indiana Univ. Press.

"Halloween at the Polls." 1988. *U.S. News & World Report* 105 (31 Oct.).

"Hallowe'en Damage Disappears with City Celebrations." 1941. *American City* 56 (Oct.): 99.

"Halloween: Pranks and Pumpkins Are Traditional." 1941. *Life* (3 Nov.).

Halpert, Herbert, and G. M. Story, eds. 1968. *Christmas Mumming in Newfoundland.* Toronto: Univ. of Toronto Press.

Hansmann, C. 1959. *Masken Schemen Larven: Volksmasken der Alpenlander.* Munich: F. Bruckmann.

Hatch, Jane, ed. 1978. *The American Book of Days.* 3d ed. New York: H. W. Wilson.

Hazlitt, W. Carew, ed. 1870. *John Brand's Popular Antiquities of Great Britain.* London: John Russell Smith.

Heath, Catherine. 1911. "Hallowe'en Tricks and Fortunes." *Delineator* 78 (Oct.): 312.

"Here's Halloween." 1950. *Women's Home Companion* 77 (Oct.).

Hole, Christina. 1976. *British Folk Customs.* London: Hutchinson.

———. 1942. *English Custom and Usage.* New York: Scribner's.

"Horrors." 1988. *People* 30 (7 Nov.).

Howe, John W. 1977. "What Is Happy About Halloween?" *Christianity Today* 22 (21 Oct.).

Hudson, Lois Phillips. 1962. "The Buggy on the Roof." *Atlantic* 210 (Nov. 1962).

Jacobson, Ethel. 1941. "Trick or Treat." *Saturday Evening Post* (1 Nov.).

"Jersey Says No Soap to Halloween." 1952. *Life* (27 Oct.).

Johnson, Helen Sewell. 1968. "November Eve Beliefs and Customs in Irish Life and Literature." *Journal of American Folklore* 81, no. 320.

Kelley, Ruth Edna. 1919. *The Book of Halloween.* Boston: Lothrop, Lee, & Shepard.

Linton, Ralph, and Adele Linton. 1950. *Halloween through Twenty Centuries.* New York: Henry Schuman.

MacCana, Proinsias. 1985. *Celtic Mythology.* New York: Peter Bedrick.

McDowell, John. 1985. "Halloween Costuming among Young Adults in Bloomington, Indiana: A Local Exotic." *Indiana Folklore and Oral History* 14, no. 1: 1–18.

Mead, Margaret. 1975. "Halloween: Where Has All the Mischief Gone?" *Redbook* 145 (Oct.).

Mechling, Jay. 1993. "Mass Media and Traditional Play at a Boy Scout Camp." Unpublished MS.

Mook, Maurice. 1969. "Halloween in Central Pennsylvania." *Keystone Folklore Quarterly* 14: 124–29.

Mooney, James. 1889. "Holiday Customs of Ireland." *Proceedings of the American Philosophical Society* 26: 377–427.

Moss, Doris Hudson. 1939. "A Victim of the Window-Soaping Brigade." *American Home* 22 (Nov.).

"A National Occasion for Merrymaking." 1933. *American City.* Rpt. in *Hallowe'en,* ed. Robert Haven Schauffler. New York: Dodd, Mead.

Nuhn, Roy. 1982. "Portfolio: Ellen Clapsaddle." *American History Illustrated* 17 (Oct.).

O'Meara, Walter. 1974. *We Made It Through the Winter.* St. Paul: Minnesota Historical Society.

Opie, Peter, and Iona Opie. 1959. *The Language and Lore of Schoolchildren.* Oxford: Clarendon.

Ó'Súilleabháin, Seán. [1942] 1970. *A Handbook of Irish Folklore.* Detroit: Singing Tree Press.

Parson, Elsie Clews, and Ralph Beals. 1934. "The Sacred Clowns of the Pueblo and Mayo-Yacqui Indians." *American Anthropologist* 36, n.s. (Oct.–Dec.): 491–516

Partridge, Bellamy, and Otto Bettmann. 1946. *As We Were: Family Life in America 1850–1900.* New York: McGraw-Hill.

Patten, Helen Philbrook. 1903. *The Year's Festivals.* Boston: Dana Estes.

Piggott, Stuart. 1938. *The Druids.* New York: Praeger.

"Prescriptions for Halloween Hoodlums." 1938. *Recreation* 32 (Oct.).

"Quaint Halloween Customs." 1912. *Harper's Bazaar* 46 (Nov.).

Rees, Alwyn, and Brinley Rees. 1961. *Celtic Heritage: Ancient Tradition in Ireland and Wales.* London: Thames & Hudson.

Ross, Anne. 1967. *Pagan Celtic Britain*. London: Routledge & Kegan Paul.

Rosten, Leo. 1976. "The Schnorrer: A Study in Piety and Paradox." In *Next Year in Jerusalem*, ed. Douglas Villiers, New York: Viking.

Santino, Jack. 1983. "Night of the Wandering Souls." *Natural History* 92 (Oct.): 42–51.

————. 1983. "Halloween in America: Contemporary Customs and Performances." *Western Folklore* 42: 1–20.

Schwartz, Alvin, ed. 1978. *When I Grew Up Long Ago*. Philadelphia: Lippincott.

Sears, Stephen, Murray Belsky, and Douglas Tunstell. 1975. *Hometown U.S.A.* New York: American Heritage.

Settle, Virginia. 1936. "An Effective Substitute for Hallowe'en Deviltry." *School and Society* 44 (24 Oct.): 541–43.

Sharp, William. 1886. "Halloween: A Threefold Chronicle." *Harper's Magazine* 73 (Nov.).

Sjoestedt-Jonval, Marie. 1940. *Dieux et heros des celtes*. Paris: Lerous.

Stone, Gregory. 1959. "Halloween and the Mass Child." *American Quarterly* 11, no. 3 (Fall): 372–79.

Sutton-Smith, Brian. 1983. "What Happened to Halloween?" *Parents* (Oct.).

Sykes, Homer. 1977. *Once a Year: Some Traditional British Customs*. London: Gordon Fraser.

"The Teaching of Citizenship and Halloween Pranks in Chicago." 1925. *School and Society* 22 (7 Nov.): 585–86.

Turner, Victor. 1969. *The Ritual Process*. Chicago: Aldine.

Vennum, Thomas, Jr. 1985. "The Ojibwa Begging Dance." In *Music and Context: Essays for John M. Ward*, ed. Anne Dhu Shapiro. Cambridge: Harvard Univ. Dept. of Music.

Walden, Keith. 1987. "Respectable Hooligans: Male Toronto College Students Celebrate Hallowe'en, 1884–1910." *Canadian Historical Review* 68, no. 1: 1–34.

Walsh, William. [1897] 1925. *Curiosities of Popular Customs*. Philadelphia: Lippincott.

Welch, Charles E., Jr. 1957–58. "Some Early Phases of the Philadelphia Mummers' Parade." *Pennsylvania Folklife* 9 (Winter).

"When the Goblins Are About." 1930. *Playground* 24 (Oct.).

Willeford, William. 1969. *The Fool and His Scepter*. Evanston, Ill.: Northwestern Univ. Press.

"Windows Bloom on Goblin Night." 1950. *Recreation* 44 (Oct.).

Wood-Martin, W. G. 1902. *Traces of the Elder Faiths of Ireland*. London: Longmans, Green.

PART II

Communities

6. Carnival, Control, and Corporate Culture in Contemporary Halloween Celebrations

RUSSELL W. BELK

The carnivalesque has not disappeared from modern Western society. It persists in numerous scattered festivals, rites, and performances ranging from ritualized, transvestite-costumed attendance at screenings of *The Rocky Horror Picture Show* to fan pilgrimages to the Super Bowl, "Dead Head" attendance at Grateful Dead concerts, the Pasadena Doo Dah Parade, and contemporary Halloween celebrations.[1] Guy Fawkes Night joins Halloween in England in continuing to display many carnival aspects,[2] and a number of countries continue to celebrate pre-Lenten carnivals. Carnival may be seen in numerous aspects of the twentieth-century North American Halloween, including pervasive humor, pranks, masks and costumes, excesses of food (treats) and drink (alcohol), role reversals, and the sense of community fostered by trick-or-treating pilgrimages and various other Halloween rituals. This chapter examines several case studies, beginning with a consideration of carnivalesque phenomena observed in three years of Halloween parties at a Salt Lake City members-only nightclub.

Halloween as Carnival

The membership nightclub remains a fixture of adult drinking in Salt Lake because state liquor laws otherwise restrict liquor by the drink to restaurant meals. Because of the dominant Mormon population, many non-Mormons see these clubs as a gathering of kindred souls on the margin of the larger society. Membership in the club studied is twenty-five dollars per year, and several thousand people currently belong. The Halloween party in the club's two-story restored building features a local rock-and-roll band and numerous bars. The crowd overflows to a large lawn tent set up in the parking lot beside the club. Approximately a thousand advance five-dollar tickets are sold to the event, and after the club fills, people—some bearing tickets—form a line at the door, awaiting entrance until they can be accommodated. All employees are in Halloween costumes, and balloons and streamers decorate the club. Those in attendance range from a minimum age of twenty-one to perhaps age sixty. The majority of those attending are in their twenties and thirties. They are primarily white and middle class. Although some people come alone or in groups, the majority attend as heterosexual couples (there are a small number of homosexual couples). A few people arrive in wheelchairs.

Although costumes are not mandatory, the best outfits are awarded prizes of dinners at various restaurants, and virtually everyone is costumed. The costumes show many carnivalesque elements. Humor and irreverence are key elements. One popular category of costume mocks religious themes. Pregnant nuns and lecherous priests are common. One "nun" danced sedately for a time until she periodically lifted her habit to dance with abandon in her garter belt, black panties, and nylons. A "priest" sported a pink cloth penis that dragged on the ground. And three gold spray-painted angels Moroni imitated the figure atop the city's Mormon temple as they "played" their long golden horns with the band on the stage. Other spoofs of local culture are more subtle: a man's graffiti-covered t-shirt read Eat Green Jello and Die (mocking local Mormon cuisine); a conservatively dressed couple (she was "pregnant") with Mormon missionary name tags pushed a stroller and carried a diaper bag (spoofing the high Mormon birth rate); and the insipid local expression "oh my heck" was transformed into "oh my fucking heck" by several patrons. Also mocked through exaggerated imitations are various public figures, including Richard Nixon, Ronald Reagan, Brian Mulroney, Margaret Thatcher, and even William Randolph Hearst and Marion Davies.

Cross-sex dress is another popular costume theme. Men sport enormous breasts beneath their dresses, nurses uniforms, and nun's habits, and women dress as combat soldiers, football players, and formally attired grooms. One woman danced in relatively normal attire until she lifted her dress to flash the band with a cloth penis and testicles beneath her skirt. More common are relatively risqué costumes, including short-skirted maids, "cigarette girls," pixies, Incredible Hulks, and various black studded-leather S&M outfits. Exhibitionism and voyeurism are especially evident in such outfits, but virtually all participants claim an intent to see and be seen. Occupational costumes show some evidence of inversion, including attorneys as convicts, bankers as burglars, a college professor as Hell's Angel, doctors as rock-and-roll stars, and retail clerks as doctors. In addition to popular media and cartoon characters (e.g., Bart Simpson, Minnie Mouse, clowns), another popular costume category involves monsters and themes of death and gore. Those who dress as monsters, corpses, and skeletons seem to be gaily celebrating the renewal of life while confronting and mocking their fears of death.

The general Halloween atmosphere at this adult club has some elements of debauchery. Two male "patients" in hospital robes exposing most of their backsides carried I-V bottles that dispensed alcohol through tubes into their mouths. During the 1990 Halloween celebration, Miller beer products were served in special orange Halloween bottles, and employees wore fluorescent buttons supplied by another beer brewer. Since 1985, beer and liquor companies have been using Halloween imagery to improve sales, and Adolph Coors sales are reported to have risen 10 percent in October as a result of such advertising and despite protests by several public-interest groups.[3] Significantly, alcohol is disinhibiting and conducive to humor—two factors that characterize the carnivalesque.[4] Drinking is a primary activity here, although the excess of alcohol and drugs is not as ubiquitous as at the outdoor Halloween celebrations on many midwestern college campuses, at the Halifax Halloween Mardi Gras, or at the Mall Crawl on the Pearl Street Mall in Boulder, Colorado (all of which have been "tamed" by law enforcement officials in recent years). More will be said about such outdoor celebrations in the next section. The general atmosphere of indulgence is present, however, and parallels the childhood desire to secure the largest possible quantity of Halloween treats and the tendency to drink to excess on Halloween, beginning during adolescence.[5]

The exaggerated size of faux sexual organs on some of the costumes also contributes to the atmosphere of indulgence and excess, if not debauchery and licentiousness. One Frankenstein's monster with four-inch platform shoes and an extended cranium ensured a woman that everything about him was huge. Another man in his twenties passed out calling cards reading "Craven Moorhead, free-lance gynecologist—There's not a vaginal problem I can't lick." Such vulgar lewdness is not only tolerated but applauded. It contrasts sharply with the more decorous behavior observed at this club on noncarnivalesque occasions. Inhibitions are also shed in dancing on a tightly packed dance floor where contact with other bodies cannot be avoided and collisions are common. Just as the mask is commonly used in traditional

societies when taboos are to be broken, it also seems to facilitate taboo violation in contemporary Halloween celebrations.[6]

    In addition to the carnivalesque features of Halloween celebrations at
this particular club, there are a number of other American Halloween celebrations involving these and other elements of carnival. Large participation
by the gay and lesbian communities is found in the Polk and Castro Street
Halloween parades in San Francisco, the Greenwich Village parade in New
York, and the street celebration in Washington, D.C.'s Georgetown.[7] There
are scatological references in both the traditional Halloween outhouse tricks[8]
and the more recent racist depictions of Arabs with toilet seats around their
necks in corporate Halloween celebrations described in a later section. Additional role reversals are found in children's use of adult occupational costumes and in other costumed transformations of people into plants, animals,
superheroes, and inanimate objects.[9] A liminal element is evident in the
"seam" between seasons that occurs on Halloween (a quarter day),[10] which
is believed to release the ghosts of the dead to roam the earth and return to
their former homes. The high frequency of Halloween costumes of ghosts,
skeletons, corpses, mummies, zombies, and various other monsters may be
seen to enact such ancient beliefs. Psychologically, Halloween also provides
a seam through which fantasies and repressed aspects of personality can
emerge. In this sense, the mask acts as an alter ego.[11] And the spirit of
communitas is present not only at parties but also in the friendly provision of
treats for trick-or-treaters on their journey into the night with fellow pilgrims.
They are greeted at the threshold by increasingly elaborate Halloween decorations, costumes, music, and other "spooky effects," as many adults transform their homes into spook houses for the occasion.[12] All of these elements
echo the spirit of carnival, even though other carnivalesque elements, such
as gambling and social class reversals (given the homogeneity of most urban
neighborhoods and parties), are lacking.

    These celebrations of Halloween, whether they are dominated by chil-
dren or adults, share a dedication to play. The carnivalesque "frame" of Halloween provides a context that suggests, in part, that the intent is playful and
should not be taken too seriously.[13] Humor, Freud noted, is directed to the
pleasure principle. However, also involved in the carnivalesque frame are
two other types of play, the joke and the comic, which Freud saw as expressing repressed hostility and obscenity (the joke) or as emphasizing differences
from others (the comic).[14] It is the comic that thrives on the incongruity of
absurd reversals and contrasts. By emphasizing differences (e.g., gender, age,
race, occupation, authority), these comic inversions serve to reinforce them.

Similarly, by venting hostilities (e.g., with leaders or dominant groups), the joke may release tensions and reinforce the status quo. All three types of playful behavior—humor, joking, and comedy—temporarily liberate participants from control by the social system.[15] This freedom frequently is seen as problematic by authorities of this social system, who may seek to reestablish control.

Efforts to Control Halloween

Two opposing models of the political impact of carnival celebrations hold that they are either a part of the revolutionary process and truly give participants a basis for power over the established hierarchy or, alternatively, that such celebrations are mere "rituals of rebellion" that act as a safety valve for feelings of injustice and, like the joke and the comic, thereby reinforce the existing power structure.[16] As Gluckman notes:

> The acceptance of the established order as right and good, and even sacred, seems to allow unbridled excess . . . for the order itself keeps this rebellion within bounds. Hence to act [out] the conflicts, whether directly or by inversion or in other symbolical forms, emphasizes the social cohesion within which the conflict exists.[17]

This safety-valve view maintains that not only is emotion vented and dissipated by carnival celebration (and thus channeled away from true rebellion), but that a small dose of disorder during carnival immunizes participants from susceptibility to the sustained disorder of revolution.[18] Thus, the ritual of rebellion is seen to paradoxically strengthen the status quo of the social structure it mocks and derides.[19] The psychological principle here is that of catharsis; the sociological principle is that of social bonding through communal celebration. The rebellion-ritual view suggests that officials encourage the celebration of carnival because they realize that the reversal is only temporary and ultimately strengthens their hegemony.

The alternate view, that carnival celebration represents real rebellion and undermines the status quo, is supported by instances in which carnival celebrations have led to bloodshed and war.[20] Castle notes numerous official attempts to ban and break up eighteenth-century English masquerades. The militant gay movement in the United States is also seen as stemming from a riot that began as an overflow of a festival celebration at the Stonewall bar in New York in 1969. Gluckman suggests that rituals of rebellion that reinforce the status quo may only be effective when people accept their social roles as unchangeable.[21] When role choice, multiple social roles, and social mobility exist, as in complex contemporary societies, carnival celebration is both less likely to occur and more likely to pose a threat to the status quo if it does occur. As a result of real or imagined potential for overthrowing authority, some analysts see most contemporary carnivalesque celebrations as having been diluted, tamed, disbanded, or otherwise brought under the control of the dominant classes.[22]

A number of Halloween celebrations offer evidence that rather than being an innocuous safety valve to dissipate the pressures of inequality, these celebrations can lead to harmful violence that goes considerably beyond harmless pranks. The most prominent example is the Halloween prelude of Devil's Night arson in the Detroit area, which seems to have peaked in 1984 with 810 fires started over a three-day period, leaving dozens homeless. The city of Detroit responded with 6:00 P.M. curfews, increased police surveillance, and citizen patrols. But Devil's Night is far from dead. Furthermore, Detroit is not alone in such incidents. Camden, New Jersey, has similar arson and vandalism on its Mischief Night. San Francisco's Castro Street Halloween celebration prompts numerous incidents of antigay violence by other celebrants.[23] On Halloween 1990, a group of New York City teenagers in Halloween costumes attacked a homeless camp, killing one and injuring nine others with knives, bats, and a meat cleaver while shouting, "Trick-or-treat!"[24] Fear of Halloween violence markedly increased school absenteeism in New York City, and in 1989 there were sixty-seven arrests for Halloween-related assaults.[25] A group of costumed youths in Boston committed a rape during Halloween 1990. And in Boulder, Colorado, where the 1989 Mall Crawl attracted forty thousand celebrants and resulted in considerable drunken fighting and vandalism, the police, on Halloween 1990, blocked major highways into town, several merchants boarded up their windows and doors, and increased police patrols reportedly reduced crowds, drunkenness, sale of hallucinogens, and violence.[26]

Efforts to suppress Halloween celebrations are not entirely new, however. Near the turn of the last century, University of Toronto students routinely held a rowdy informal parade over the two miles of main street leading to downtown Toronto. Their mild vandalism and curses led campus and police officials to restrict them to campus, which led to the end of fifteen years of these celebrations.[27] A longer-standing enmity toward Halloween celebrations has been that of the Christian church, which opposes Halloween's emphasis on such anti-Christian symbols as the Devil, witches, and ghosts. Inasmuch as the Celtic predecessor Samhain festivities were centered on the return of the dead and may have involved human sacrifice by

Druid priests,[28] Vatican authorities instructed that the holiday be supplanted by a similarly timed Christian holy day. In 731 All Saints' Day was added to the Christian calendar on 1 November, and about 1006 All Souls' Day was added on November second. However, these holy days have not successfully replaced the desire for a non-Christian carnival, and northern North America continues to celebrate All Saints' (All Hallows) Eve as Halloween (Hallows evening), whereas Mexico continues to celebrate the pre-Columbian festival now known as el Día de los Muertos, the Day of the Dead.[29] Just as the Vatican tried to supplement Samhain masquerades by encouraging parishioners to dress as their favorite or patron saint on All Saints' Day, contemporary parochial schools often forbid nonreligious Halloween costumes at school. And some religious leaders continue to battle Halloween as an evil manifestation of the Devil.[30] At the same time, contemporary practitioners of the occult claim the night as their own.[31] Nevertheless, most occult and New Age mystics try to keep a low profile on Halloween in order to avoid provoking responses like a 1987 suit to bar Halloween celebrations from Arkansas schools.[32]

A more subtle suppression of Halloween has occurred in the past two decades as adults have effectively reduced and institutionalized children's celebrations through rumors of Halloween sadists who put poison, razor blades, and hallucinogens in children's candy.[33] There is widespread belief in these urban legends, even though they have little or no basis in fact.[34] As a result, in place of wide-ranging unsupervised trick-or-treating, children are being more closely supervised by parents, restricted to smaller neighborhood areas, or redirected to indoor parties, fairs, spook houses, and shopping mall trick-or-treating.[35] Paradoxically, as children's traditional Halloween celebrations have been controlled, adult celebrations have markedly increased.[36] Hunter asks:

> Are the adults accompanying the children in the performance of their children's rituals, or are the children accompanying the adults in the performance of the adults' rituals? Ownership of the Halloween ritual is at stake.[37]

If so, adults seem to be gaining (or regaining) possession of the ritual.

Alternating cautious support and efforts to control adult Halloween celebrations can be seen clearly in another research site: Halifax, Nova Scotia. Prior to the First World War, *Halloween* was a familiar term, but Halloween was better known in Halifax and surrounding areas as *Cabbage-Stump-Night.*[38] Cabbages at the time were sold on their long stalks, or stumps, which were saved and used that night to make a loud drumlike noise when banged against people's doors by small groups of young people (primarily male) looking for mischief. The mischievous pranks of Cabbage-Stump-Night included breaking windows, moving college football goalposts, exploding firecrackers, whitewashing formerly black horses, stealing front gates, stuffing rags into auto exhaust pipes, and overturning outhouses. During World War I these activities subsided. When they resumed after the end of the war, they increased in vigor. There was also an unsolved murder reported involving a storekeeper who had stayed up on Cabbage-Stump-Night to protect his Halifax store.[39] Police were said to have chased the murderer into a cemetery where he disappeared.

Sometime after World War I, trick-or-treating also started in Halifax, sometimes involving the song:

> Tramp, tramp, tramp, the boys are marching,
> We are the witches at your door.
> If you will not let us in
> We will bash your windows in
> And you'll never see us goblins any more.[40]

Costumes became common on trick-or-treaters and soaping windows became more common than breaking them. By the 1980s, Halifax religious leaders, parents, and civic leaders had provided Halloween parties and other indoor amusements to try to minimize vandalism, but their effect was reportedly minimal.[41] In 1981 two Halifax businessmen staged a masquerade at a large downtown tavern on the Saturday night before Halloween, and it was so popular that a line wound around the block waiting to get in. Unlike most pranksters and trick-or-treaters of prior Halloweens, the participants were adults of drinking age (nineteen and older). The next year, the party became a street party with a stage set up in a vacant lot between two bars. Together with a local radio station, the event was presented with the misnomer of "Mardi Gras." By 1984 an entertainment promoter had added an indoor costume competition at a large downtown convention center.[42] Although the city council had previously refused to close the streets, the lack of problems the previous year convinced them that they should do so in 1984.[43] That year the Mardi Gras attracted nearly fifteen thousand partiers, mostly in costume. The convention-center party offered costume prizes of a weekend for two in Quebec City and a five-hundred-dollar gift certificate for records, but it allowed no liquor inside, and as a result most people preferred to remain in the street.[44]

In 1985 the indoor costume competition featured a band and allowed liquor, but the majority of the twenty-five thousand participants still preferred to stay on the streets. The promoter's attempts to turn the Mardi Gras into a three-day party met with little success, however.[45] Nevertheless, the Halloween festival was attracting people from all over Nova Scotia and other Maritime provinces, as well as a few from the United States. By 1986 the city of Halifax, although voting not to sponsor Mardi Gras, had taken over security and clean-up responsibilities. Local newspaper coverage, which until this time had been uniformly positive, began to issue some cautions about the party, such as this:

> However, the party is no recess for drugs and liquor. Police will be in full force, keeping an eye out "for any damage, fights, or anything out of the ordinary," said Sergeant Ken MacKenzie, in charge of community relations and crime prevention, Halifax Police Department. Pubs and lounges will also be on the look out for illegal drinking.[46]

The same source reminded readers that there had been a disastrous riot in Halifax following the end of the Second World War. But the mayor and local businesses were cognizant of the positive effect of the Mardi Gras on business and remained supportive. The 1987 Mardi Gras attracted forty thousand people and was touted as the nation's largest Halloween celebration and second on the continent only to New York's Greenwich Village Halloween parade.[47] The indoor party drew two thousand people, and the costume grand prize was a pair of tickets to the Caribbean or Europe. Although illegal fireworks, drunkenness (accounting for virtually all of the 105 arrests), fights, great quantities of broken beer bottles, people throwing bottles at and urinating on the walls of a downtown church, and occasional excessively frightening costumes—such as a man operating a (chainless) chain saw in the crowd—presented some problems, there was only a single broken store window in 1987.

Nevertheless, following the 1987 Mardi Gras, the Halifax City Council met "to try to keep the Halloween Mardi Gras from getting out of hand again."[48] The mayor specified his goals: "We don't want to have any incidents and we don't want to have any public intoxication . . . [we want] to insure everything is under control . . . [and] we don't want any broken glass." At the meeting, the city council discussed starting with a parade and costume competition (those in costume were believed to cause fewer problems), providing multiple bands in order to spread the crowd over a larger area, installing portable lavatories ("although unfortunately the tradition is to knock these down on Halloween"), better lighting, better public transportation, first-aid stations, and closing liquor stores earlier.[49] The basic fear was that the party was growing too quickly and spontaneously and needed to be organized and controlled. A committee of six city officials was formed to meet shortly before the 1988 Mardi Gras in order to coordinate events, but the city was reluctant to get more involved than this.

Several of the events planned by the city for the 1988 Mardi Gras, such as a large beer tent, were canceled due to high insurance costs. This was all right with some members of the press, who felt that the event was getting too commercialized anyway.[50] Both the crowds and the number of arrests were about the same as in the previous year. A sexual assault and a robbery and assault were linked to the Mardi Gras. By 1989 crowds were estimated at forty-five to fifty thousand, and 136 arrests were made (all but seven were men, all but four were for drunkenness).[51] Before the Mardi Gras the mayor proclaimed: "If [the festival] was structured or too well-organized, some of the spontaneity would certainly be missing. No one owns the Mardi Gras, it belongs to the people of Halifax."[52] Following the event, however, the press reported a number of negative incidents, including three sexual assaults, store owners holed up in their shops to protect them, and a mood transformed "from a rather family-oriented group to that of a drunker, nastier and wilder mob."[53] The papers also said that "Halifax police were barely able to control the busiest Mardi Gras yet" and that "Halifax police, even with a bolstered force of an extra 40 officers, had a hectic night dealing with numerous assaults, liquor offenses, bottle-throwing and rowdy partiers."[54] The chairman of the city's Special Events Committee said, "There is no problem with people having fun. But the city is not going to put up with unacceptable behavior."[55]

During the 1990 Mardi Gras, the city of Halifax made good on this promise with a policy of zero tolerance for alcohol, whereas previously, open alcohol and drunkenness on the street were tolerated as long as they were not disruptive. More than 240 arrests were made, despite crowds of only twenty to twenty-five thousand, and only about 30 percent of the crowd came in costume.[56] The dramatic drop in attendance and costuming was attributed to both negative publicity and cold temperatures.[57] Both causes were commonly cited by those I interviewed. There was agreement that police and city officials had overreacted to a relatively harmless event and had robbed it of much of its fun.

The ten-year history of the Halifax Halloween Mardi Gras has been one of alternating official efforts to both support and control the event. Although no major violence or riot has occurred, public officials remain fearful of this possibility, given the size of the crowd, the amount of drinking, and the general carnival spirit of the masked celebrants. The process of increasing civil control and striving for "decent" middle-class behavior has been in ascendance since the middle ages.[58] An unexplicated fear in the present case may also involve the reversal and mocking attitude of the participants. During the 1990 Mardi Gras, for instance, several people dressed as pigs and wore tags bearing the names of prominent local officials. Others dressed as police and sheriffs, and one man in a police uniform attempted to direct traffic down a one-way street the wrong way. A chainsaw (with chain) was used to dismember a mannequin in imitation of the film *The Texas Chainsaw Massacre*. The tension between control and chaos was greatest following the 1989 Mardi Gras. Partly as a result of official efforts to control the 1990 celebration, there was a feeling that the original spontaneity of the event had been lost. Similar fears have been expressed concerning the Doo Dah Parade in Pasadena, Brazilian *carnival*, Trinidad's carnival, Toronto's caribana, and Philadelphia mumming.[59]

Corporate and Commercial Cultures
Enter Halloween Celebrations

For thousands of years Halloween and its predecessor celebrations have resisted various "takeover" attempts by organized religion, governments, and other institutions. In recent years however, there is some evidence that businesses have made some subtle gains in taking over the holiday. These takeovers are occurring not so much in overt control of the celebrations as in harnessing existing celebrations in ways that are beneficial to corporate interests. For adults, this encroachment has occurred mainly in the workplace, whereas for children, it has occurred primarily in the marketplace. The following discussion focuses on a case study in the workplace and comments more briefly on changes occurring in the marketplace.

During the past ten years in the United States and Canada, it has become increasingly common to see employees in retail positions in costumes on Halloween day. One of the more heavily costumed businesses has been banking. Given the extremely conservative image of banking, reversal has great surprise potential in this context—the feature that Castle found most desirable for a successful masquerade.[60] At the same time it has not been lost upon bank management that Halloween costumes on employees may do much to humanize the public image of their institutions. A similar effect is found in the Halifax Mardi Gras, in which downtown chartered banks and trust company branches compete for best costumes, and in the Doo Dah Parade, in which one of the most popular units has long been the Synchronized Briefcase Drill Team, composed of First Interstate Bank trust officers in three-piece suits. The bank initially refused to support this group, but when a photograph of the team appeared in the *Los Angeles Times* following the first parade, the bank quickly became an enthusiastic supporter.[61]

The focus of a case study I conducted during Halloween 1990 was the regional office a large international financial institution I will call FinCorp. The office currently employs more than two thousand people and has since 1984 encouraged all employees to dress in costume for Halloween. Not only are most employees costumed, but there are costume and skit competitions and each department and subdepartment picks a theme and then decorates their office and encourages workers to dress in costumes that are consistent with this theme. For instance, in 1990 (during the buildup for the Gulf War) one corridor was decorated as the "Sleazee Saloon," with employees in Western attire; another was the "Get Lucky Brothel," with a "nun" and males in drag as prostitutes; and in a Saddam Hussein–theme area of the office there were numerous paper camels, Hussein's face framed by toilet seats, and a sign reading Shi'ite Happens. In an area decorated as the "Spiders' Den Lounge" the dark, low-ceiling cave that had been constructed of sheets and artificial spider webs necessitated crawling to desks where computer screens were, nevertheless, lit up. Another area chose Saturday Night Live as a theme, and besides character costumes and a "Quiet on the Set!" sign, a television and VCR continually played reruns of the "Saturday Night Live" television show. In another area with tombstones on each desk, a filing cabinet "squashed" a dummy wearing the name tag of one supervisor, and a headless dummy sat at the desk in another supervisor's office. Skits included "Linus" playing his piano (an electronic keyboard inside a miniature cardboard grand piano) and an office that played "Wheel of Fortune," complete with host "Pat Sajak," assistant "Vanna White," a contestant, a wheel, and employees in large blocks acting as letters in the slogan that the contestant was to guess (YOUR JOB IS A PRESENT). Performances have sometimes overflowed into the outside patio and parking lot.

The large lunchroom was also decorated, and a "witch" served hot cider from a steaming cauldron. Employees make it a point to parade through the executive offices in costume, and one year a sixties theme resulted in a sit-in outside these offices with guitars, peace music, and hippie costumes. Anti-establishment hippie and punk rocker costumes continue to be popular. Many employees bring their children to see the celebrations on Halloween day, and the night before Halloween a number of people voluntarily and enthusiastically work into the night setting up the decorations in their offices. All this goes on with the support and encouragement of the top management of this high-security firm. However, it is clear from their expenditures and exuberance that employees feel very much a part of the celebration and enjoy themselves.

An executive vice-president of the corporation is responsible for this celebration. He says he came to this office in early 1984 and found it "was a damn disaster area." Nevertheless, some progress was made in turning around the operation during his first year there:

> So along came the first Halloween and I said, hey, you know, this place needs a little rest, and for no good reason other than instinct, I guess in the beginning, I said, "We're going to have a Halloween; we're going to have a costume day for Halloween." Well, maybe 200 people came in costumes and there was nothing elaborate; uh, no themes any place. . . . But it was a lot of fun. The people who didn't said, "Oh, I should've done that." Every time this happened, more people got involved. And it was clear that a lot of business problems were being solved at the same time, so the tension issues were less than they had been at the beginning. . . . They have plays; they've got skits down there. They've had MASH groups; they had an operating tent one year using a chain saw. But they did all these things, and I walked down there and I said, "By God, we've solved the problem," 'cause it was clear that people . . . had gotten into this theme business, and people who are uncomfortable are not likely to go off and do crazy things.

The executive himself makes it a point to wear a costume Halloween day (and for several lesser costume days he has since instituted) and to walk around the entire building. The Halloween celebration has been so successful in improving both office performance and morale that other divisions around the country have begun to emulate this division's Halloween activities. By midmorning on Halloween, computers and fax machines in each division have received tips on unusual and "hot" costumes in other divisional offices. Even employees at the corporate headquarters in Manhattan have started donning Halloween costumes, and at yearly meetings of top executives in exotic locations around the world costumes are also now worn. The executive who came up with the idea says, "I see this as a morale booster, as a productivity booster, as a message." He also describes these activities as "an investment," and adds, "I don't know how to buy that. You can't write a check for it. You've gotta be, I don't know, maybe semi-crazy." The success of this "craziness" is shown in the fact that the corporate headquarters is nominating this divisional office (out of more than thirty) for a prestigious quality award given by the United States government to one business each year. And out of a total employee special-benefits budget of nearly half a million dollars for this office, Halloween activities cost no more than a few hundred dollars for prizes.

What is going on here? At one point the executive responsible for these FinCorp Halloween celebrations referred to the "culture" he perceived had developed in this office. Probably most corporations have cultures that involve certain shared beliefs, rituals, expectations, and folklore.[62] But recently attention has been given to the concept of trying to "manage" or manipulate corporate culture in ways that are beneficial to the organization.[63] For instance, Van Maanen and Kunda describe the activities of executives of the "Tandem Computer Corporation" who spend most of a corporation-sponsored vacation in Hawaii drinking together, playing children's picnic games, wearing corporate t-shirts, and singing corporate songs.[64] Trophies are awarded and the executives achieve a feeling of heightened positive emotion toward "their" company. Similar activities can be observed in corporations ranging from Tupperware to IBM. However, what FinCorp is doing with Halloween appears more subtle and more ingenious. Employees are able to perform a ritual of rebellion and enact rites of reversal in ways that they themselves appear to choose. If a theme is imposed, it is done by their immediate work group. Moreover, these days of craziness have the blessing of top management but, seemingly, have not been engineered by them. No one is forced to become involved, and either peer pressure or the genuine fun of these Halloween activities are the primary motivations for participating. As several employees spontaneously expressed in their most recent Halloween celebration, "This is a fun place to work!" The executive originating their corporate Halloween has received thank-you letters from employees saying, directly or indirectly, "We trust you." The effect is fully consistent with what Van Maanen and Kunda term "emotional mobilization" for the good of the corporation.[65] Kertzer notes that "rituals do have value for the many people who otherwise feel impotent before the powers that rule over them. The value of rites is psychological; they reduce people's anxiety level and give them the healthier impression that they do have some control over their lives." As Sutton-Smith and Kelly-Bryne put it, this is a case of play as a mask for work.[66]

Nor is FinCorp alone in finding Halloween a vehicle for enhancing corporate culture. For instance, state office buildings in the same city as the divisional office studied have also followed FinCorp's lead and sponsor costume parades and competitions during the Halloween workday. Numerous other offices, banks, retailers, and service companies seem to be following suit in decorating for Halloween and in allowing and encouraging their employees to don costumes for the day. Another large business in the healthcare field with offices in the western United States, recently decided to find a way to make Halloween a "special event," in order to "help put some spark back in the company" and to "motivate people, show them they're recognized and appreciated."[67]

Humor in the workplace can take various forms. Roy first noted that fooling around helped to make monotonous work fun for a physically isolated group of machine workers. Such fooling around consisted of joking, kidding, pranks, and horseplay, which integrated the group and gave a sense of liminality and *communitas*. This bonding also has been observed by Vinton, who advises managers to resist the temptation to tell employees to cut out the funny business and get to work.[68] Abramis distinguishes between "play as game" and "play as goofing around" in the workplace and argues that only the former is conducive to improving work and employee morale, because it makes the work itself a challenge, like a game or puzzle. But Santino sees that practical jokes, pranks, and stories about these events can have an important function in expressing emotions normally forbidden in the workplace and in releasing tensions that otherwise build up.[69] In contrast, the emotions that are normally encouraged on the job are "managed emotions" that present an agreeable front but require the suppression of true emotions.[70] The Halloween celebrations at FinCorp are much closer to sanctioned goofing around than they are to making the job a game. As such, even though they involve few pranks or practical jokes, they still allow symbolic rebellion against institutional decorum by inviting employees to become convicts, hippies, punk rockers, clowns, gypsies, or other symbolic trickster figures for a day, and even to squash or behead an effigy of their bosses if they desire. In this way tensions are eased and FinCorp becomes associated with the positive emotions generated by fun and play. By sanctioning the temporary deviance of Halloween humor, the corporation increases employee dedication to its objectives.[71]

Whereas adult Halloween celebrations are increasingly channeled toward the interests of corporate culture, children's Halloween celebrations are increasingly channeled toward the interests of consumer culture. Soliciting sweets or money in trick-or-treating, besides celebrating the excess of superabundance, has long carried the message that gluttonous indulgence in forbidden foods is good—at least during the inversion of Halloween.[72] Young children band together and make a pilgrimage into the unknown darkness, using masks, costumes, and vague threats of vandalism to ostensibly extort candies from neighbors who ostensibly do not recognize them through their disguises. When, as is increasingly true, the threats of vandalism are hollow,[73] Sutton-Smith observes that this is a reassuring ritual:

We say to our children, in effect, that your neighbors are to be trusted.
They are nice people. If you go up to their scary door along their scary
path dressed up as a scary person, nevertheless they will treat you nicely
and give you candy and food.[74]

Recently, however, fears of Halloween sadists and Halloween violence have
created a popular new venue for trick-or-treating: the shopping mall. Numerous shopping malls in the United States now encourage merchants to
dress in Halloween costumes and to hand out treats to costumed child trick-
or-treaters during a several-hour prescribed period early on the night of Halloween. Most retailers comply, whether they are Victoria's Secret, Hickory
Farms, or B. Dalton. For a large mall, making the rounds to collect such
treats can require one or two hours and result in a large bag full of candy.
Given this change in trick-or-treat practices, we might paraphrase Sutton-
Smith's interpretation as follows:

We say to our children, in effect, that your retailers are to be trusted.   .
They are nice people. If you go up to their scary store in the scary mall
dressed up as a scary person, nevertheless they will treat you nicely and fill
your shopping bag full of candy and food.

The lesson in consumer socialization here is clear: good things no longer
come from neighbors (who are increasingly likely to be out participating in
adult Halloween celebrations anyway), but from the mall. Just as the squares
and streets of the city are the focus of the traditional carnival, the mall acts
as the new cultural community.[75] But it provides a sterilized pseudo-public
space devoted to promoting consumption in a safe environment that excludes
"undesirables" (e.g., the poor, beggars, prostitutes, and racial minorities) just
as it does the weather. And whereas the traditional city closes itself to normal business during carnival,[76] the shopping mall is clearly open for business
during Halloween. This substitution of the commercial community for the personal community of neighbors at Halloween may thus be seen as the childhood
counterpart of the uses of Halloween to foster corporate culture among adults.

Conclusions

Neither official ambivalence nor the association of the marketplace with carnival are new developments. In fact, Bakhtin saw the boisterous exaggerat-
ing spirit of the vulgar marketplace and the celebration of superabundance
as being central to the carnival of Rabelais.[77] Gluckman found that the rituals of rebellion in southeast Africa are also timed to the harvest in order to

diffuse envy and anxiety by delaying the orgy of consumption until the crops are in and survival is assured. But in spite of associations with the marketplace and abundance, as Santino observed, Halloween has long remained an essentially uncommercialized folk holiday.[78] This observation is now being challenged. It is clear that the contemporary North American Halloween, though it retains many significant folk elements, has been considerably transformed in its present manifestations. After centuries of continuing ambivalence toward Halloween celebrations, emerging trends in the workplace and the marketplace suggest that Halloween may be becoming co-opted in subtle ways by being transformed into a vehicle for nurturing corporate and consumer cultures. The trends discussed in this chapter suggest that the folk character of Halloween may be diminishing in the face of increasing corporate and commercial control.

Countertrends may be seen in the widely heralded increase in adult participation in Halloween outside of the workplace. As adults increasingly participate in carnivalesque Halloween parties and festivals, corporate appropriation becomes more difficult. Whereas both the workplace and the mall may expect something in return for their Halloween largesse and permissiveness, this is not the case in more spontaneous adult celebrations. In these celebrations, play and humor dominate, and for this reason, they are unlikely to act as vehicles for political revolution. When North Americans are seriously dissatisfied with their economic, social, or political situation, they are unlikely to embrace Halloween play. This is seen in the decline of Cabbage-Stump-Night during World War I, the delay in adult celebrations of Halloween until after the Vietnam War, and the FinCorp executive's observation that people who are uncomfortable are unlikely to celebrate with abandon. If this thesis is correct, we may see the intensity of adult Halloween celebrations as an index of the health of the economy, society, and government.

Even with increasingly vigorous adult Halloween celebrations, it is unlikely that commercial and corporate inroads into the folk aspects of Halloween will diminish. Mall trick-or-treating by children and workplace celebrations by adults both appear to be part of a continuing shift in Halloween control from children to adults to corporations. Though Halloween is becoming more controlled and institutionalized, we must be careful not to become too nostalgic in idealizing Halloweens past.[79] Despite recent changes, one essential element of the carnivalesque persists. The key feature of carnival detected by Bakhtin was humor. And humor remains central to the carnivalesque Halloween.[80] If child and adult humor differ in their subtlety and sophistication, the contemporary Halloween may be our strongest current opportunity to display guileless childlike humor. So long as humor predominates, Halloween celebrations are innocuous and reinforce rather than oppose the power structure that would otherwise seek to control them. And it is this humor that may ultimately be the most effective antidote to the institutional elements beginning to pervade Halloween. For although Halloween may no longer be free from commercialization, its celebrants remain active jokesters and tricksters rather than passive consumers of entertainment. It is this participative humor that invigorates Halloween and contributes to its longevity.

Notes

1.   Carnivalesque elements include humor (especially satires of public institutions and figures of authority, comic amusements involving fools, clowns, or animals, and ludicrous inversions of the normal power structure), images of birth, growth, death, and dirt, rituals of excessive consumption and conspicuous display, and sexual liberation. See Mikhail Bakhtin, *Rabelais and His World*, trans. Helene Iswolsky (Cambridge, Mass.: MIT Press, 1968); Terry Castle, *Masquerade and Civilization: The Carnivalesque in Eighteenth-Century English Culture and Fiction* (Stanford, Calif.: Stanford Univ. Press, 1986); Alessandro Falassi, "Festival: Definition and Morphology," in *Time Out of Time: Essays on the Festival*, ed. Alessandro Falassi (Albuquerque: Univ. of New Mexico, 1987), 1–10; Victor Turner, *The Ritual Process* (Chicago: Aldine, 1969); Umberto Eco, "The Frames of Comic 'Freedom,'" in *Carnival*, ed. Umberto Eco, V. V. Ivanov, and Monica Rector (New York: Mouton, 1984), 1–9; and V. V. Ivanov, "The Semiotic Theory of Carnival as the Inversion of Bipolar Opposites," trans. R. Reeder and J. Rostinsky, both in *Carnival*, 11–35.

2.   See Ervin Beck, "Children's Guy Fawkes Customs in Sheffield," *Folklore* 95, no. 2 (1982): 191–203 and "Trickster on the Threshold: An Interpretation of Children's Autumn Traditions," *Folklore* 96, no. 1 (1985): 24–28.

3.   Amy E. Gross, "Beer Marketers Brew Brands for Halloween," *Adweek's Marketing Week* 31 (24 Sept. 1990): 37; Thomas R. King, "Brewers Hope for Treat from Promotion Tricks," *Wall Street Journal*, 5 Oct. 1989, B1; Michael Matza, "It's Halloween with a Chaser as Alcohol Ads Haunt Holiday," *Philadelphia Inquirer*, 31 Oct. 1990, G1.

4.   Frank J. MacHovec, *Humor: Theory, History, Applications* (Springfield, Ill.: Charles C. Thomas, 1988).

5.   See Russell W. Belk, "Halloween: An Evolving American Consumption Ritual," in *Advances in Consumer Research*, ed. Marvin Goldberg, Jerry Gorn, and Richard Pollay (Provo, Utah: Association for Consumer Research, 1990), vol. 17: 508–17; and Stacey Levinson et al., "Halloween as a Consumption Experience," in *Advances in Consumer Research*, ed. John Sherry and Brian Sternthal, (Provo, Utah: Association for Consumer Research, 1992), 19: 219–28.

6.   Laura Makarius "The Mask and the Violation of Taboo," in *The Power of Symbols: Masks and Masquerade in the Americas,* ed. N. Ross Crumrine and Marjorie Halpin (Vancouver: Univ. of British Columbia Press, 1983), 195–203.

7.   See, for instance, Jack Kugelmass "The Greenwich Village Halloween Parade and the Culture of New York City," paper presented at 87th Annual Meeting of the American Anthropological Association, Phoenix, Ariz., 1988; Mary O'Drain, "San Francisco's Gay Halloween," *International Folklore Review* 4 (1988): 90–95; Jeffrey Schmatz, "Homosexuals Unmask on a Night of Costumes," *New York Times,* 31 Oct. 1988, 7, and Don Shirley, "Halloween for Grown-Ups," *Washington Post,* 2 Nov. 1978, rpt. in *The Folklore of American Holidays,* ed. Hennig Cohen and Tristram Potter Coffin (Detroit: Gale Research, 1987), 310–11.

8.   Gregory Stone, "Halloween and the Mass Child," *American Quarterly* 13, no. 3 (1959): 372–79.

9.   See Theodore Caplow et al., *Middletown Families: Fifty Years of Change and Continuity* (Minneapolis: Univ. of Minnesota Press, 1982), 231–233, and Belk, "Halloween."

10.   Each season has at least one major holiday celebration in the United States (Easter, Fourth of July, Halloween and Thanksgiving, Christmas), but only Halloween falls on a quarter day between two seasons. Glassie makes the same point about Halloween in the Irish seasonal calendar; see Henry Glassie, *All Silver and No Brass: An Irish Christmas Mumming* (Bloomington: Indiana Univ. Press, 1975), 97.

11.   See Peter T. Markman and Roberta H. Markman, *The Masks of the Spirit: Image and Metaphor in Mesoamerica* (Berkeley: Univ. of Calif. Press, 1989), and Victor Turner, "*Carnival* in Rio: Dionysian Drama in an Industrializing Society," in *The Celebration of Society: Perspectives on Contemporary Cultural Performance,* ed. Frank E. Manning (Bowling Green, Ohio: Bowling Green Univ. Press, 1983), 103–24.

12.   See Belk, "Halloween."

13.   See Richard Alford, "Humor Framing Conventions: Techniques and Effects," in *Play as Context: 1979 Proceedings of The Association for the Anthropological Study of Play,* ed. Alyce Taylor Cheska (West Point, N.Y.: Leisure Press, 1981), 268–78, and Erving Goffman, *Frame Analysis* (New York: Harper and Row, 1974).

14.   Sigmund Freud, *Character and Culture* (New York: Collier, 1963); Sigmund Freud, *Jokes and their Relation to the Unconscious,* trans. James Strachey (1905; New York: W. W. Norton, 1963).

15.   Marvin R. Koller, *Humor and Society: Explorations in the Sociology of Humor* (Houston: Cap and Gown Press, 1988); Harvey Mindess, *Laughter and Liberation* (Los Angeles: Nash, 1971).

16.   See Max Gluckman, *Politics, Law and Ritual in Tribal Society* (Chicago: Aldine, 1965); Eco, "The Frames of Comic 'Freedom'"; and Peter Stallybrass and Allan White, *The Politics and Poetics of Transgression* (Ithaca, N.Y.: Cornell Univ. Press, 1986).

17. Max Gluckman, *Order and Rebellion in Tribal Africa* (London: Cohen & West, 1963), 124.

18. Castle, *Masquerade and Civilization*, 89.

19. Max Gluckman, *Custom and Conflict in Africa* (Glencoe, Ill.: Free Press, 1959), 109.

20. Such was the case, for instance, in certain sixteenth- to nineteenth-century carnival celebrations in Switzerland, the Netherlands, Italy, and France, and resulted in banning of carnival rites by both twentieth-century Spanish dictators; see David I. Kertzer, *Ritual, Politics, and Power* (New Haven: Yale Univ. Press, 1988) and Emmanuel Le Roy Ladurie, *Carnival in Romans* (originally published in France as *Le Carnival du Romans,* 1979; New York: Braziller, 1979).

21. Castle, *Masquerade and Civilization;* Gluckman, *Custom and Conflict in Africa.*

22. "Halloween-Masked Gang Attacks Homeless Camp," *San Francisco Chronicle,* 1 Nov. 1990, A11.

23. Clarence Johnson, "Rain Won't Spook Halloween Revelers," *San Francisco Chronicle,* 31 Oct. 1990, A2.

24. See Kertzer, *Ritual, Politics and Power;* Marianne Mesnil, "Place and Time in the Carnivalesque Festival," in *Time Out of Time,* ed. Alessandro Falassi, 184–96; and Christel Lane, *The Rites of Rulers: Ritual in Industrial Society—The Soviet Case* (Cambridge, England: Cambridge Univ. Press, 1981). Similarly, the Pasadena Doo Dah Parade, established as a carnivalesque inversion of the conservative Rose Parade, is slowly being co-opted by bureaucratic authority, according to Denise Lawrence, "Parades, Politics, and Competing Urban Images: Doo Dah and Roses," *Urban Anthropology* 11 (Summer 1982): 155–76, and "Rules of Misrule: Notes on the Doo Dah Parade in Pasadena," in *Time Out of Time,* ed. Alessandro Falassi, 123–36.

25. Craig Wolff, "Youth Packs Rampage in 3 Boroughs: 67 are Held by Police in Halloween Assaults," *New York Times,* 1 Nov. 1989, B1.

26. Keith McCullen, "Halloween Festivities Quieter in Boulder," *Rocky Mountain News,* 1 Nov. 1990, 1.

27. Keith Walden, "Respectable Hooligans: Male Toronto College Students Celebrate Hallowe'en, 1884–1910," *Canadian Historical Review* 68 (March 1987): 1–34.

28. Robert J. Myers, *Celebrations: The Complete Book of American Holidays* (Garden City, N.Y.: Doubleday, 1972), 257–64.

29. See Joanne F. Hernandez and Samuel R. Hernandez, *The Day of the Dead: Tradition and Change in Contemporary Mexico* (Santa Clara, Calif: Triton Museum of Art, 1979); María Teresa Pomar, *El Día de los Muertos: The Life of the Dead in Mexican Folk Art* (Fort Worth: Fort Worth Art Museum, 1987); Lourdes Portillo and Susana Munoz, directors, *La Offrenda: The Days of the Dead,* film, 1989; and Chloë Sayer, *Mexico: The Day of the Dead, An Anthology* (London: Redstone Press, 1990).

30. For example, Miranda Ewell, "Gays, 'Prayer Warriors' in Battle of Shrieks," *Anchorage Times,* 1 Nov. 1990, A1; Mike Flemming, "Devil Warning Precedes Trick-or-Treat Scramble," *Memphis Commercial Appeal,* 1 Nov. 1990, B1; and Jack Kelley, "Satanist 'Revival' Rumors Stir a Furor," *USA Today,* 29 Oct. 1990, 3A.

31. For example, Steve Silk, "Halloween Is High Season for Salem's Witches," *St. Louis Post Dispatch,* 31 Oct. 1990, 1, 5.

32. Rick Boling, "Devil's Advocate," *Omni* 9 (Apr. 1987): 113.

33. D. Wemhamer and Richard Dodder, "A New Halloween Goblin: The Product Tamperings," *Journal of Popular Culture* 18 (Winter 1984): 21–24.

34. See Joel Best, "The Myth of the Halloween Sadist," *Psychology Today* 19 (Nov. 1985): 14–19; Joel Best and Gerald T. Horiuchi, "The Razor Blade in the Apple: The Social Construction of Urban Legends," *Social Problems* 32 (June 1985): 488–99; and Sylvia Grider, "The Razor Blades in the Apples Syndrome," in *Perspectives on Contemporary Legend: Proceedings of the Conference on Contemporary Legend,* ed. Paul Smith (Sheffield, England: Center for English Cultural Tradition and Language, 1984), 129–40.

35. Kelly W. Kelly and William M. Wentworth, "A Structural Reinterpretation of Responsibility, Risk, and Helping in Small Collectives of Children," *American Sociological Review* 49 (Oct. 1984): 611–19; Sabina Magliocco, "The Bloomington Jaycees' Haunted House," *Indiana Folklore and Oral History* 14 (Jan.–June 1985): 19–28.

36. Michael Demarest, "Halloween as an Adult Treat: An Escapist Extravaganza Dazzle Mardi Gras," *Time* 122 (31 Oct. 1983): 110; Jack Santino, "Halloween in America: Contemporary Customs and Performances," *Western Folklore* 42 (Jan. 1983): 1–20; and "Night of the Wandering Souls," *Natural History* 92 (Oct. 1983): 43–51; Shirley, "Halloween for Grown-Ups"; and USA Today, "Party Night Isn't Just for Kids Anymore," *USA Today,* 31 Oct. 1988, 1A.

37. Daryl M. Hunter, "'No Malice in Wonderland': Conservation and Change in the Three Halloweens of Ann Mesko," *Culture and Tradition* 7 (1983): 37–53.

38. Nova Scotia Chronicle-Herald, "Cabbage-Stump-Night of Not So Long Ago," *Nova Scotia Chronicle-Herald,* 31 Oct. 1961, 5, 23; F. H. MacArthur, "Those Awful Hallowe'en Pranks," *Nova Scotia Chronicle-Herald,* 27 Oct. 1966, 1; and Michael Punch, "Hallowe'en: It is Centuries Old," *Halifax Mail-Star/Herald Chronicle,* 31 Oct. 1984, 13.

39. Nova Scotia Chronicle-Herald, "Cabbage-Stump-Night of Not So Long Ago."

40. MacArthur, "Those Awful Hallowe'en Pranks."

41. Punch, "Hallowe'en: It is Centuries Old."

42. Sara Holland, "Mardi Gras: The Weird and Wonderful Walk the Streets in the Second Largest Halloween Party in North America," *Where, Halifax/Dartmouth,* 15 Oct.–15 Nov. 1990, 18–21.

43. Halifax Daily News, "Halloween Party Bigger Than Ever," *Halifax Daily News,* 11 Oct. 1986, 1.

44. Sheryl Grant, "Mardi Gras to be Inside," *Halifax Mail-Star*, 23 Oct. 1984, 1; Sheryl Grant and Michael Doyle, "Halifax Mardi Gras Draws Nearly 15,000," *Halifax Chronicle-Herald*, 29 Oct. 1984, 1.

45. Helen Densmore, "Halifax Mardi Gras Bash is Unique," *Halifax Mail-Star*, 23 Oct. 1985, 1, 2; Halifax Daily News, "Halloween Party Bigger Than Ever."

46. Charlene Sadler, "Party-Goers Gear Up for Mardi Gras," *Halifax Chronicle Herald*, 10 Oct. 1986, 1.

47. Mike Coleman and Steve Proctor, "Mardi Gras Draws 40,000 Revellers," *Halifax Chronicle Herald*, 2 Nov. 1987, 1, 12; and Keith Mano, "The New York Halloween Parade," *National Review* 41 (24 Nov. 1989): 56–57.

48. Rob Roberts, "Mayor Seeks Better Mardi Gras Control," *Halifax Daily News*, 2 Nov. 1987, 1.

49. Joel Jacobson, "Mardi Gras to Get Help: Officials Feel Semblance of Organization Needed," *Halifax Mail-Star*, 5 Nov. 1987, 1, 2; Lionel Wild, "The Party's Over: City Will Run Halloween Bash Next Year," *Halifax Daily News*, 5 Nov. 1987, 2.

50. Tanya Miller, "Mardi Gras a Popular Haunt," *Halifax Chronicle Herald*, 29 Oct. 1988, 1-O, 6-O; Tim Carlson, "It's Canada's Biggest Party," *Halifax Daily News*, 28 Oct. 1988, 19.

51. Halifax Mail-Star, "Mardi Gras Halloween Bash: Thousands of Costumed Revellers Pack Bar District," *Halifax Mail-Star*, 31 Oct. 1988, 1, 2; Barbara Bateman, "Cops Round Up 136 During Mardi Gras," *Halifax Daily News*, 30 Oct. 1989, 3.

52. Parker Robinson, "Commercial Sponsor Planned for 1990 Mardi Gras," *Halifax Mail-Star*, 26 Oct. 1989, 1.

53. Barbara Bateman, "Cops Round Up 136 During Mardi Gras"; Ian Johnston, "Night Creatures," *Halifax Daily News*, 28 Oct. 1989, 23.

54. Parker Robinson, "Mardi Gras Mayhem Barely Contained," *Halifax Mail-Star*, 1 Nov. 1989, A1, A2; Mark Blanchard, "Spooks, Kooks Revel at Mardi Gras Bash," *Halifax Mail-Star*, 29 Oct. 1989, 1.

55. Johnston, "Night Creatures."

56. Cathy Krawchuk, "Mardi Gras: Jail Cells Crowded, Streets Not," *Halifax Mail-Star*, 29 Oct. 1990, A1, and Sandra Porteous, "Ooh, It's Cold: Crowds Down for Mardi Gras," *Halifax Daily Sunday News* , 28 Oct. 1990, 5.

57. Pam Sword, "Mardi Gras Turns Downtown Halifax into Theatre," *Halifax Mail-Star*, 29 Oct. 1990, 1.

58. Norbert Elias, *The Civilizing Process: The History of Manners*, trans. Edmund Jephcott (Basel: Haus zum Falken, 1939; New York: Urizen Books, 1978.

59. Lawrence, "Rules of Misrule: Notes on the Doo Dah Parade in Pasadena"; M. Taylor, "The Politics of Aesthetic Debate: The Case of Brazilian Carnival," *Ethnology* 21 (Oct. 1982): 301–11; John Stewart, "Patronage and Control in the Trinidad Carnival," in *The Anthropology of Experience*, ed. Victor W. Turner and Edward M. Bruner (Urbana: Univ. of Illinois Press, 1986), 289–315; Frank E. Manning, "Carnival in Canada: The Politics of Celebration," in *The Masks of Play*, ed.

Brian Sutton-Smith and Diana Kelly-Byrne (New York: Leisure Press, 1984), 24–33; Susan G. Davis, "Making the Night Hideous: Christmas Revelry and Public Order in Nineteenth Century Philadelphia," *American Quarterly* 34 (Summer 1982): 185–99.

60. Castle, *Masquerade and Civilization.*

61. Lawrence, "Parades, Politics, and Competing Urban Images."

62. Jack Santino, "The Outlaw Emotions: Narrative Expressions on the Rules and Roles of Occupational Identity," *American Behavioral Scientist* 33 (Jan. 1990): 318–29.

63. For example, Desmond Graves, *Corporate Culture—Diagnosis and Change: Auditing and Changing the Culture of Organizations* (New York: St. Martin's Press, 1986); Linda A. Krefting, and Peter J. Frost, "Untangling Webs, Surfing Waves, and Wildcatting: A Multiple-Metaphor Perspective on Managing Organizational Culture," in *Organizational Culture*, ed. Peter J. Frost et al., 155–68 (Beverly Hills: Sage, 1985); and Caren Siehl, "After the Founder: An Opportunity to Manage Culture," in *Organizational Culture*, 125–40.

64. John Van Maanen and Gideon Kunda, "'Real Feelings': Emotional Expression and Organizational Culture," *Research in Organizational Behavior* (Greenwich, Conn.: JAI Press, 1989), vol. 11: 43–103.

65. Van Maanen and Kunda, "'Real Feelings.'"

66. Kertzner, *Ritual, Politics and Power*, 131–32; Brian Sutton-Smith and Diana Kelly-Byrne, "Conclusion," in *The Masks of Play*, 184–99.

67. Charles Despres, field notes, 15 Oct. 1990, Dept. of Anthropology, David Eccles School of Business, Univ. of Utah.

68. Donald F. Roy, "'Banana Time': Job Satisfaction and Informal Interaction," *Human Organization* 18, no. 4 (1960): 158–68; Don Handleman, "Re-Thinking 'Banana Time': Symbolic Integration in a Work Setting," *Urban Life* 4 (Jan. 1976): 433–48; Karen L. Vinton, "Humor in the Workplace: It is More Than Telling Jokes," *Small Group Behavior* 20 (May 1989): 151–66.

69. David J. Abramis, "Play in Work: Childish Hedonism or Adult Enthusiasm?," *American Behavioral Scientist* 33 (Jan. 1990): 353–73; Santino, "The Outlaw Emotions."

70. Aline R. Hochschild, *The Managed Heart* (Berkeley: Univ. of California Press, 1983); Anat Rafaeli and Robert I. Sutton, "The Expression of Emotion in Organizational Life," in *Research in Organizational Behavior*, 11: 1–42.

71. Chris Powell, "Humour as a Form of Social Control: A Deviance Approach," in *It's a Funny Thing, Humor*, ed. Antony J. Chapman and Hugh C. Foot (Oxford: Oxford Univ. Press, 1977), 53–55.

72. Belk, "Halloween."

73. Maurice A. Mook, "Halloween in Central Pennsylvania," *Keystone Folklore Quarterly* 14 (Fall 1969): 124–29; Stone, "Halloween and the Mass Child."

74. Brian Sutton-Smith, "What Happened to Halloween?" *Parents* 58 (Oct. 1983): 63–64.

75. H. L. Goodall, *Casing a Promised Land: The Autobiography of an Organizational Detective as Cultural Ethnographer* (Carbondale: Southern Illinois Univ. Press, 1989).

76. Turner, "*Carnival* in Rio"; Roberto Da Matta, "Carnival in Multiple Planes," in *Rite, Drama, Festival, Spectacle: Rehearsals Toward A Theory of Cultural Performance,* ed. John J. MacAloon (Philadelphia: Institute for the Study of Human Issues, 1984), 208-40.

77. Bakhtin, *Rabelais and His World.*

78. Gluckman, *Order and Rebellion in Tribal Africa;* Santino, "Night of the Wandering Souls."

79. E.g., Catherine Harris Ainsworth, "Halloween," *New York Folklore Quarterly* 29 (Sept. 1983): 163–93.

80. Bakhtin, *Rabelais and His World.*

References

Abramis, David J. 1990. "Play in Work: Childish Hedonism or Adult Enthusiasm." *American Behavioral Scientist* 33 (Jan.): 353–73.

Ainsworth, Catherine Harris. 1983. "Halloween," *New York Folklore Quarterly* 29 (Sept.): 163–93.

Alford, Richard. 1981. "Humor Framing Conventions: Techniques and Effects." *Play as Context: 1979 Proceedings of The Association for the Anthropological Study of Play,* ed. Alyce Taylor Cheska, 268–78. West Point, N.Y.

Bakhtin, Mikhail. 1968. *Rabelais and His World.* trans. Helene Iswolsky. Cambridge, Mass.: MIT Press.

Beck, Ervin. 1984. "Children's Guy Fawkes Customs in Sheffield." *Folklore* 95, no. 2: 191–203.

———. 1985. "Trickster on the Threshold: An Interpretation of Children's Autumn Traditions." *Folklore* 96, no. 1: 24–28.

Beimler, Rosalind Rosoff. 1991. *The Days of the Dead.* San Francisco: Collins Publishers.

Belk, Russell W. 1990. "Halloween: An Evolving American Consumption Ritual." *Advances in Consumer Research* 17, ed. Marvin E. Goldberg, Gerald Gorn, and Richard Pollay, 508–17. Provo, Utah: Association for Consumer Research.

Belk, Russell W., and Wendy J. Bryce. Forthcoming. "Christmas Shopping Scenes: From Miracle to Mall." *International Journal of Research in Marketing.*

Best, Joel. 1985. "The Myth of the Halloween Sadist." *Psychology Today* 19 (Nov.): 14–19.

Best, Joel, and Gerald T. Horiuchi. 1985. "The Razor Blade in the Apple: The Social Construction of Urban Legends." *Social Problems* 32 (June): 488–99.

Boling, Rick. 1990. "Devil's Advocate." *Omni* 9 (Apr.): 113.

Caplow, Theodore, Howard M. Bahr, Bruce A. Chadwick, Reuben Hill, and Margaret Holmes Williamson. 1982. *Middletown Families: Fifty Years of Change and Continuity.* Minneapolis: Univ. of Minnesota Press.

Carmichael, Elizabeth, and Chloë Sayer. 1991. *The Skeleton at the Feast.* London: British Museum Press.

Castle, Terry. 1986. *Masquerade and Civilization: The Carnivalesque in Eighteenth-Century English Culture and Fiction.* Stanford, Calif.: Stanford Univ. Press.

Crader, Kelly W., and William M. Wentworth. 1984. "A Structural Reinterpretation of Responsibility, Risk, and Helping in Small Collectives of Children." *American Sociological Review* 49 (Oct.): 611–19.

Da Mata, Roberto. 1984. "Carnival in Multiple Planes." In *Rite, Drama, Festival, Spectacle: Rehearsals toward a Theory of Cultural Performance,* ed. John MacAloon, 208–240. Philadelphia: Institute for the Study of Human Issues.

Davis, Susan G. 1982. "Making the Night Hideous: Christmas Revelry and Public Order in Nineteenth Century Philadelphia." *American Quarterly* 34 (Summer): 185–99.

Demarest, Michael. 1983. "Halloween as an Adult Treat: An Escapist Extravaganza Outdazzling Mardi Gras." *Time* 122 (31 Oct.): 110.

Despres, Charles. 1990. Field notes, 15 Oct. Dept. of Anthropology, David Eccles School of Business, Univ. of Utah.

Eco, Umberto. 1984. "The Frames of Comic 'Freedom.'" In *Carnival,* ed. Eco et al., trans. R. Reeder and J. Rostinsky, 1–9. New York: Mouton.

Elias, Norbert. 1939. "The Civilizing Process: The History of Manners." In *Basel: Haus zum Falken,* trans. Edmund Jephcott. New York: Urizen Books.

Falassi, Alessandro. 1987. "Festival: Definition and Morphology." In *Time Out of Time,* ed. Falassi, 1–10.

Freud, Sigmund. 1963. *Character and Culture.* New York: Collier.

———. 1963. *Jokes and Their Relation to the Unconscious,* trans. James Strachey. New York: W. W. Norton.

Glassie, Henry. 1975. *All Silver and No Brass: An Irish Christmas Mumming.* Bloomington: Indiana Univ. Press.

Gluckman, Max. 1959. *Custom and Conflict in Africa.* Glencoe, Ill.: Free Press.

Gluckman, Max. 1963. *Order and Rebellion in Tribal Africa.* London: Cohen & West.

Gluckman, Max. 1965. *Politics, Law and Ritual in Tribal Society.* Chicago: Aldine.

Goffman, Erving. 1974. *Frame Analysis.* New York: Harper and Row.

Goodall, H. L. 1989. *Casing a Promised Land: The Autobiography of an Organizational Detective as Cultural Ethnographer.* Carbondale: Southern Illinois Univ. Press.

Graves, Desmond. 1986. *Corporate Culture—Diagnosis and Change: Auditing and Changing the Culture of Organizations.* New York: St. Martin's Press.

Grider, Sylvia. 1984. "The Razor Blades in the Apples Syndrome." In P. Smith, *Perspectives on Contemporary Legend.* 129–40.

Gross, Amy E. 1990. "Beer Marketers Brew Brands for Halloween." *Adweek's Marketing Week* 31 (24 Sept.): 37.

Handleman, Don. 1976. "Re-Thinking 'Banana Time': Symbolic Integration in a Work Setting." *Urban Life* 4 (Jan.): 433–48.

Hernandez, Joanne F., and Samuel R. Hernandez. 1979. *The Day of the Dead: Tradition and Change in Contemporary Mexico.* Santa Clara, Calif.: Triton Museum of Art.

Hochschild, Aline R. 1983. *The Managed Heart: Commercialization of Human Feeling.* Berkeley and Los Angeles: Univ. of California Press.

Holland, Sara. 1990. "Mardi Gras: The Weird and Wonderful Walk the Streets in the Second Largest Halloween Party in North America." *Where Halifax/Dartmouth* (15 Oct.–15 Nov.): 18–21.

Hunter, Darryl M. 1983. "No Malice in Wonderland: Conservation and Change in the Three Hallowe'ens of Ann Mesko." *Culture and Tradition.* 7: 37–53.

Ivanov, V. V. 1984. "The Semiotic Theory of Carnival as the Inversion of Bipolar Opposites." In Eco et al., *Carnival,* trans. R. Reeder and J. Rostinsky, 11–35.

Kertzer, David I. 1988. *Ritual, Politics, and Power.* New Haven: Yale Univ. Press.

Koller, Marvin. 1988. *Humor and Society: Explorations in the Sociology of Humor.* Houston: Cap and Gown Press.

Krefting, Linda A., and Peter J. Frost. 1985. "Untangling Webs, Surfing Waves, and Wildcatting: A Multiple-Metaphor Perspective on Managing Organizational Culture." In *Organizational Culture,* ed. Frost et al., 155–68.

Kugelmass, Jack. 1991. "Wishes Come True: The Greenwich Village Halloween Parade." *Journal of American Folklore* 104 (Fall): 443–65.

Ladurie, Emmanuel Le Roy. 1979. *Carnival in Romans.* New York: George Braziller. (Originally published in France as *Le Carnival du Romans.* Paris: Editions Gallimard, 1979.)

Lane, Christel. 1981. *The Rites of Rulers: Ritual in Industrial Society—The Soviet Case.* Cambridge, England: Cambridge Univ. Press.

Lawrence, Denise. 1982. "Parades, Politics, and Competing Urban Images: Doo Dah and Roses." *Urban Anthropology* 11 (Summer): 155–76.

Lawrence, Denise. 1987. "Rules of Misrule: Notes on the Doo Dah Parade in Pasadena." In *Time Out of Time,* ed. Falassi, 123–36.

Levinson, Stacey, Stacey Mack, Dan Reinhardt, Helen Suarez, and Grace Yeh. 1992. "Halloween as a Consumption Experience." *Advances in Consumer Research* 19, ed. John Sherry and Brian Sternthal, 219–28. Provo, Utah: Association for Consumer Research.

MacHovec, Frank J. 1988. *Humor: Theory, History, Applications.* Springfield, Ill.: Charles C. Thomas.

Magliocco, Sabina. 1985. "The Bloomington Jaycees' Haunted House." *Indiana Folklore and Oral History* 14 (Jan.–June): 19–28.

Makarius, Laura. 1983. "The Mask and the Violation of Taboo." In *The Power of Symbols: Masks and Masquerade in the Americas,* ed. N. Ross Crumrine and Marjorie Halpin, 195–203. Vancouver, B.C.: Univ. of British Columbia Press.

Manning, Frank E. 1984. "Carnival in Canada: The Politics of Celebration." In *The Masks of Play,* ed. Sutton-Smith and Kelly-Byrne, 24–33.

Mano, Keith. 1989. "The New York Halloween Parade." *National Review* 41 (24 Nov.): 56–57.

Markman, Peter T., and Roberta H. Markman. 1989. *The Masks of the Spirit: Image and Metaphor in Mesoamerica.* Berkeley: University of California Press.

Mesnil, Marianne. 1987. "Place and Time in the Carnivalesque Festival." In *Time Out of Time,* ed. Falassi, 184–96.

Mindess, Harvey. 1971. *Laughter and Liberation.* Los Angeles, Nash.

Mook, Maurice A. 1969. "Halloween in Central Pennsylvania." *Keystone Folklore Quarterly* 14 (Fall): 124–29.

Myers, Robert J. 1972. *Celebrations: The Complete Book of American Holidays.* Garden City, N.Y.: Doubleday.

O'Drain, Mary. 1986. "San Francisco's Gay Halloween." *International Folklore Review* 4: 90–95.

Pomar, María Teresa. 1987. *El Día de los Muertos: The Life of the Day of the Dead in Mexican Folk Art.* Fort Worth: Fort Worth Art Museum.

Portillo, Lourdes, and Susana Munoz, directors. 1989. *La Offrenda: The Days of the Dead.* Film. San Francisco: Xochitl Film Productions.

Powell, Chris. 1977. "Humour as a Form of Social Control: A Deviance Approach." In *It's a Funny Thing, Humor,* ed. Antony J. Chapman and Hugh C. Foot, 53–55. Oxford: Oxford Univ. Press.

Rafaeli, Anat, and Robert I. Sutton. 1989. "The Expression of Emotion in Organizational Life." In *Research in Organization Behavior* 11, ed. L. L. Cummings and Barry W. Straw, 1–42. Greenwich, Conn.: JAI Press.

Roy, Donald F. 1960. "'Banana Time': Symbolic Integration in a Work Setting." *Urban Life* 18, no. 4: 158–68.

Santino, Jack. 1983a. "Halloween in America: Contemporary Customs and Performances." *Western Folklore* 42 (Jan.): 1–20.

———. 1983b. "Night of the Wandering Souls." *Natural History* 92 (Oct.): 43–51.

———. 1990. "The Outlaw Emotions: Narrative Expressions on the Rules and Roles of Occupational Identity." *American Behavioral Scientist* 33 (Jan.): 318–29.

Sayer, Chloë. 1990. *Mexico: The Day of the Dead: An Anthology.* London: Redstone Press.

Shirley, Don. 1978. "Halloween for Grown-Ups." *Washington Post* (2 Nov.). Rpt. in *The Folklore of American Holidays,* ed. Hennig Cohen and Tristram Potter Coffin, 310–11. Detroit: Gale Research Company.

Siehl, Caren. 1985. "After the Founder: An Opportunity to Manage Culture." In *Organizational Culture,* ed. Frost et al., 125–40.

Stallybrass, Peter, and Allan White, *The Politics and Poetics of Transgression.* Ithaca, N.Y.: Cornell Univ. Press, 1986.

Stewart, John. 1986. "Patronage and Control in the Trinidad Carnival." In *The Anthropology of Experience,* ed. Victor W. Turn and Edward M. Bruner, 289–315. Urbana: Univ. of Illinois Press.

Stone, Gregory. 1959. "Halloween and the Mass Child." *American Quarterly* 13, no. 3: 372–79.

Sutton-Smith, Brian. 1983. "What Happened to Halloween?" *Parents* 58 (Oct.): 63–64.

————, Brian, and Diana Kelly-Byrne. 1984. "Conclusion." In *The Masks of Play*, ed. Sutton-Smith and Kelly-Byrne, 184–99.

Taylor, J. M. 1982. "The Politics of Aesthetic Debate: The Case of Brazilian Carnival." *Ethnology* 21 (Oct.): 301–11.

Turner, Victor. 1969. *The Ritual Process: Structure and Anti-Structure*. Chicago: Aldine.

Turner, Victor. 1983. "*Carnival* in Rio: Dionysian Drama in an Industrializing Society." In *The Celebration of Society: Perspectives on Contemporary Cultural Performance*, ed. Frank E. Manning, 103–24. Bowling Green, Ohio: Bowling Green Univ. Press.

Van Maanen, John, and Gideon Kunda. 1989. "'Real Feelings': Emotional Expression and Organizational Culture." *Research in Organizational Behavior* 11. Greenwich, Conn.: JAI Press.

Vinton, Karen L. 1989. "Humor in the Workplace: It is More Than Telling Jokes." *Small Group Behavior* 20 (May): 141–166.

Walden, Keith. 1987. "Respectable Hooligans: Male Toronto College Students Celebrate Hallowe'en, 1884–1910." *Canadian Historical Review* 68 (March): 1–34.

Wemhamer, J. D., and Richard Dodder. 1984. "A New Halloween Goblin: The Product Tamperings." *Journal of Popular Culture* 18 (Winter): 21–24.

7. Day of the Dead
The Tex-Mex Tradition

KAY TURNER AND PAT JASPER

"Day of the Dead—The Tex-Mex Tradition," for which this essay was originally developed, was the first art exhibit of its kind in Texas to present traditional artistic expressions of All Souls' Day as they are maintained and practiced by Mexican American families and communities in South Texas. A major objective of the exhibit was to create public awareness of All Souls' Day traditions as they have been carried on by generations of Mexican Americans in Texas. These traditions are related to, but markedly differ from, those encountered in Mexican celebrations of the Day of the Dead, an annual ceremony with obvious roots in indigenous and pre-Conquest traditions of remembering and honoring the deceased. Mexican-derived Day of the Dead traditions are currently enjoying immense popularity in galleries and museums north of the border, but the meaning and significance of family-based Texas-Mexican folk traditions—even knowledge of their existence—are largely unknown to the public.

Beginning in the late 1970s, the Mexican celebration of Day of the Dead achieved a new status as a tourist attraction, especially in south and central Mexico. People from all over the world now stream into these and other areas of Mexico to observe the celebration. Simultaneous with this phenomenon was the rise of interest in the Day of the Dead on this side of the border. About fifteen years ago, Chicano galleries (e.g., Galería de La Raza in San Francisco; Xochil Gallery in Mission, Texas; LUChA in Austin; and more recently MexicArte in Austin and Centro Cultural Aztlan in San Antonio) began holding Day of the Dead exhibits in November. The trend continued to grow—in fact, it exploded—and by the late 1980s, Day of the Dead exhibits were being held in such diverse places as New York City, Chicago, Houston, and Miami. Although the majority of these exhibits are based in Mexican American art centers, the celebration has been taken up by other Hispanic groups and even by Anglo establishments.[1]

For the most part such exhibits feature the work of fine artists who bring their personal aesthetic sensibilities and skills to bear in liberal interpretations of the Mexican *ofrenda* (a domestic altar made especially for the Day of the Dead to hold offerings for deceased loved ones) tradition. Some of the treatments are personal, some are political, some are fanciful, but all of them remove the *ofrenda* tradition from its original Mexican folk context by making use of the altar not as a religious and familial site primarily but as a sculptural form that generates the potential for a multilayered assemblage of images, objects, and meanings. Appropriated expressions of the tradition are celebratory, extravagant, and theatrical in their mix of popular with traditional materials, sacred with secular, and personal with national and political agendas.

Within the American gallery setting, Day of the Dead exhibitions become emblems of the tradition in Mexico and vehicles for memorialization, but they also achieve new meaning as artistic statements that knowingly appropriate aspects of the celebration for purposes beyond its original intent. In these new environments, the spectacle aspects of Day of the Dead in Mexico are imitated or refigured, but they are ultimately framed and generally received as unfamiliar and exotic renderings. Perhaps this is because Mexico is a country in which the spirit world is still alive, whereas the United States is, in the modern era, a country characterized by absence of belief in the spirit world. As it is presented in American galleries, the Day of the Dead becomes a *reinvented* tradition used to explore the notion of death and spirituality in a national milieu that is essentially uncomfortable with both.[2]

It should be noted as well that Mexican Day of the Dead traditions are increasingly being linked to Halloween. Halloween (All Hallow Even, the eve of All Saints' Day) is associated with All Souls' Day, but its derivation is European, not Mexican. Halloween celebrations in Texas, New York, and other parts of the United States have grown significantly in the past ten years. What was once limited to a children's holiday customarily celebrated in neighborhoods has now become a much more public celebration that includes the participation of adults in parades, large parties, sponsored dances, and other events. Both the display and sale of Mexican skeleton toys and miniatures and the making of *ofrendas* in galleries and museums add components of traditional Mexican Day of the Dead celebrations to the increased exuberance in celebrating Halloween. In this way—especially in the Southwest—the two celebrations have become somewhat conflated, at least in the public eye.

All of this is clearly in contrast to the traditional Mexican American celebration in Texas of All Souls' Day, which retains its character as a holy day, and most essentially as a family day wherein deceased relatives are honored and remembered not through the excess of festivity, but through a more somber and reflective process of visiting and attending to the graves of the dead. Mexican American All Souls' Day traditions are maintained traditions; that is, they are rooted in a legacy of obligations and practices that retain a continuity of remembrance from generation to generation.

The Texas-Mexican celebration of All Souls' Day is primarily informed by the living descendants' sense of responsibility to their dead. Mexican American All Souls' Day is foremost an expression of family continuity, an expression of the "work of kinship" that, on this day, is centered on the annual renewal of ties between the living and the dead.[3] As one woman in San Antonio expressed it: "This day is very special for us. On this day we remember those who are there in the earth. They expect us to come to remember them."

The Tex-Mex Tradition

Traveling in the far west end of San Antonio's Avenida Guadalupe in late October and early November, one notes the almost-overnight appearance of public vendors crowded into parking lots along the street. Making the quick jog from Guadalupe to Castroville Road and continuing, the side-by-side vendors' wares create an uninterrupted line of color and texture. Tin cans full of fresh flowers—mostly marigolds, some zinnias, brilliant cockscomb, miniature yellow and purple poms—form the front row of each display. Behind the profusion of fresh flowers stand rows of wreaths and artificial flower arrangements of varying heights and degrees of ornamentation. Close by each display is an attendant, ready to bargain about prices for the available styles of wreaths, arrangements and fresh flowers. The occasion these vendors turn out for is All Saints' Day (1 November, the feast day that honors the lives of all the saints) and All Souls' Day (2 November, a day given over to remembrance of family members and friends who have died), and the wares they sell are used to decorate Mexican American graves in cemeteries throughout San Antonio and surrounding communities during this period. Their customers are individuals and family groups intent on honoring and remembering deceased friends and relatives at this special time of year (fig. 7.1).

Fig. 7.1. Family saying graveside rosary in honor of deceased relatives at San Fernando II Cemetery in San Antonio, Texas. Photograph by Kathy Vargas, 1988.

Most of the vendors lining Guadalupe and Castroville sell to people on their way to visit the graves of family members buried in the sprawling San Fernando II Cemetery, San Antonio's largest Mexican American cemetery. Although it depends on when All Souls' and All Saints' days fall during the week, the vendors usually set up the weekend before 1 November and conduct sales until the holy days of commemoration occur. Some years the vendors remain set up after 2 November, hoping to benefit from sales to individuals who have postponed their grave-site visits until the following weekend. On the busiest days surrounding All Souls' Day, the vendors do so much business that traffic is stopped or slowed to a crawl. Most people looking for decorating materials cruise slowly down the street, then pull up alongside vending sites to admire wreaths and collect information on competing prices. Once the buyers decide on a purchase, they park and pay for their selection. The transaction occurs quickly and smoothly; it's one that has taken place many times before and will take place again and again.

Having made an appropriate selection of materials, people then move on to visit the grave site of a loved one. Lines of cars slowly enter San Fernando cemetery, and the broad landscape of the site is dotted throughout with individuals and families attending the graves of their departed. Some of the visitors come but once a year at this time and spend however long it takes to pay their respects and attend to the graves. Others return several times over the year, spending perhaps a few hours each time to clear and clean away decorations that have been exposed to the weather, replacing them with new ones, watering and maintaining live plants, praying, talking, and relaxing in the presence of their loved ones last resting place.

Years ago, when private transportation was rare and San Fernando II sat at the rural outskirts of the city, families rode the bus to this corner of San Antonio. They spent the entire day at the grave, combining a family outing with the opportunity to visit, remember, and groom the grave sites of relatives and friends. Up until the early 1960s, it was not uncommon for people to bring food for themselves to eat and to leave as offerings for the dead, as is customary in Mexico. Many of the grave-site visitors brought their own handmade floral arrangements with which to decorate; others cut flowers at home or collected them along the way to adorn and beautify the burial place. It was just such activity that led the matriarch of the Elizondo family, whose home is located at the northeast corner of the cemetery, to plant flowers to sell to passersby on their way to the graveyard. From that simple act a year-round, multigenerational family floral business was born, initially spawning and finally competing with the overflow of vendors who now line Castroville and Cupples roads. Nowadays, the demand for decorating materials—both fresh and artificial—far outweighs the ability of one business or one family to supply it.

On a smaller scale, scenes like those on Cupples and Castroville roads are repeated at cemeteries around the city and in small towns throughout South Texas. The tradition of family grave-site visitation and decoration is typical in the region, but occasionally a community will commemorate their dead in a more collective manner. A small village outside San Antonio, for example, has been the site for at least a century of an annual candlelight procession from the local parish to the area cemetery. There, as darkness descends, current and former residents gather at graves, which they clean, decorate and generously appoint with candles. Amidst the brilliance of colorful flowers and the soft yellow glow of hundreds of burning tapers, the Catholic Mass is said by the local priest, graves are blessed, and the small community renews its social ties with the living and its spiritual bonds with the dead. In this cemetery, as in others, the depth of the tradition and its continuity across generations is realized in viewing the freshly decorated graves of family members who have been dead for half a century or more (fig. 7.2).

From place to place throughout South Texas, variations on the All Souls' tradition have evolved over time. In a border community outside of Rio Grande City, selected residents begin working weeks in advance of the holy day to collect money and buy materials in preparation for their distinctive

Fig. 7.2. Family grave plot decorated and lighted with candles on the night of All Souls. Photograph by Kathy Vargas, 1988.

version of the celebration. On the morning of November second or the closest weekend day designated by the organizers, community members—past and present—arrive at the cemetery. Some former residents travel from as far away as Corpus Christi and Dallas. In addition to the conventional and family-based task of grave maintenance and adornment, the group together undertakes the decoration of the entire cemetery. Multiple strands of brightly colored ribbon are braided along the entire length of the fence surrounding the graveyard, and the archways and gates at each entry are wrapped and hung with handmade floral baskets made with the same material. The cemetery remains decorated in this manner year-round, reminding residents and visitors of the community's connection to, and involvement with, the memory of its deceased loved ones.

Texas and Mexican Traditions: A Brief Comparison

To a large extent, the All Souls' Day traditions described above find their legacy in Mexico. Yet in Texas the practice of these traditions is marked by differences that reflect the circumstances of cultural divergence, assimilation, and exchange experienced by *mexicanos* in the multicultural environment of the Lone Star State. Mexican-based celebrations have taken on distinct forms and meanings in Texas in response to the political, social, and cultural domination of Mexicans by Anglo elites throughout much of this century.[4] Mexican Americans' freedom to express their faith through folk religious practices was curtailed—though not extinguished—by pressures put upon them to assimilate Anglo norms and to abandon traditions that could be construed as non-Christian. This resulted in an expression of the tradition that is quieter, more insular and reliant on the family directly.

This explains, in part, why the character of the celebration of All Souls' Day in Texas, though deeply felt and value laden, is generally less direct and less dramatic than it is in Mexico. For example, traditional names for the holiday reflect the difference between Mexican and Mexican American versions of the celebration. In Mexico, All Souls' Day is called *Día de los Muertos* (Day of the Dead), but here in Texas such frankness is eschewed through the substitution of euphemistic phrases such as "*el día de los difuntos*" (the day of the deceased) or "*el día de los finados*" (the day of the "finished" and/or "departed"). As one woman told us, "*Día de los Muertos* sounds so *dead*. All right, I'm dead, but don't say it so ugly."

In Mexico, *el Día de los Muertos* combines practices drawn from pre-Columbian indigenous cultures and Spanish Catholic influences. The holiday in Mexico adheres to age-old traditions that link the living and the dead through both community and family-based celebrations; spirits of the dead are believed to return to their families and communities, and they are appropriately greeted and fêted with their favorite foods and other worldly pleasures such as cigarettes and liquor. In Mexico the emphasis on the actual return of the dead makes this day an occasion for a show of hospitality to spirits who annually come home to enjoy certain earthly pleasures no

longer available to them. *El Día de los Muertos* marks a special time—a time
when spirits are invited back to their families to act out a remembrance of
their humanness.[5]

In contrast, the Texas-Mexican remembrance of the dead acknowledges
their importance by marking their separation from this world. In Texas-Mexican terms, acts of remembrance delineate and demarcate the differences
between the living and the dead. Texas-Mexican celebrations center in acts
that symbolically affirm the separation of the dead from the living while ac-
knowledging reconnection with the deceased through memory.

Although the tradition in Texas is certainly centered on religious practice and belief, it is also largely informed by a social impulse that broadens
the meaning and richness of the celebration. For many Texas-Mexican communities the day has the character of a social gathering and includes family
and community reunions. Memories of the dead are often framed by
graveside encounters between old friends and relatives: seeing each other
again, they tell stories about themselves in the present and in the past, re-
counting memories of deceased loved ones who once were a part of their
social universe, momentarily reengaging them in that universe again.

The chairwoman of the parish cemetery association in La Coste, a rural
community south of San Antonio, has observed time and time again the kind
of reunions that occur there on All Souls' Day (fig. 7.3):

> Yes, I find that they talk first more generally about how you're doing,
> how's your family, how's your job . . . And then it's well "Who do you have
> here?" "Well, I have my mother or my father or my uncle or aunt or who-
> ever." Then they start to remember. First one, then the other person re-
> members . . . And she might ask "Whatever happened to so and so?" And
> the other one tells her "Oh, he's dead already." And so on and so on . . . it
> goes on and on . . . it's really amazing. But they don't talk much about how
> people died. They remember old times.

If the grave site is the central meeting ground for All Souls' Day in Texas, in
Mexico the center of the tradition is found at the *ofrenda,* a special altar
made at home, at church, or outside cemeteries. *Ofrendas* are arranged with
flowers, candles, incense, and offerings of favorite foods for the departed.
Traditionally, an altar is a threshold; it marks a sacred site between heaven
and earth that provides access of each to the other.[6] An *ofrenda* partakes of
the altar's general definition as an active threshold between earth and
heaven, but the *ofrenda* is specifically created as a site of encounter between
the living and the dead. All the things on an *ofrenda* have a quality of action

Fig. 7.3. Grave site in La Coste, Texas, is cleaned and raked into a patterned design by family members. Photograph by Kathy Vargas, 1988.

that makes them able communicators between humans and the spirits of the deceased. The smoke of incense, the flicker of candles, the aroma of food and intense color of flowers—these are sensual indicators that draw the spirits of the dead home to briefly enjoy the comforts and pleasures of family and community life.

Although Mexican American fine artists recently have initiated gallery-based showings of *ofrendas* for Day of the Dead, these altars are rarely seen as a part of family-based traditions in the Texas-Mexican community. However, some Texas families, originally from parts of Mexico where the tradition is common, continue to make simple *ofrendas* with the limited materials available to them here. In the Crabbs Prairie home of Margarita Ramos de Vasquez, for example, a temporary *ofrenda* is created just below the home altar she maintains year-round in her dining room. Incense, candles, and flowers (often paper ones of her own making) are placed on a hand-crocheted and embroidered cloth made by her mother. Homemade tamales are set out as an offering to the spirits of deceased loved ones and then consumed later in the day by her and her family.

Still, the preparation of a traditional *ofrenda* in Texas is uncommon; here, the All Souls' Day tradition centers on the grave site, the place that traditionally represents and actually is the final resting place of the dead. North of the Texas-Mexican border the grave site is an ending place. Here, the physical body is interred in the earth, and the spirit or soul is freed from its worldly labors to cross a threshold to the other side from which there is no expected return.

Grave-site cleaning and decoration—usually by the family of the dead, sometimes by a friend—is the primary activity that marks All Souls' Day observations in Texas. In select instances, some graves are maintained and groomed at frequent intervals throughout the year or on holidays that are especially relevant to the deceased loved one (such as a birthday, Mother's Day, or Father's Day). And due to its increasing conflation with Halloween, more and more graves are decorated in the fall with mass-produced materials such as orange and black balloons, plastic pumpkins, paper ghosts, and other images of the holiday.

Most graves receive their single annual refurbishment at this time of year, with the removal of old flowers, pots, and other paraphernalia, followed by the thorough raking and weeding of the site. Then fresh flowers are set out, and additional long-lasting decorations such as plastic flower wreaths, spangled Styrofoam crosses, and vases filled with silk or curled-ribbon flowers are newly arranged on the grave. Sometimes single individuals undertake this commemorative responsibility, but often several cars full of family members may be seen pulling up, piling out and praying at the grave of a family patriarch or matriarch. Such an observance may last only a few minutes or cover the course of a day with relatives coming and going, carrying away weathered materials, and returning with fresh, new supplies for the grave site.

The favorite fresh flower for decorating Texas-Mexican graves is the golden-yellow marigold. The tradition of using marigolds originated in Mexico, where for centuries a type of marigold has been the traditional flower for Day of the Dead. In Mexico, the flower is still called by its *Nahuatl* (Aztec) name *zempasuchitl*, suggestive of the possibility that it was used in association with death before the Conquest. The marigolds used in the San Antonio area are grown locally by several farming families of Belgian descent. This network of growers has supplied flowers for All Souls' Day for decades. Although marigolds dominate their harvests, they also grow rows of zinnias, poms, cockscomb, and chrysanthemums.

In addition to the farmers, an entire Mexican American folk industry has grown up around the tradition of grave decorating associated with All Souls' and All Saints' days. Local vendors who sell fresh cut stems contract with the Belgian farmers by the row, and each row is identified by a stake with the vendors' name on it. Every morning vendors or their helpers harvest a portion of their contracted plot before each sales day begins. The vendors then return to the sales stations they have set up around the cemeteries and divide the washtubs full of harvested flowers into coffee can–sized containers that have either been scrubbed or covered with foil wrapping paper. A successful week of sales in November means that farmers must plant their crop in late summer, whereas vendors begin stocking nonperishable materials, such as cans and frames, several months in advance.

Part of the economy that has grown up around the tradition of grave decoration includes several simple handcraft forms such as paper-flower making and the fashioning of special arrangements known as *coronas* (wreaths) and *cruces* (crosses). These craft traditions were formerly practiced by individuals making them specifically for private use, but lack of time and the desire for convenience have now made them largely the province of vendors. And, although the practice is rarely encountered now, in recent times flowers were handmade of paper, then dipped in wax to preserve their color and form.[7] Mass-produced artificial flowers or handmade ones crafted from durable materials such as ribbon have made the wax-dipped varieties obsolete, but there are still flower sellers in San Antonio and the Rio Grande Valley who remember and occasionally practice these older forms.

To have an adequate inventory ready for display and sale, vendors must begin stockpiling both materials and the finished products well in advance. Like the advance contract they undertake with the flower farmers, planning for vendors involves a risky mix of approximation and luck. Weather conditions, the location of the holy day within a given week, and even the state of local economies can combine to make any year's sales a resounding success or a dismal failure. Of course, certain nonperishable supplies gathered over the year in anticipation of this sales period can be saved and used later if they are not consumed immediately.

One asset that can be employed to defray the cost of building an inventory of sales items, while decreasing financial risk, is the use of family-based labor. After work and school and on the weekends, spouses, children, parents, in-laws, and other extended family members are an available resource of essentially free labor. Everything—from unskilled jobs such as scrubbing out tin coffee cans, transporting and moving inventory, and cutting flowers to technically more demanding tasks such as wreath making and flower arranging—is distributed among relatives.

Because relatives constitute the essential unit of production associated with the customs and crafts surrounding All Souls' Day, the family base of this tradition is effectively maintained from year to year. Most of the activities undertaken by vendors, both in preparation for and in the course of sales, encourage family cooperation and sharing. Even the youngest children assist and learn something new in the process. Women talk and tell stories as they fill their homes to bursting with brightly colored arrangements. Male in-laws come and go from the sales locales with fresh inventory and food. In fact, the occasional character of this economic activity and its place within the preexisting rhythms of Mexican American family life has been so successful that it has spread to other holidays such as Palm Sunday and Mother's and Father's Day.

For the most part, women undertake the skilled chores and the sales activity, whereas men provide the muscles and machines to lift, move, and transport supplies and sales products. Most vendors note that they learned both the craft and the commercial aspects of the business from a female relative, such as their mother, their grandmother, or, often, an aunt. Working outside the home less frequently than men, women are more able to convert their time to such seasonal activities as this. As a result, this home-centered economy promotes the woman's role in family economic life. Women are empowered by a form of financial independence that, in itself, can benefit the family as a whole. As one vendor noted, "My husband helps me, but all the money I earn is mine. One year I made enough money to buy a whole living room suite."

At the center of this entire tradition, both in Mexico and in Texas, are issues of ephemerality and consumption. In both cultures, All Souls' Day is the most important day for memorializing the dead, and for many it is the only day in the year such specific and ritualized attention is given to the deceased. Ephemerality and the way it is manifested on each side of the border is a key to understanding the difference in Mexican and Texas-Mexican practice. In keeping with the transitory nature of the celebration in Mexico (i.e., that spirits of the dead are present only for a short, if intensive, period of time), material expressions of the tradition are markedly ephemeral. Candles, food, flowers, and other offerings on *ofrendas* and graves are meant to be *consumed* by the dead—used up in the time span of their brief return. Mexican expressions of the celebration are framed in a cyclical sense of time; the spirits of the dead return every year, and they are welcomed back through acts of hospitality that are repeated year after year.

In Texas, ephemeral expressions such as flowers and candles certainly play a role in the celebration, but they are found in relation to more long-lasting decorations (plastic flower wreaths, etc.). This results, in part, from a distinct intention associated with the day. Many items brought to decorate Texas grave sites are intended to last throughout the year as a sign of remembrance. North of the border, Day of the Dead celebrations are enacted within a more linear, historical sense of time. Perishable items such as fresh flowers are indicators of respectful attention paid, but these things eventually will be discarded or destroyed by the elements. In essence, in Texas, participants in the tradition know that their offerings inevitably will be consumed by time and nature. Someone who buys an impermanent product will have reason to return and buy more; a family member who decorates the grave of a loved one with fresh flowers will have additional motivation for further visits. In this way ephemerality is echoed in the very character of the Texas tradition: the repeated act of remembering is mirrored in the refurbishment of the grave site.

The issues of consumption and ephemerality surrounding the Day of the Dead are particularly heightened in Mexico by the eating of a range of festival foods made only for these days. *Pan de muerto* (bread of the dead) and various sweets such as candy skulls and tombstones molded from a sugar-based dough appear for sale in *panaderías* (bakeries) and marketplaces as the last days of October approach. These foods, especially bread, play a central role in the Mexican celebration. In inviting the spirits of the dead back to their homes food is the main symbolic enticement. As the most important source of human sustenance, food is used to gift the spirits, to remind them of the pleasure of human life.

Traditional All Souls' Day celebrations in Texas do not make use of food or eating as a central symbol. Some Mexican American bakers do, however, carry on the tradition of creating *pan de muerto*. These bakers, most of them trained in Mexico, make and sell the distinct shapes and designs of *pan* they learned to create in different regions of their native land. *Muertos* (figures representing dead men and women) are made throughout Mexico, but they vary in style from place to place. For example, those made by San Antonio baker Manuel Bedoy, who hails from Guadalajara, are typical of the style of "dead bread" found in that region: they are large—approximately two feet long—and elaborately detailed with fine curlicues of dough (fig. 7.4). On the other hand, Lux Bakery, owned by the Alvarez family, also of San Antonio, is well known for its smaller, cross-shaped variations of the *muerto* and Raymond Torres of Los Cocos Bakeries makes a distinctive headless *muerto* that is colored red. Other

Fig. 7.4. Master baker, Manuel Bedoy of San Antonio, making large decorative male and female *muertos* (figures of the dead). Photograph by Kathy Vargas, 1988.

traditional shapes for *pan de muerto* made in Texas include the *calabaza,* or squash, with bones on top in place of stems, and skull-shaped cookies.

Although *pan de muerto* is made in San Antonio and occasionally along the border, the tradition is not a widespread one in Texas. In fact, the production of *pan de muerto* in San Antonio is in itself a reinvented tradition. Manuel Bedoy reports that a number of years ago a local priest who had recently visited Mexico came to him requesting the kind of bread he had seen there during these same holy days. Bedoy, working from memory, made the breads for the priest and has continued to do so for a widening market up to the present day. In effect, the burgeoning interest in Mexican traditions associated with Day of the Dead has brought about a revitalization of the availability of *pan de muerto* in San Antonio. Bedoy comments that with the exception of more recently arrived Mexicans, it is often Anglos—especially schoolteachers—who place orders for it. North of the border, *pan de muerto* simply is not an active symbol in All Souls' Day celebrations. It has taken on an emblematic use by representing but not actively promoting the intentions of Day of the Dead. Moreover, the bakers of *pan de muerto* in San Antonio increasingly expand their markets by appropriating images associated with Halloween. Breads and cookies are made in the shape of bats, ghosts, and smiling pumpkins. To a large extent "dead bread" has been absorbed into the Halloween tradition of giving and getting treats. At least in San Antonio, eating the special *pan* at this season is as much an adjunct aspect of Halloween as it is of traditional All Souls' Day.

Another Mexican-derived Day of the Dead tradition has been maintained in San Antonio for at least the past seventy-five years, perhaps longer. The tradition of printing up and distributing short poems called *calaveras* (literally, "skulls") aimed at mocking, chastising, or kidding the living began in Mexico City in the nineteenth century and continues there today. The tradition is primarily an urban-centered one, used to make the Day of the Dead an occasion for politically motivated jesting and for the "killing" of both heroes and villains, the famous and the infamous. In some ways, the tradition of writing and publishing *calaveras* is as ephemeral an activity as the others related to Day of the Dead, in that the incidents that spur them, their street-based medium of quick distribution, and even the notoriety of individuals who merit them may be entirely transitory, constituting a momentary part of local history and memory.

The salient symbols for the *calaveras* are, of course, the skull and skeleton, and much wordplay is given over to images of loose bones and cavorting cadavers. The animated skeleton—a liminal figure between the living body and the disembodied dead spirit—is an apt symbol for realizing the playful antics that are characterized in the *calaveras*. The broadsides are often illustrated with simple drawings of fiendishly laughing skeletons dressed in fancy suits, gowns, or recognizable attire worn by the person being addressed. Whereas the more serious, rural celebrations of Day of the Dead acknowledge the living spirits of the dead and their cyclical return to earth, the urban *calavera* tradition is aimed at historical personages and their participation in historical events. The laughing skeleton becomes an appropriate figure for disembodying the power of history at a time when the spirit world rules.

In San Antonio the *calavera* tradition first appeared in local newspapers, especially the Spanish-language daily *La Prensa*. Mexican American journalists such as Romulo Munguia and Feliciano Rodarte, familiar with the practice in Mexico, used their positions on local papers to publish a limited selection of *calaveras* about notable area personalities. Generally speaking, the writers and their targets were and are members of the Hispanic community; hence, they are familiar with and even flattered by the attention such a poetic lampoon creates. A decidedly literary form of satirical harassment, the contemporary tradition of *calavera* composition in San Antonio has largely become the domain of the better-educated and elite members of the community.

Fig. 7.5. Cleaning and decorating graves is a family activity. Photograph by Kathy
Vargas, 1988.

In the early 1970s, Moises Espino del Castillo, a local professor emeri-
tus of Spanish, began publishing an annual booklet of *calaveras,* inspired by
Munguia and Rodarte's earlier work. Encouraged by friends, Espino del
Castillo raised the money for the publication, wrote most of the *calaveras*
himself, and oversaw all aspects of the booklet's layout, printing, and distribution. For sixteen years, pages of these short, satirical poems were broken
up only by advertisements of local businesses and business people (who
would then often earn a poetic jibe for their participation in the publication)
and by line drawings done in the style of Jose Luis Guadalupe Posada of
skulls, skeletons, and other images of death. The *calaveras* aimed their
barbed compliments at a range of San Antonians, including Mayor Henry
Cisneros, various city council members, and local florists and *panaderos*
(bakers) whose businesses flourish at this time of year. The publication's success has spawned some imitators over the years, but none with the vitality,
widespread support, and long history of Espino del Castillo's efforts.

Conclusion

The Texas-Mexican commemoration of All Souls' Day is above all a family-
based tradition that has its place among other traditions that celebrate and
solidify the meaning of kinship (fig. 7.5). Family traditions are at the core of

the Mexican American experience. These traditions are pervasive, vital, ongoing, and highly visible, but because of their special focus in family life, they have remained largely undocumented and their importance underappreciated. Yet if there is something critical for all to learn from the Texas-Mexican observance of Day of the Dead, it is the way families and communities use the tools of tradition to externalize their encounter with death and loss through the physical expression of connection. Ephemeral materials and momentary activities continually reinvest a lifetime of devotion to memory of the deceased. The annual decorating and refurbishment of graves, finally, are acts of regeneration.

Notes

This essay originally was written for the catalog accompanying the exhibit "Day of the Dead—The Tex-Mex Tradition" held in 1988 at the Guadalupe Cultural Arts Center in San Antonio, Texas. Pat Jasper and Kay Turner of Texas Folklife Resources curated the exhibit with the help of photographer Kathy Vargas, visual arts director at the center, who also documented South Texas All Souls' Day traditions for the exhibit.

    1.   The extent to which the Day of the Dead has become a widely celebrated and variously meaningful event in Chicano culture requires further study. Catalogs, programs, and ephemera are the major sources of information on the subject at this time. See, for example, publications from annual exhibits at the Alternative Museum in New York City and Galería de la Raza in San Francisco.

    2.   The idea of reinvented traditions, also selective traditions, reflects scholarship that seeks to understand the evolving and adaptive nature of certain national and local traditions that may be reformulated to meet changing social, political, and cultural circumstances. In the United States, the Day of the Dead has been reinvented or selected out as a cultural and aesthetic event of a nature very different from the religious and familial heritage of the Mexican holiday. For further reading on the remaking of tradition in modern cultures, see Williams 1977; Shils 1981; Handler and Linneken 1984; and Santino 1986.

    3.   The concept of the "work of kinship" was first explored in Micaela Di Leonardo's book on the gendered aspects of Italian American family traditions, *The Varieties of Ethnic Experience* (1984). Di Leonardo's work focuses on cross-family and cross-generational kinship ties as they are solidified through women's maintenance of holiday traditions. The "work of kinship" in Mexican American culture also is largely women's work and women's maintenance of relational ties with the dead during the All Souls' Day season is but one example on a continuum of tasks that reinforce family ties.

4.   Several important works by scholars attend to the contestative and adaptive aspects of Mexican American folk traditions in relation to the social and political history of South Texas. See, for example, Paredes 1958, Limón 1983, Peña 1985, Montejano 1987, and Seriff 1989.

5.   For further information and details concerning traditions associated with the Mexican Day of the Dead, see Toor 1947; Green 1969, 1983; Seriff 1984; and Griffith 1985.

6.   For contrast, see Turner 1990 for a discussion of traditional home altars and their place in daily Mexican American folk religious practices.

7.   The making of paper flowers for Mexican American grave decorations in west Texas is thoroughly discussed in Tunnell and Madrid 1991.

References

Di Leonardo, Micaela. 1984. *The Varieties of Ethnic Experience*. Ithaca: Cornell Univ. Press.

Green, Judith Strupp. 1969. *Laughing Souls: The Days of the Dead in Oaxaca, Mexico*. San Diego Museum of Man Popular Series No. 1.

——. 1983. *Día De Los Muertos: An Illustrated Essay and Bibliography*. Santa Barbara, Calif.: Center for Chicano Studies.

Griffith, James S. 1985. *Respect and Continuity: The Arts of Death in a Border Community*. Tucson: Southwest Folklore Center, Univ. of Arizona.

Handler, Richard, and Jocelyn Linneken. 1984. "Tradition: Genuine or Spurious?" *Journal of American Folklore* 97: 193–210.

Limón, Jose. 1983. "Folklore, Social Conflict, and the United States Mexico Border." In *Handbook of American Folklore*, ed. Richard Dorson, 216–26. Bloomington: Indiana Univ. Press.

Montejano, David. 1987. *Mexicans in the Making of South Texas, 1836 -1986*. Austin: Univ. of Texas Press.

Paredes, Americo. 1958. *With His Pistol In His Hand: A Border Ballad and Its Hero*. Austin: Univ. of Texas Press.

Peña, Manuel. 1985. *The Texas Mexican Conjunto*. Austin: Univ. of Texas Press.

Santino, Jack. 1986. "The Folk Assemblage of Autumn: Tradition and Creativity in Halloween Folk Art." In *Folk Art and Art Worlds*, ed. Vlach and Bronner, 151–69.

Seriff, Suzanne. 1984. "Laughing Death: A Critical Analysis of the Days of the Dead Celebration in Oaxaca, Mexico." Master's thesis, Univ. of Texas, Austin.

——. 1989. "'Este Soy Yo:' The Politics of Representation of a Texas-Mexican Folk Artist." Ph.D. diss., Univ. of Texas, Austin.

Shils, Edward. 1981. *Tradition*. Chicago: Univ. of Chicago Press.

Toor, Frances. 1947. *Mexican Folkways*. New York: Crown Publishers.

Tunnell, Curtis, and Enrique Madrid. 1991. "Coronas para los Muertos: The Fine Art of Making Paper Flowers." In *Hecho en Tejas: Texas-Mexican Folk Arts and Crafts,* ed. Joe Graham, 131–45. Denton: Univ. of North Texas Press.

Turner, Kay F. 1990. "Mexican-American Women's Home Altars: The Art of Relationship." Ph.D. diss., Univ. of Texas, Austin.

Williams, Raymond. 1977. *Marxism and Literature.* Oxford: Oxford Univ. Press.

8. Adult Halloween Celebrations on the Canadian Prairie

MICHAEL TAFT

The phenomenon of adult masquerading at Halloween is either rare in North America or, more likely, it has rarely been reported by observers of modern calendar customs. Certainly the children's dress-up tradition of trick-or-treating is common, in both practice and reporting. Halloween masquerading also has become a widespread tradition among urban gay populations,[1] and is somewhat common among teenagers and young adults in the form of costume parties and balls.[2] But to what extent do adults in mainstream North American society practice this tradition?

In examining my own background, I would have to conclude that adult masquerading is rare. In my middle-class, New York City neighborhood of the 1950s, children's trick-or-treating was a yearly event, but I can remember only one occasion where an adult dressed up for Halloween: a neighbor and good friend of my parents once dressed in disguise and went from door to door. Initially we were shocked—our amusement coming only after some reflection on the incident. This man dressed up for only one Halloween and visited only his immediate friends in the neighborhood, but his solitary and peculiar action remained in the minds of his neighbors ever after.

But are my childhood experiences (and my memories of them) typical of those in other North American cultures? As McDowell has written, "We know more about the . . . costume traditions in far-flung areas of the world than about the Halloween costuming that takes place right in our houses and on our streets."[3] I became especially aware of this fact when I first encountered the adult Halloween traditions of rural Saskatchewan.[4]

The southern half of the Canadian province of Saskatchewan—an area the size of California—is made up of hundreds of small towns and hamlets, most with populations of less than five hundred, and some consisting of less than twenty-five souls. These communities are the focuses of the agrarian population surrounding them: family-run, large-production grain farms that have given the province the appearance of a vast, flat checkerboard. These small communities serve the business and social needs of the farm families; the banks, stores, grain elevators, churches, community halls, schools, cafés, hockey rinks, and retirement homes draw together farmers and ranchers from their far-flung homesteads in the countryside.

The one million people of Saskatchewan are a varied lot; most are second- or third-generation descendants from Northern and Eastern European immigrants—Scandinavians, Germans, Poles, Russians, Ukrainians, Hungarians, Romanians—along with some French, Belgian, and Dutch descendants. The province also includes a substantial native population (mostly Cree, Sioux, Chipewayan, Assiniboine, and Ojibwa), British migrants from eastern Canada, American immigrants from a variety of ethnic backgrounds, and a considerable number of Chinese. In short, Saskatchewan can claim a rich ethnic diversity.

These groups have each contributed their ethnic traditions to the folklore of the province, but despite the perceptions of most who have studied Saskatchewan culture, the entirety of the province's expressive heritage is greater than the sum of its individual ethnic traditions. In other words, the people of the province have readily taken up and adapted popular, mainstream North American customs that may have no direct equivalencies in the Old World cultures from which these people are descended. Among these transient, non-ethnic customs is the celebration of Halloween.

As Hunter has observed, Saskatchewan children dress in disguise at Halloween and make the rounds of their neighbors in their quest for treats.[5] What is more unexpected, however, is that adults also engage in disguised house visiting at Halloween. Hunter's description of this adult custom, based as it is on a single informant from an especially isolated Ukrainian settlement in Saskatchewan, might seem anomalous, rather than representative of any province-wide tradition. In my own early investigations of adult Halloween masquerading in a French Saskatchewan community, I too thought that the custom was rather peculiar to this ethnic enclave on the prairies—a transference of the French Mardi Gras.[6] But I soon learned that this adult tradition was common to many communities in the province, that no one ethnic group could claim this custom as its own, and that this tradition was certainly one manifestation of Halloween as celebrated by mainstream North American society.

This celebration, as outlined by Hunter and as I will further describe below, conforms in its general structure to Halpert's mumming category, the "informal visit".[7] Adults dress in costumes that conceal their identity, gather in small groups, visit homes (as well as outlying farmsteads) in their community where they disrupt the household and demand drinks, and then often congregate at the local pub or attend a masked ball. In short, the custom is a form of mumming (and I will refer to it as such), but the exact details of this practice vary from community to community, and indeed from group to group within these communities.

What is a "typical" adult mumming tradition in Saskatchewan? Usually a month or two before Halloween, people will begin thinking about whether they will "go out this year." They will discuss the possibilities with their friends and relatives, and begin planning their costumes. Of course, Halloweening (as it is often called) might also occur on the spur of the moment, usually at the urging of others:

> Glenna: Yeah, you know, people can come to your house at about two in the morning and roust you out of bed and say, "Come on, get up! We're going Halloweening!" I mean, that has happened to us a couple of times. And by the time—five or six in the morning—and you're visiting the third house, or whatever, since they picked you up—you know, they're already pooped out and asleep in the car. And you're just getting going. (Lintlaw, Saskatchewan, 14 August 1985)

As Hunter has shown, there is often an evolution of involvement in Halloween house visiting. Community members might begin the custom as children—trick-or-treating in a traditional North American fashion. As teenagers and young adults, they might turn to pranking, but they might also form their own groups—based on friendship and kin—and continue their house visiting in a more rowdy, "adult" manner. Young parents will often forego adult house visiting in favor of accompanying their children on trick-or-treat rounds; however, as their children grow older, they might reform their cohorts and become true adult mumming troupes.

Childhood friends, co-workers, siblings, married couples, drinking buddies—the associations between members of a particular mumming group take a number of forms. In some cases, a husband and wife, or two particularly close friends, will purposely *not* go mumming together, for fear that if one member of the troupe is recognized, then the other's identity will become clear through association; thus, for example, a wife might go with someone else's husband.

Amelia, of Lintlaw, Saskatchewan, revealed a number of variables which determined whether or not a house was visited by her group of mummers. On the one hand, she would go to the house of close friends, even if they lived miles away from her, in order to honor them with her visit, but on the other hand,

> I think, too, it depends on the people you associate with, you know. Like you got your close circle of friends and then you got your extended circle of friends. It might be that Halloween night might be one of the nights you might visit some of your extended friend's places that you wouldn't maybe hit [on other occasions]. Because you don't want to go to people's places that will know you right off. (Lintlaw, Saskatchewan, 14 August 1985)

In other words, she might prefer to visit those "extended friends" who would be less likely to guess her true identity than would her more intimate friends.

The interplay among the different networks of friendship, association, and hospitality account for the somewhat contradictory descriptions of house-visit itineraries that people in the province give. Yet whatever the reasons for choosing a particular co-participant and itinerary, the heart of the Halloween tradition is the house visit itself:

> Rita: If we just want to surprise someone, we'll stop at their door, and they'll look at us. They don't have a clue who we are. And we're not saying anything. We'll say, "Trick or treat," and they'll say, "Do we know you?" And we just nod, or whatever we do. And then they'll say, "Do you want to come in?" And we go [in]. And then they'll say, "Do you want some candy? What do you guys want?" Oh we don't say anything. And then they go into the liquor cabinet and come out: "You want this?" And then finally they say, "Well you have to tell us who you are." And then we'll say, "No." "Then you can't have any drinks; you can just have candy." . . . In the end, like, we end up telling them who you are. (Ponteix, Saskatchewan, 9 February 1983)

Both visitors and hosts endure the pressure of an everyday reciprocity shattered by the special rules of Halloween behavior, because at any other time of year, visitors readily identify themselves and hosts readily oblige their guests with food and drink.

This hospitality "game" may end in a number of ways. The mummers might wear down their hosts and receive the asked-for drinks; the hosts might break the will of the mummers, forcing them either to leave without refreshment or to reveal their identities in order to be treated as normal guests. In most reported cases, however, the mummers will not reveal their identities under any circumstances, even if offered drinks and even if their identities are guessed by their hosts. Throughout Halloween night, most mummers remain strangers.

Regarding costumes: escaped prisoners, tramps, witches, ghosts, characters from film and television, Indians, blacks, Chinese, politicians, even an entire wedding entourage—the list of possibilities is endless, and imaginative Halloweeners will readily transform their appearance (and sometimes their behavior) to fit these character types. A particularly common false identity requires the simple act of cross-dressing: as in other mumming traditions, men will dress as women and women will don the clothes of men:[8]

> Brad: So I had a real big bust, eh? I walked in, just prancing around. Got up to the pool table with this little short skirt to about here. So I spread my legs. And everybody's looking. Nobody knew who I was. They figured everybody else out—or some of the guys—but they didn't know who I was, okay? Guys are on patrol—Halloween night—driving up and down. Apparently, they tell me, I jumped into a vehicle with these two bachelors, driving around town. (Lintlaw, Saskatchewan, 14 August 1985)

If one of the games of Halloween concerns hospitality, perhaps the more important game requires that the hosts try to discover the true identities of their disguised visitors. That the largest body of memories and stories about Halloween night concerns this guessing game indicates the significance of this part of the Saskatchewan mumming custom. Guisers delight in recalling how they tricked their friends and family, for the stories told with most relish concern the tricking of the very people who would be most able to recognize them:

> Amelia: Dora came along. She was dressed from home when she got this far. And she changed her clothes and used some of our costumes. And went on her way and went home. And her husband didn't know her. He thought that somebody else had come in. He was having a great time trying to figure out who this was, because she had changed when she left, but he never thought of her doing that. So when she got home, she had to be another person. (Lintlaw, Saskatchewan, 14 August 1985)

This guessing game sometimes continues well after Halloween, because Saskatchewan mummers often will not reveal their identities even weeks, months, or years after their house visits; and former hosts might continue their quest for the true identities of their visitors long after Halloween is over.[9]

Variations on this game abound. A member of a household who guesses the identities of the mummers has the choice of telling or not telling the others in the house, blackmailing the mummers with his or her information, following the mummers to other homes to see who else can guess, revealing the identities of the mummers sometime after Halloween night, or in some other way making use of this privileged information. Conversely, mummers might reveal their identities to selected individuals in the community whom they favor in some way:

> Rita: My mother's generation. Now that they're all grandmothers—like they're all grandmothers.
>
> Enid: They're a "grandma club." And they do that. They get dressed up.
>
> Rita: They do more than some of the kids. And I didn't know who any of them were. The only reason why I knew was because they came up to me, when I came in in the afternoon, and said, "When we see you we'll call you: 'Hi sexy.' Or something. That's—you'll know that's us." And then we went to the bar and it was fine. We were having a good time. And these ladies come up and: "Hi sexy!" And I thought, "Grandma Oldfield! Is that you?" I thought, "Holy moly!" (Ponteix, Saskatchewan, 9 February 1983)

Pub owners are, of course, aware of local Halloween customs and will decorate their establishments accordingly (in recent times, this means paper witches, ghosts, and other popular North American Halloween motifs) and readily give mummers free range in the pub. The hospitality game is certainly more difficult to play in a pub, but patrons might still bribe the mummers with drinks, or the mummers might hint that they should be treated to drinks, as a way of playing with the normal rules of sociability in pubs. The game of guessing identities, however, is as popular in the pub as in the home, but pub celebrants often dress in costumes that do not necessarily hide their identities. In this respect, the pub acts as a venue for a masked ball, where some of the participants are more intent on showing off their ingenuity in costuming than in hiding their features. Thus, apart from the house-visiting mummers who drop into the pub—and who will usually have their identities hidden—there are often another group of maskers whose faces, at least, are recognizable, and whose costumes are clearly representative of some character type: witches, devils, monsters, and other motifs associated with the supernatural aspects of North American Halloween, or characters with no particular relationship to a "scary" theme, such as clowns, priests, members of one or another ethnic group, Siamese twins, and the like.

Besides house visiting and masked pub dances or balls, the third element of Saskatchewan Halloween customs is pranking. This custom, however, has become increasingly restricted in its classic form. One or two generations ago, Halloween pranking was common, and generally involved turning the agricultural world upside down. Thus, pranksters would hoist farm wagons onto barn roofs; they might harness and saddle a rancher's cattle; and tractors, balers, and other farm machinery might find their way out of the fields and onto the streets of town. A favorite prank, both in Saskatchewan and throughout North America, involved tipping over an outhouse, often when its owner was busy inside.[10] Other pranks included petty vandalism, such as soaping windows, throwing eggs at cars, deflating car tires, burning hay bales, and even moving around parts of the town's streetscape. What characterizes most of this type of pranking activity is that it was generally the preserve of young adults and teenagers, usually boys rather than girls.[11]

The demise of the outhouse, agricultural machinery that is too expensive and complicated to tamper with, a change in the attitudes toward pranking, and perhaps—as some whom I've interviewed have observed—a diminishing work ethic have made the strenuous work of such pranking less fashionable that it once was. Where people once tacitly condoned petty vandalism and adolescent misrule on Halloween, they now work against the continuance of this custom. Street patrols at Halloween are now common.

Not all pranking, however, is perceived as destructive. The general rambunctiousness of mummers and the small tricks they occasionally play on their hosts is both accepted and expected behavior at Halloween. The mummer is a trickster, who may in turn be tricked. As tricksters, therefore, Halloween mummers, whatever their ages or status in the community, perform certain types of pranks:

> Sandra: The senior citizens in this district are notorious. There's about five couples that gather and they dress up and they go out, every year, usually to each other's places. But I know, I know she didn't find her coffee pot for two weeks, one year, after Halloween. It was in a dresser drawer.

> Taft: So they go around and visit each other's houses and play tricks?

> Sandra: They put clothes on the line, and then everyone found out whose clothes they were. The longjohns even had a name in them.

> Paula: Just like some of the younger ones do, too. (Glentworth, Saskatchewan, 24 January 1991)

Mummer's pranks are mischievous but harmless; they disrupt everyday household and community life, but they avoid maliciousness or the destruction of property. What these pranks lack in destructiveness, however, they often make up for in taboo activity. Mummers break the normal prohibitions against overt scatological and sexual display:

> Betty: Oh we've got to tell about the time the girls went to the drugstore, Grisdale's drugstore.
>
> Kelly: Yuckadoo! What were they dressed like though?
>
> Betty: I don't know what they were dressed like.
>
> Kelly: They went in with a pot—a pee pot.
>
> Betty: A kid's [pot], wasn't it a kid's?
>
> Kelly: A pee pot.
>
> Betty: Wasn't it a chamber pail?
>
> Kelly: A chamber pail. I think it was a chamber pail with yellow jello [inside], you know, that hadn't [hardened] and a couple of sausages.
>
> Betty: Oh it was terrible. And they went into a drugstore. And the worst of it was, this druggist was—he was absolutely—he was just very squeamish, you know. Just about threw up, I guess.
>
> Kelly: This strict, straight-faced person.
>
> Betty: They just had to do it to him. (Midale, Saskatchewan, 11 July 1990)

The antisocial atmosphere of the Saskatchewan Halloween, however, rarely creates problems within the community. The roles people play—mummers and hosts, alike—are usually well understood, and there is generally an agreed suspension of the rules by all concerned. Yet if the normal rules of behavior are suspended, Halloween creates its own special rules of propriety: after all, Halloween night in these small towns is not a time of unrestrained anarchy. There is no criminal intent in the Halloween customs, nor does criminality occur. In effect, the celebrants do not break the rules of society; they only play with the idea of breaking the rules.

Several people used the word "scary" to describe the unease that accompanies the antisocial aspects of Halloween mumming, but they would often pair this word with "fun," which indicates the purposely ambivalent nature of the game mummers and hosts play. Playing with unease allows the celebrants to examine the whole question of social discomfort in a safe way.

By placing social discomfort within the confines of the "world" of Halloween night, mummers and hosts can feel the real unease of socially tense situations without ultimately worrying about the consequences of this unease—nobody is going to be intentionally hurt. Thus the "fun" is partly in the "scariness" of Halloween night.

Catharsis is certainly a function of the Saskatchewan Halloween celebration—a release from the everyday social constraints through ritual reversal and misrule.[12] The times of the year when one can step out of character are few, and Halloween is one of those times. As a mummer, one must step out of character in order to remain unrecognized, but beyond the necessity of hiding one's true identity, stepping out of character is pleasing in itself—a chance to try new forms of social interaction without being accused of "not being oneself."

The question remains, however, as to why people in small-town Saskatchewan celebrate Halloween in the manner I have described. After all, mumming and masquerading (as well as hosting such visitors) take considerable planning and energy. Catharsis and the release from social constraints are not reasons for the celebration—they are results of the celebration. There are, in fact, several occasions throughout the year when people in the province replace the workaday world with a playful, perhaps even cathartic or carnivalesque, atmosphere. Community meals—fowl suppers, wild game suppers, pancake breakfasts—are common, especially as fund-raisers; and sports such as rodeos, hockey and softball tournaments, and curling bonspiels bring the community together several times a year. Parades and festivals of various sorts are a regular seasonal feature in many prairie towns, and birthdays, anniversaries, retirements, weddings, funerals and church services are all part of the yearly calendar of community rituals.

Certainly prairie folk have a penchant for dressing in costume, and in this respect, Halloween is part of the more general practice of masquerading in Saskatchewan. In past generations, for example, the one-room school would produce a yearly Christmas concert in which community children would put on a variety of skits, and in which a community member would dress as Santa Claus and give gifts to the children.[13] Costuming at wedding and baby showers is common, and skits—especially mock wedding skits—are a regular part of anniversary celebrations in the community.[14] As well, certain ethnic traditions demand disguise and house visiting in somewhat the same manner as Halloween mumming: the Ukrainian Christmas tradition of the Malanka and the German Christmas custom of belsnickling are both practiced in Saskatchewan.[15] Thus most people in the province are familiar with masquerading in one form or another.

The difference between Halloween and these other community celebrations, however, lies in the lack of associations this celebration has with other rituals. It is not a fund-raiser, nor is it part of the celebration of some rite of passage, such as a wedding, birth, or anniversary. It has no religious connotations in the minds of the participants, nor is it tied to major sacred and secular celebrations such as Christmas or Easter. (Compare the European carnival and Mardi Gras, which have obvious associations in the minds of the celebrants with Easter and Lent.) Halloween stands alone as a time for revelry, unattached to any greater significance.

Some have certainly argued that Halloween is a rite of harvest whose origins go back at least as far as ancient Celtic traditions.[16] But the people of Saskatchewan are, for the most part, neither aware of this history nor particularly interested in it. (The popular media care, however, and virtually every year they ask me to explain to them, once again, the origins of Halloween. But the media have as little interest in the indigenous customs of the Saskatchewan Halloween as the Saskatchewan people have in the historical origins of the holiday.) Kuhn has put this case succinctly: "It is quite doubtful if one in ten thousand even ventures a random guess as to why he goes out in the street of town or village in grotesque disguise. He does it from sheer force of custom."[17]

The people are aware that Halloween falls near the end of harvest; in fact, in Saskatchewan, harvest usually ends at the beginning of October, while farmers spend the remainder of the month hauling their grain and hay. After the hard work of harvest, Halloween is definitely a time to celebrate. But few farmers would go so far as to associate Halloween with symbolic death or the awakening of souls or spirits.

The proper harvest celebration in Saskatchewan is Thanksgiving, which falls appropriately on 14 October—in contrast to its later date in the United States. Special church services, a feast, and the associated symbolic decorations of harvest (wheat sheaves, dried ears of corn) mark this celebration as the acknowledged descendant of ancient rituals:

> Kelly: It is different from Halloween, that's for sure.
>
> Betty: Thanksgiving is a more serious time of the year, you know.
>
> Kelly: That's right. Halloween is a joke.
>
> Betty: That's probably the most fun time of the year, you know, for doing stupid things. That's about it—once a year, you're allowed to do it that night. (Midale, Saskatchewan, 11 July 1990)

The symbolic and historical significance of Thanksgiving, its mixture of sacred and secular traditions, is lost on nobody in Saskatchewan. The same cannot be said of Halloween.

By contrast, Halloween celebrations in many parts of the United States seem more closely tied to the harvest than the holiday described here. The warmer climate of the United States calls for a late October or early November harvest, coinciding more closely with Halloween than with American Thanksgiving, which occurs well after Halloween and takes on certain associations with Christmas. Thus American Thanksgiving is not nearly as appropriate a harvest ritual as is its Canadian counterpart. Perhaps as an indication of the lack of any general association of Halloween with harvest on the Canadian prairie is that the harvest and nature/culture symbolism Santino ascribes to urban and suburban American celebrations of Halloween—pumpkins, shocks of corn, and the like—is not nearly as prevalent in the communities of rural Saskatchewan.[18]

The historical and sacred emptiness of Halloween is partially explained by the fact that it is, essentially, a modern, introduced bit of popular culture in Saskatchewan. The ethnic mixture of the province's population allows for few universally recognized Old World traditions. The Halloween that people in Saskatchewan celebrate is very much a North American one, just as the Halloween in Newfoundland is a relatively modern tradition, and the trick-or-treat and masking customs on 31 October in England and Finland have been introduced from the United States and Canada.[19]

The relationship between Halloween and harvest celebrations in Saskatchewan, then, is more coincidental than anything else. The significance of this holiday, beyond its important function as a celebration of nonsense and reversal, lies in another direction. Certainly, the Saskatchewan Halloween is some kind of commentary on stranger/neighbor, insider/outsider relationships in the community. Firestone, among others, has understood the importance of Newfoundland Christmas mumming in this respect.[20] In both Newfoundland and Saskatchewan, mummers act the part of strangers when they intrude in at least a mock-threatening way into people's homes.

Although it is instructive to compare Newfoundland mumming with its counterpart in Saskatchewan, the meaning of these outwardly similar traditions is not identical. For Newfoundlanders, mumming is a fundamental statement of island identity and has taken on strong symbolic significance in the island's nativist movement; it is a powerful and aggressive commentary on what "belonging" means in the context of a Newfoundland outport.[21] By contrast, mumming is not nearly as loaded with cultural significance for people in Saskatchewan. For one thing, Christmas—the time of Newfoundland mumming—is a fundamentally more serious celebration than the secular holiday of Halloween.

But a more important point of difference lies in the fact that mumming in Saskatchewan is not the double-edged sword that it seems to be in Newfoundland. Newfoundlanders not only honor each other through mumming visits (showing acceptance of a family as a good community member and a friend), but they can also punish community outcasts through mumming. The best example I have of this activity is from my own experience as a Newfoundland mummer in the early 1980s; but in order to understand this story, it is important to know that in Newfoundland mumming, the mummers usually remove their masks and act in a normal, sociable manner, once they have been given food or drinks, or once their real identities have been discovered.[22]

In a community (that I shall not name), I went mumming with a local family and some mutual friends. Before visiting one house, the leader of our group made jokes about the single mother who lived there. We entered her home in disguise, saying nothing, in traditional mumming style. Even after she gave us drinks, however, we continued our silence. Suddenly, the leader of the group signaled for us to leave, which we did; the woman remained mystified and undoubtedly troubled about who we were. It became clear to me that the leader meant to play a cruel joke on this woman (who, for whatever reasons, seemed to be a community outcast) by not fulfilling his expected role as a mummer. I have heard of no similar experiences in Saskatchewan.

If Saskatchewan mumming, then, is not a particularly strong symbol of harvest, stranger/neighbor relations, nativism, or social divisions and tensions, where does its significance lie? The answer may be that, by default, Halloween is the most important *community* holiday of the year for people in Saskatchewan. Christmas, especially with the demise of the school Christmas concerts, is now a family, rather than community, get-together, as is Thanksgiving and Easter. Because of the peculiarities of Canadian identity, Canada Day (1 July) has never become a strong community celebration in the way the Fourth of July is in the United States. Fund-raising suppers, parades, and other such celebrations do not support a wide range of festive behaviors, nor do all members of the community participate in them. Halloween is the only day in the year when everyone in the community is free to contribute to a celebration in whatever way they wish: as mummers, as hosts, as onlookers, as pranksters, or even minimally as an audience for stories about the night's activities.

The acts of mumming, house visiting, and pub crawling lend themselves to community cohesiveness. Mummers display themselves to their neighbors and challenge them to identify the mummers as members of the community. House visiting strengthens neighborly ties by its very nature, even if the mummers remain strangers and never reveal their identities. Assembling at the pub celebrates a town gathering spot, and in the process, highlights the importance of such centers of community activity. In this one respect, the function of Saskatchewan mumming is similar to that of Newfoundland mumming, when "the community celebrates its identity."[23]

The people themselves realize this function. Many who have left their small-town homes in Saskatchewan make sure to return for at least two occasions: Christmas and Halloween. At Christmas, they renew their ties with family; at Halloween, they reintegrate themselves into their local community:

> Rita: I think everyone goes home for Halloween. That's the thing. I don't know, because if you go—like if you stay up here in Saskatoon for Halloween, you don't know anybody at the bar anyways. And what's the fun of trying to guess who it is, when you don't even know the person anyways? It's not the same at all. (Ponteix, Saskatchewan, 9 February 1983)

Guessing identities or fooling friends—both aspects of mumming reestablish ties; both allow friends and neighbors to say, "I know who you are" in an especially creative and symbolic way.

What makes Halloween particularly significant in this respect is that the small communities of the province are under threat. The precariousness of prairie dry-land farming and the historical migration of Saskatchewan people to other provinces and to the cities has always threatened the existence of prairie villages, and, indeed, there are many ghost towns in Saskatchewan. Recently, times have been especially hard on the prairies, with international economic trends and government policies driving people off the farms and away from rural towns.[24]

Halloween will do nothing to prevent Saskatchewan communities from dying, if they do indeed die, but through its function of bringing people together and giving them a renewed sense of community, Halloween acts as a commentary on community continuity and cohesiveness. Similarly, adult Halloween traditions in other parts of North America have been strongest among those who feel a special communal affinity, whether urbanites who live on cul-de-sacs, parents whose children attend the Montessori School, or members of an American Sign Language Deaf Club (to name three recent studies).[25]

The complexities of any community celebration are considerable. The reasons why people perform such rituals are many and often contradictory. Adult Halloween festivities in Saskatchewan exhibit all of this complexity, and for this reason, if for no other, deserve our attention.

Notes

1.   Mary O'Drain, "San Francisco's Gay Halloween," *International Folklore Review* 4 (1986): 90–95; Jack Kugelmass, "Wishes Come True: Designing the Greenwich Village Halloween Parade," *Journal of American Folklore* 104 (1991): 443–65.

2.   John H. McDowell, "Halloween Costuming Among Young Adults in Bloomington, Indiana: A Local Exotic," *Indiana Folklore* 14, no. 1 (1985): 1–18.

3.   McDowell, "Halloween Costuming," 1. This same observation has been made by Sylvia Grider, "The Razor Blades in the Apples Syndrome," in *Perspectives on Contemporary Legend: Proceedings of the Conference on Contemporary Legend, Sheffield, July 1982*, ed. Paul Smith (Sheffield: CECTAL, Univ. of Sheffield, 1984), 129, and Darryl M. Hunter, "No 'Malice in Wonderland': Conservation and Change in the Three Hallowe'ens of Ann Mesko," *Culture & Tradition* 7 (1983): 50, among others.

4.   My sources for the following information on Saskatchewan traditions (unless otherwise noted) are a number of interviews I conducted with people from various parts of the province between the years 1983 and 1991. I would like to thank all the people who gave their time to my investigations (and whose names I have decided to change for the purpose of this article). I would also like to thank the Social Sciences and Humanities Research Council of Canada for its financial support for parts of my research.

5.   Hunter, "No 'Malice in Wonderland,'" passim; see also Edith Lindquist, "Penny-Lynne Micklewright's Hallowe'en Customs from 1959 to 1981 in Yorkton, Saskatchewan," unpublished student paper, Taft Folklore Collection, Saskatchewan Archives Board, accession 82-20c.

6.   Michael Taft, "Unmasking Hallowe'en: A Preliminary Look at a Small Town Celebration," paper presented at the Folklore Studies Association of Canada annual meeting in Quebec City, 1983.

7.   Herbert Halpert, "A Typology of Mumming," in *Christmas Mumming in Newfoundland: Essays in Anthropology, Folklore, and History*, ed. Herbert Halpert and G. M. Story (Toronto: Univ. of Toronto Press, 1969), 34–61.

8.   Cross-dressing is common in Newfoundland Christmas mumming—see Margaret R. Robertson, *The Newfoundland Mummer's Christmas House-Visit* (Ottawa: National Museums of Canada, 1984), 27–29; Nova Scotia belsnickling—see Richard Bauman, "Belsnickling in a Nova Scotia Island Community," *Western Folklore* 31 (1972): 234; the Miss Funny character in the Christmas mumming of Ballymenone, Northern Ireland—see Henry Glassie, *All Silver and No Brass: An Irish Christmas Mumming* (Bloomington: Indiana Univ. Press, 1975), passim, to name but three examples.

9.   This extension of the one-night custom is similar to that of the Nova Scotia belsnickling tradition—see Bauman, "Belsnickling," 238.

10.   Steve Siporin's chapter in the present volume gives the best description of these rural pranks. On the illicit functions of outhouses, including pranking, see

Gerald Thomas, "Functions of the Newfoundland Outhouse," *Western Folklore* 48 (1989): 233–42.

11. Social sanctioning of youthful pranking at Halloween is a widespread custom. Siporin describes it in relation to American rural Halloween; Henry Glassie describes similar youthful pranking in Northern Ireland in *Passing the Time in Ballymenone: Culture and History of an Ulster Community* (Philadelphia: Univ. of Pennsylvania Press, 1982), 778, as was also found in the Republic of Ireland—see, Sean O Suilleabhain, *A Handbook of Irish Folklore* (Detroit: Singing Tree Press, 1970), 345. Misconduct by college boys at Halloween is also part of this same pranking custom—see Keith Walden, "Respectable Hooligans: Male Toronto College Students Celebrate Hallowe'en, 1884–1910," *Canadian Historical Review* 68 (1987): 1–34.

12. The starting point for most studies of reversal and misrule is Mikhail Bakhtin's examination of the carnivalesque, *Rabelais and His World,* trans. Helene Iswolsky (Cambridge: MIT Press, 1968).

13. The fullest description of the Christmas concert in the Canadian prairies is John C. Charyk, *The Biggest Day of the Year: The Old-Time School Christmas Concert* (Saskatoon: Western Producer Prairie Books, 1985).

14. For a description of showers, see Colleen Kanhai, "Wedding Showers at Weldon, Saskatchewan," unpublished student paper, Taft Folklore Collection, Saskatchewan Archives Board, accession 82-13c; for mock weddings, see Michael Taft, "Folk Drama on the Great Plains: The Mock Wedding in Canada and the United States," *North Dakota History* 56, no. 4 (1989): 16–23.

15. For the Malanka tradition, see Robert B. Klymasz, "'Malanka': Ukrainian Mummery on the Prairies," *Canadian Folk Music Journal* 13 (1985): 32–36, and Robert B. Klymasz, *Svièto: Celebrating Ukrainian-Canadian Ritual in East Central Alberta Through the Generations,* ed. Radomir B. Bilash (Edmonton: Historic Resources Division, Alberta Culture & Multiculturalism, 1992), passim; for belsnickling, see Andrew Murray, "From Peltznickel to Belsnickle," unpublished student paper, Taft Folklore Collection, Saskatchewan Archives Board, accession 87-39.

16. Jack Santino, "Halloween in America: Contemporary Customs and Performances," *Western Folklore* 42 (1983): 3–8; Siporin, "American Halloween Pranks," 13.

17. Alvin Boyd Kuhn, *Hallowe'en: A Festival of Lost Meanings,* 2d ed. (Wheaton, Ill.: Theosophical Press, 1966), 4.

18. Jack Santino, "The Folk *Assemblage* of Autumn: Tradition and Creativity in Halloween Folk Art," in *Folk Art and Art Worlds,* ed. John Michael Vlach and Simon J. Bronner (Ann Arbor: Univ. Microfilms Research Press, 1986), 151–69.

19. For the introduction of Halloween to Newfoundland, see Philip Hiscock, "Hallowe'en Guys Come to Newfoundland," *The Folklore Round Table* 9 (Fall 1989): 28–36; for England, see E. Beck, "Children's Halloween Customs in Sheffield," *Lore and Language* 3, no. 9 (1983), 83; for Finland, see Mary-Ann Elfving, "Varför studera innovativa ideer? Valentindagen och Halloween," *Meddelanden från folkultursarkivet* 7 (1981): 116–23.

20. Melvin M. Firestone, "Mummers and Strangers in Northern Newfoundland," in *Christmas Mumming in Newfoundland,* ed. Halpert and Story, 63–75.

21. See Gerald L. Pocius, "The Mummers Song in Newfoundland: Intellectuals, Revivalists and Cultural Nativism," *Newfoundland Studies* 4, no. 1 (1988): 57–85.

22. See Robertson, *The Newfoundland Mummer's Christmas House-Visit,* 85–87. On the violent and antisocial nature of Newfoundland mumming, see the synopsis of the considerable scholarship on this subject given by Don Handelman in his *Models and Mirrors: Towards an Anthropology of Public Events* (Cambridge, England: Cambridge Univ. Press, 1990), 146. I do not feel good about the particular experience that I relate, as it raises serious ethical questions about my role as a participant observer. My only excuse is that I did not realize what was happening until the incident was over.

23. Louis J. Chiaramonte, "Mumming in 'Deep Harbour': Aspects of Social Organization and Drinking," in *Christmas Mumming in Newfoundland,* ed. Halpert and Story, 103; see also Bauman, "Belsnickling," 243.

24. I have discussed these factors in more detail in "The Mock Wedding in Western Canada: A Sense of Continuity," paper presented at the California Folklore Society annual meeting, Los Angeles, 1991.

25. Barbara B. Brown and Carol M. Werner, "Social Cohesiveness, Territoriality, and Holiday Decorations: The Influence of Cul-de-Sacs," *Environment and Behavior* 17 (1985): 539–65; Nancy Klavans, "A Halloween Brunch: The Affirmation of Group in a Temporary Community," in *"We Gather Together": Food and Festival in American Life,* ed. Theodore C. Humphrey and Lin T. Humphrey (Ann Arbor: UMI Research Press, 1988), 43–51; and Stephanie Aileen Hall, "'The Deaf Club is Like a Second Home': An Ethnography of Folklore Communication in American Sign Language (Pennsylvania)" (Ph.D. diss., Univ. of Pennsylvania, 1989), respectively.

References

Bakhtin, Mikhail. 1968. *Rabelais and His World,* trans. Helene Iswolsky. Cambridge: MIT Press.

Bauman, Richard. 1972. "Belsnickling in a Nova Scotia Island Community." *Western Folklore* 31: 229–43.

Beck, E. 1983. "Children's Halloween Customs in Sheffield." *Lore and Language* 3, no. 9: 70–88.

Brown, Barbara B., and Carol M. Werner. 1985. "Social Cohesiveness, Territoriality, and Holiday Decorations: The Influence of Cul-de-Sacs." *Environment and Behavior* 17: 539–65.

Charyk, John C. 1985. *The Biggest Day of the Year: The Old-Time School Christmas Concert.* Saskatoon: Western Producer Prairie Books.

Chiaramonte, Louis J. 1969. "Mumming in 'Deep Harbour': Aspects of Social Organization and Drinking." In *Christmas Mumming in Newfoundland,* ed. Halpert and Story, 76–103.

Elfving, Mary-Ann. 1981. "Varför studera innovativa ideer? Valentindagen och Halloween." *Meddelanden från folkultursarkivet* 7: 116–23.

Firestone, Melvin M. 1969. "Mummers and Strangers in Northern Newfoundland." In *Christmas Mumming in Newfoundland,* ed. Halpert and Story, 63-75.

Glassie, Henry. 1975. *All Silver and No Brass: An Irish Christmas Mumming.* Bloomington: Indiana Univ. Press.

———. 1982. *Passing the Time in Ballymenone: Culture and History of an Ulster Community.* Philadelphia: Univ. of Pennsylvania Press.

Grider, Sylvia. 1984. "The Razor Blades in the Apples Syndrome." In *Perspectives on Contemporary Legend,* ed. P. Smith, 128–40.

Hall, Stephanie Aileen. 1989. "'The Deaf Club is Like a Second Home': An Ethnography of Folklore Communication in American Sign Language (Pennsylvania)." Ph.D. diss., Univ. of Pennsylvania.

Halpert, Herbert. 1969. "A Typology of Mumming." In *Christmas Mumming in Newfoundland,* ed. Halpert and Story, 34–61. Toronto: Univ. of Toronto Press.

Handelman, Don. 1990. *Models and Mirrors: Towards an Anthropology of Public Events.* Cambridge: Cambridge Univ. Press.

Hiscock, Philip. 1989. "Hallowe'en Guys Come to Newfoundland." *Folklore Round Table* 9: 28–36.

Hunter, Darryl M. 1983. "No 'Malice in Wonderland': Conservation and Change in the Three Hallowe'ens of Ann Mesko." *Culture & Tradition* 7: 37–53.

Kanhai, Colleen. 1982. "Wedding Showers at Weldon, Saskatchewan." Unpublished student paper, Taft Folklore Collection, Saskatchewan Archives Board, accession 82-13c.

Klavans, Nancy. 1988. "A Halloween Brunch: The Affirmation of Group in a Temporary Community." In *"We Gather Together": Food and Festival in American Life,* ed. Theodore C. Humphrey and Lin T. Humphrey, 43–51. Ann Arbor: Univ. Microfilms International Research Press.

Klymasz, Robert B. 1985. "'Malanka': Ukrainian Mummery on the Prairies." *Canadian Folk Music Journal* 13: 32–36.

———. 1992. *Svièto: Celebrating Ukrainian-Canadian Ritual in East Central Alberta Through the Generations.* Ed. Radomir B. Bilash. Edmonton: Historic Resources Division, Alberta Culture & Multiculturalism.

Kugelmass, Jack. 1991. "Wishes Come True: Designing the Greenwich Village Halloween Parade." *Journal of American Folklore* 104: 443–65.

Kuhn, Alvin Boyd. 1966. *Hallowe'en: A Festival of Lost Meanings.* 2d ed. Wheaton, Ill.: Theosophical Press.

Lindquist, Edith. 1982. "Penny-Lynne Micklewright's Hallowe'en Customs from 1959 to 1981 in Yorkton, Saskatchewan." Unpublished student paper, Taft Folklore Collection, Saskatchewan Archives Board, accession 82-20c.

McDowell, John H. 1985. "Halloween Costuming Among Young Adults in Bloomington, Indiana: A Local Exotic." *Indiana Folklore* 14, no. 1: 1–18.

Murray, Andrew. 1987. "From Peltznickel to Belsnickle." Unpublished student paper, Taft Folklore Collection, Saskatchewan Archives Board, accession 87-39.

O Suilleabhain, Sean. 1970. *A Handbook of Irish Folklore.* Detroit: Singing Tree Press.

O'Drain, Mary. 1986. "San Francisco's Gay Halloween." *International Folklore Review* 4: 90–95.

Pocius, Gerald L. 1988. "The Mummers Song in Newfoundland: Intellectuals, Revivalists and Cultural Nativism." *Newfoundland Studies* 4, no. 1: 57–85.

Robertson, Margaret R. 1984. *The Newfoundland Mummer's Christmas House-Visit.* Ottawa: National Museums of Canada.

Santino, Jack. 1983. "Halloween in America: Contemporary Customs and Performances." *Western Folklore* 42: 1–20.

———. 1986. "The Folk *Assemblage* of Autumn: Tradition and Creativity in Halloween Folk Art." In *Folk Art and Art Worlds,* ed. Vlach and Bronner, 151–69.

Siporin, Steve. 1987. "American Halloween Pranks: 'Just a Little Inconvenience.'" Paper presented at the American Folklore Society annual meeting, Albuquerque.

Taft, Michael. 1982. "Unmasking Hallowe'en: A Preliminary Look at a Small Town Celebration." Paper presented at the Folklore Studies Association of Canada annual meeting, Quebec City.

———. 1989. "Folk Drama on the Great Plains: The Mock Wedding in Canada and the United States." *North Dakota History* 56, no. 4: 16–23.

———. 1991. "The Mock Wedding in Western Canada: A Sense of Continuity." Paper presented at the California Folklore Society annual meeting, Los Angeles.

Thomas, Gerald. 1989. "Functions of the Newfoundland Outhouse." *Western Folklore* 48: 233–42.

Walden, Keith. 1987. "Respectable Hooligans: Male Toronto College Students Celebrate Hallowe'en, 1884–1910." *Canadian Historical Review* 68: 1–34.

9. The Seasonal Context of Halloween
Vermont's Unwritten Law

A. W. SADLER

This is an examination of the bi-seasonal calendar of rural north-western Vermont, whose major transition point, as you go from summer to winter, is marked by the old festival of Hallowe'en. It is also a kind of bio-graphical sketch of my principal informant, whom I shall call Frank Briggs. He is a man of the land, a man who belongs to the farm and the village of his birth—not quite in the way his forefathers did, but as he settles into middle age, the land again begins to assert its hold over him, as it perhaps does over all of us.

It is not the man I wish to begin with, however, but the landscape of his world, and his village, Fairfield. It lies well north of the "big city" of Burlington, amid the rolling green hills that skirt Mount Mansfield and its neighbors, Belvidere, Haystack, and Tillotson. Standing with the Green Mountains to their back, the people of Fairfield look westward to the waters of Lake Champlain and the craggy Adirondacks beyond.

The land is dotted with dairy farms: acres of open pasture, fields of hay and corn, barns and silos, ruminating cows, and stands of maple, pine, and birch. Summers are sunny, with azure skies and cool nights. Autumn is a blaze of color, the air crisp and fragrant with the scent of leaves. But winter is the critical season, and the great lake to the west is critical to winter. The oranges and reds of October give way to the subdued browns and purples of November, as a fading sun filters through the barren woodlands and chilly breezes drift across a lake reluctant to let go of summer's warmth. The terrain is bleak, the skies overcast. Then, about the last week of January or the first week of February, the lake's surface freezes solid from shore to shore. The Green Mountain boys used to cross over to New York on foot. In Fairfield, people speak of it as "the closing of the lake." The conflict between the lingering echoes of summer and the depth of winter has been resolved, and the skies overhead suddenly become blue and the air icy dry. Fishing shanties pop up on the ice, and fresh smelt and perch turn up in farmhouse fry pans.

The year's first frost occurs early in September, and the snow begins to fall in November, as a rule—though flurries may come in October or even September. Subzero temperatures are common after January, with dazzling sunshine on the mounting groundcover of snow. The deer-hunting season opens after the first week of November, and the hunters look forward to the first snowfall, which they call a "tracking" snow.

Frank Briggs was working in Burlington when I knew him, but his thoughts had never left Fairfield for long. His father was a dairy farmer there, and he had spent his boyhood there, along with a dozen or so brothers and sisters. Several of his brothers and sisters still live in Fairfield and manage farms; but he and the others entered the professions and left the family homestead. One became an architect, another worked with the state agricultural bureaucracy, and so on. None ever left the state, and most were clustered within fifty miles of Fairfield and never ceased to feel a close tie with the family and the land.

One autumn evening, I was talking with Frank about the change of the seasons and the festivals that sometimes mark them. I had come across an old Kwakiutl saying, "In summer, the sacred is on the bottom, and the profane is on the top; in winter, the sacred is on top, the profane on the bottom." I asked him if there wasn't a similarity in Vermont's calendar: two very different seasons, summer and winter, with the transition point marked by a festival: Hallowe'en. And then I made the mistake of remarking that in some cultures with a bisected calendar of this sort, the entire winter is thought of as a festive time. He chuckled and said:

> I wouldn't think of winter as a festival so much; more as an ordeal. Summertime was a time of relaxation: a time when you could slip out of your clothes and have a swim when you felt like it. Oh, there was work to be done, and some of it hard work. But it was not monotonous work, like winter's work, and that made all the difference. Winter is an oppressive season, and the chores are dull and steady. Summer is a time of vigorous work and vigorous play, a time of variety. Your planting doesn't take very long, a few weeks at most, and then you're into haying, and that's hard work, but it's over soon enough. And then there's harvesting, and that's

hard work but it's over before long. And then you set into the first of November and you're gonna have to milk those cows and you're gonna have to feed those cows and you're gonna have to clean the manure out from behind those cows every day from the first of November till the first of May, and that is *one long chore time.*

In summer, the cows are out to grass. You might put them in the barn to milk them at five o'clock in the morning (we'd have them out by 6:30 or 7, and have the rest of the day to ourselves); and we'd put them in again at five o'clock at night, and have them out to grass again by 6:30 or 7, and be free again. In the summertime all your work is outdoors. You just go in the barn to milk at night, and it may be hot, but you're only there for an hour or so. In the wintertime, you're in the barn all the time.

You'd always put the cows in the barn for the winter the first of November. It's kind of an Unwritten Law. If you don't get them in by the first of November, you make sure to get them in before the first day of deer season, because they're gonna get shot if they're not in by that time. So November is your orientation toward winter, and the cows going into the barn on the first of November is a tremendous change. You're gonna have to do a lot of things after the first of November because the cows are in the barn that you don't have to do during the summertime. And one of them isn't too pleasant a thing. It's to clean the gutters and bring the manure out to the fields, and either *pile* it or *spread* it.

That recollection of the odor of the barns in winter, and his bondage to the cows and the closeness of the barn in his boyhood days, gave him pause. It is one of the weaknesses in our understanding of the human condition, I think, that we give so little attention to the sense of smell and always seem surprised to discover that some of our deepest impressions lie deep in our memories, associated not with sights and sounds but with smells.

Wintertime, to Frank Briggs, meant monotony, enclosure, suffocation. But there were opportunities for escape—hunting, trapping, even chopping wood. Anything to be outdoors and free again. And always when he spoke of these chances for escape, he spoke of his father. His father never ceased to be a father to his children. Frank recalls him as a taskmaster, a man who never relaxed his dominant role within the family, even in moments of play. He was to be admired, but never quite reached or equaled. Frank never speaks of the best times of his childhood without recalling his father. When he and his brother went off to college, and then he off to seminary (he is today a priest), they came back to the farm for the Christmas holidays and were promptly sent out to chop wood. Chopping wood, he recalls, was almost a sport:

It meant you were out away from the smell of the manure and the cows
and the closeness of being inside, and you were out in the fresh air.

They always chopped wood during those winter vacations, figuring on getting up enough wood for sugaring, and enough wood for the house, to last
the winter:

> 'Course, we were eight boys in the family; Dad used to take advantage of
> the Christmas vacation. But really it wasn't that bad, because it meant you
> were out of doors, and you were active, and you had the freedom of the
> outdoors and the fresh air. One Christmas vacation it was *below* 45 below
> zero three days in a row, and we worked in the woods every day. Dad was
> a kind of taskmaster. I felt I learned more discipline at home than I ever
> did in the seminary or anywhere else. But, really, the cold didn't bother
> you. It was nice to get out. You did the things you had to do. You didn't
> have much time, between sunup and sundown, with getting the chores
> done. But it was nice to get out into the woods, and do the chopping, and
> get the wood up for the rest of the winter, and the following sugaring.

And then there was trapping, and hunting. Muskrat pelts became prime as
the cold weather set in. He and his brother, from age nine or so, spent an
hour and a half each morning "walking their traps"—in late November, and
again in springtime, before the first of May. At two dollars apiece, they
might net thirty or forty dollars in the fall season, and have some spending
money for Christmas.

There was no deer hunting in those days; the large deer herds of our
day were unknown then. He was already in high school when he saw his first
deer. The sport then was fox hunting. The season began the first of November. His father was an avid fox hunter:

> We'd go to the early Mass, and then take the dog and go. It was a tremen-
> dous sport. We'd eat a real big breakfast, especially when we'd be fox
> hunting. It was the only time I ever knew him to cook. You hunted with a
> hound, and the hound making big circles, following the scent, and eventu-
> ally, hopefully, driving the fox by one of us. And we'd be posted on run-
> ways; they usually run in a pattern. My father was great like that; he'd con-
> centrate on trying to outsmart the foxes. So that you would be on a runway
> where you figured that the fox was gonna come. And, really, dad's gener-
> osity showed. If he had one of the boys that was home from school that
> didn't get to hunt very much, he'd always get the choice runway, and my
> father would take one somewhere else, where the fox was less apt to go.
> Usually the way it would work out, though, was that we would miss it, and
> the darn fox would run over to my father anyway.

Frank Briggs took what he had learned on the farm and, as a student in a
Catholic college in Vermont, as a seminarian in Boston, and finally as a priest
in the Burlington diocese, applied it to a life of religious discipline.

As a Christian, he follows the Christian calendar, which has two beginnings, one at Christmas and the other at Easter. But as a man of the land, he
has inherited another calendar. It also has two beginnings, one in November
and the other in May. His work life follows the Christian calendar, with its
round of saints' days and fast days. Yet the consciousness that flourishes
within his boyhood memories vibrates to a different harmonic. The dairy
farmer's yearly round echoes the old calendar of the pastoral Celts, who celebrated their New Year on the first of November, and who believed that the
souls of all who die must find a lodging in the woodlands and await year's
end, when all haunting spirits are abroad on that dangerous night of the last
of October. The church transformed Samhain into All Hallows' Eve, and
marked the old Celtic transitional date with the dual festivals of All Saints
and All Souls. Thus did the church reduce a calendric milestone to a rather
minor observance in the calendar of the New Consciousness. But Vermont's
dairyland still resonates to the mysticism of the old calendar, even as its
priests and ministers teach the mythology and morality of the new.

That is the deeper meaning, I think, of Frank Briggs's oft-repeated expression "it's a sort of an Unwritten Law." The code he lives by, outwardly,
is the code of his church; the Unwritten Law is the rhythm of his inner, his
old self, the self that lives in his earliest memories. The Unwritten Law is for
him "just a natural way of doing things"—a way that has lived on through
two thousand years of Christianization, miraculously untouched by that presumably higher consciousness.

Some years back, having served his apprentice years, Frank Briggs was
invited to establish a new parish in a small city. Soon after, his thoughts more
and more on Fairfield, he bought himself an abandoned farm near the old
family homestead, and started to, as he said, "fool around with it." It became
a place of retreat for him, on his days off and vacations; a place of quiet, a place
to be closer to his roots, a place to get the feel of the mud under his boots again.

One year in mid-November he mentioned that he had told his hired
man, before the first snowfall and before the beginning of deer season, to
open all the gaps in all his fences,

> not because I'm particularly charitable, and not because I'm anxious to
> have everybody and his brother come up ski-dooing, but because if I don't
> open the gaps, well, they carry fence-cutters with them in the ski-doo [he
> chuckled good-naturedly at their foresight], an' if you don't open your

gaps, you lose your fence. Anyway, your cows are in the barn for the winter, so you can leave your fences down. Just from a sort of natural Vermont way of doing things, I feel a lot better about leaving my gaps open in the wintertime, because I feel people'd be honest enough so that if they see a gap open, then they're gonna go down and go through the gap, rather than cut the fence to go through. But if you leave your gap closed, they might cut the fence to go through, and then cut it somewhere else to go back.

Opening your gaps means opening your land on November first and leaving it open until May first, offering open access to hunters, hikers, snowmobilers, and snowshoers—to sportsmen of all kinds. It means recognizing winter as an open season, a season without boundaries, when people can live as free as the animals of the wild live. Then, when the May change of seasons comes, you mend your fences and begin the other season, a season of land enclosure, when growing crops and grazing cows require that people accept the expedient of fences.

The alternative to opening your gaps is posting your land. The controversy over posting represents one battle line between the written law and the Unwritten Law; one area where the special ethic of the Vermont dairyman is in conflict with the legal code of the outside world, which rests, among other things, on the principle of property ownership in perpetuity. The true Vermonter seems to have no such notion of land ownership. Fences are necessary to keep the cows in, not to keep others out.

The free crossing of boundaries in summer is simply not done. Once the season changes, though, the world changes, the rules change, and the countryside becomes open land, and the landsman becomes a creature who yearns to live free in the open land, unbound by superfluous restrictions.

The laws, the written laws of posting, require that anyone who wants his land to remain "private" (however contrary to nature that may be) must place signs that read "No Hunting and No Trespassing" every four hundred feet, around the entire perimeter of the land, accompanied by a single strand of wire. Furthermore, the land must be specially registered with the town clerk and the Fish and Game Department as posted land. Unless these requirements are strictly met, the land is not truly posted and is therefore open to all who care to use it. The law is intended to discourage posting, by making it complicated and costly. The land owner is not automatically entitled to the command of his land; he must go out of his way to establish his year-round proprietorship. If he chooses nonetheless to do so, he puts his land and his reputation at risk; true Vermonters will regard him as mean and selfish, a Scrooge in the midst of all the rustic Pickwickians. Frank Briggs puts it this way:

I never gave it a thought, really—crossing a fence when we were hunting—when I come to think about it. Unless it was posted. And then I'd
be apt to just take the posting sign down. You just weren't supposed to
post your land. We always figured that anybody that posted his land
against hunters was one of the meanest persons that ever could be imagined. You didn't have a right to, somehow or other. The kind of people
that would post their land, in Fairfield for instance, was somebody that
came up from New York, and bought a farm, and just decided they
didn't want anybody on it. And so the local boys used to go around and
take the posting signs down, just before deer season. In the summertime, you couldn't have this kind of openness, because the cattle were in
the pastures, and the fences had to stay up, to keep the cows in. And
then when the cows went into the barn, there wasn't that need for keeping the gaps closed. And you sorta had the freedom to cross fences, and
cross meadowlands and cross woodlands. During the summertime, you
wouldn't think of walkin' through somebody's hayfield, or cornfield, or
oatfield, really, unless you had a good reason to. But during the wintertime, there's no harm done; the grass isn't growing, and the fields are
usually covered with snow.

The falling snow blurs the boundaries. They reemerge from under the
snowcover just as the sap starts to flow, and sugaring time comes to the
north country, and people begin to think again of restoring their boundaries. Frank Briggs again:

You'd finish up your winter season by fixing your fences, the last part of
April. The snow will knock fences down, and posts get broken over. Here
again, I've never seen it in law, but—it's easy to determine whose fence is
whose on a boundary line, an' it's determined by both owners standing
face to face at the midpoint of the fence that's between 'em, an' each takes
the fence on his right hand. So that's if we're standin' face to face, then
this [indicating right] is my fence an' that's your fence. An' if you don't fix
your fence, an' my cows get through your fence, I can sue you for dam-
ages. But I don't necessarily have to bring the lawsuit to you. I can fix your
fence an' send the bill to the selectmen of the town, and they have to pay
it, and they'll then add it to your tax bill.

So in the May to November cycle, "good fences make good neighbors." In
the November to May cycle, it's just the opposite: intact fences are just plain
unneighborly. The sense of private property is at best seasonal, and when
the ground freezes, and the cows go into the barn, and the snow starts to

fall, and the menfolk feel that perennial urge to hunt and trap, true neighbor-liness requires that there be no boundaries. The land must become open land.

There is one exception. Your dooryard remains forever yours. Your home has front steps, and a front door. But your dooryard

> is where all the action takes place. Now, it's where the cars drive up. Usu-ally it's the kitchen door. I think of it in terms not so much of a grassy plot, as a well worn path up a set of well worn steps into a well worn door, into the kitchen. As I was growing up, there might be wagon tracks, now auto-mobiles, and probably a pair of boots or two on the steps.

> You'd have three yards, really. You had the dooryard, the front yard and the back yard. The dooryard was where everyone came in. That was the nuts and bolts of the place, the heart of the place. The front door was where you might have shrubbery and flowers. We'd use the front door really very, very, very seldom. You'd know it was a stranger comin' to the house if he came to the front door. You'd use it for weddings and funerals.

> And then the back door was the door where we went out to the garden. Mother had some flowers in the back yard. And that's where we might sit at night, in the evening, with lawn chairs. Kind of a family place, picnic on Sunday, that kind of thing.

> You can tell what kind of a family it is pretty much by the dooryard. If you find parts of old motors or something like that, you know that they're not too neat, and probably not too prosperous. An' if you find the steps swept clean, then you can pretty well expect that you're gonna find a neat kitchen and a neat house when you go in.

> And the dooryard could extend a long ways, too. My brother's dooryard might take up an acre of land. His machinery would be out there, and that all would be classified as dooryard.

Your dooryard is an extension of your home into the open space without, and is as inviolable as your home or your person. It is sanctuary. Any unwar-ranted intrusion into it is a violation of the Unwritten Law. If a deer is shot on your lands during the winter season, it belongs to the hunter; but if the wounded deer enters your dooryard, ownership is a moot point. Poachers had best keep their distance from your dooryard; they have no business there. Frank Briggs tells one of his stories: a neighbor of his up in Fairfield had been out hunting all day and hadn't had any luck. It was a Sunday, toward the end of deer season:

Well, he got home, and he was in the house watching the football game, just before dark, and two of his boys heard some shooting out in back of the house. They've got a big open pasture there in the woods up there. So anyway they saw this deer coming down, they saw that it was shot, and they went out, and they saw the hunters coming down out of the woods. But the deer was actually closer to the house than it was to the woods. Naturally the boys got excited—you don't see deer shot very often—and they barreled out there, and they got there, and all of a sudden the hunters stopped coming down from the woods. It was an illegal deer, you see, an antlerless deer, either a doe or a buttonhorn buck. Didn't have any horns on it. So they came back and told their dad, that they'd just shot a doe down in back there. "Well," he says, "go down and get it!" An' he said, "If they're gonna shoot a doe, at least they might not do it in my own dooryard." That was sorta stealin' from him, in a way. So he had the boys go down and drag the deer up to the house, and he put it in and dressed it off, and so on. He felt he had just as much right to it as the people that shot it, and he knew they couldn't say anything about his having gotten it. They were the only ones that knew he had it, and—oh, it was tender and nice!

I pause here in my account of life in Vermont's dairyland to give a brief mention of how the materials for this essay came to be collected—where in fact I came by the notion that there was something here that had to be written about. I suppose it began, in a way, in far-off Japan. I had been living there for a time with my family, exploring the festival life of the Japanese. Celebration is an important part of the lives of the people of Japan, and indeed of all the varied peoples of Asia.

The project finished, we returned to our home in Vermont. Life was in many ways easier, more comfortable, filled with conveniences; but the smell of roasting chestnuts in the air, mixed with the sounds of a distant drum and the shouts of youths carrying the sacred ark of the neighborhood shrine in the street procession, all was sadly missed. Life without festive renewal is colorless and flat for those who have known the alternative. Then, one late October evening, the doorbell rang, and I opened to a very short devil, with a bright red face and black horns. He was an *oni*, a devil of Japan's north country. It was Hallowe'en in Vermont.

Of course, he was not a devil at all. He was the little boy from across the street, wearing a "made in Japan" mask he had bought at the local five-and-dime. How had this imported devil gotten to Vermont? And why in October, when he belongs to the early January rites that mark the calendric year-change in the Far East? Was Hallowe'en truly a festival, and comparable with Asian festivals? I began to explore Hallowe'en customs in that corner of

the world, not knowing where the search would take me. There were pleasant discoveries of a bookish nature; for example, Ralph and Adelin Linton's
little book, *Halloween through Twenty Centuries,* now unfortunately long
out of print.[1] And there were long walks down country lanes, the leaves above
orange and sometimes red and yellow, and the leaves underfoot all wrinkled
and crunchy, with the smell of burning in the air. Well and good. The ancient Celts (the Lintons had reassured me) celebrated the day with bonfires
and dancing, sometimes dispensing of their captives (outsiders, all) by box-
ing them in wicker cages and setting them to the torch.[2] Occasionally a black
cat was thrown into the fire for good measure. Bonfires were a part too of
the November fifth Guy Fawkes revelries, along with the gleeful hanging of
effigies of the Guy.

In my walks in late October, there were plenty of effigies to be seen,
and some were hanging effigies, suspended from a porch roof or a low tree
limb in a dooryard. More often they were slouched under trees or, in suburban areas, daintily seated in aluminum tube chairs. They had cloth heads
with a suggestion of a face painted on; or more often their heads were pumpkins—an open invitation to roving boys on Cabbage Night (the night before
Hallowe'en) to lift them off and smash them on the street. Here the prop-
erty-conscious suburban child has the advantage; he or she can lift that
chaired vegetable-man and park him in the garage overnight for safe-keeping.

I found no common name for these figures in the Burlington area. Some
called them scarecrows, though they bore no resemblance to scarecrows; in
any case the crows had all gone, along with the harvest. One child called his
a *funny man,* and others (for example in the Rutland area, to the south)
called them *Jack O'Lantern.* In the literature, I have seen them referred to
as *harvest figures.*[3] In Fairfield, they are uniformly called *Jack O'Lantern,*
after the familiar legend of the trickster Jack who outwits the Devil but, having no place in Heaven, is condemned to wander the earth, seeking his way
through the night with a lighted coal from the hellfires set inside a turnip.
(The pumpkin is New England's contribution to the tale.)

These harvest figures are made by raking up the leaves in the dooryard and
stuffing them into an old pair of pants and an old shirt (checkered and flanneled,
preferably), and then perching the pumpkin, symbol of the harvest, on top.

One year we had a houseguest about the time of the changing seasons,
and I took him for a walk in the countryside. I especially wanted him to see
one of the hanging effigies, unknown in his part of the country. I had spot-
ted a fine example in the dooryard of a farmhouse not far from home, and
we headed in that direction. The effigy was gone; November had come, and

with it, deer season. The effigy had been replaced by the bloody carcass of a freshly killed buck, hanging from the limb of the old maple. The sight came as a shock, and a revelation. The hanging of effigies, the immolation of pumpkins, the wearing of ghoulish masks, all bespoke an anxiety about death somehow appropriate to the ending of the season of personal independence: now here before our eyes was death itself, complete with the glassy eyes, the ooze, and the smell. Death itself, hung out in the old tree of the dooryard, for all to see: a trophy, a display. The summertime is dead; now is the time to raise the fist of defiance against the restrictions of winter. Let death be an answer to death. The hanging carcass invites us to look upon death, and having seen it, to exult over it. Life and death do not exist, the one without the other, but combined, to form the entity that moves the cosmos. Hallowe'en and deer season go hand in hand. It is a time when whisky is drunk, to add to our sobriety. It is a time to confront the brute facts of our existence. Men revive their animal spirit by killing innocent beasts in the wild.

That is what I think I saw on the face of a small child, peering out at me through the tinted glass of a big car that was just leaving the state weighing station in deer season. The two men in the front seat had driven in, hauled their deer carcass over to the scale, and watched as state officials took all their official measurements, their "facts an' figgers." That done, the deer was loaded back into the trunk of the car, and the lid closed as far as it would go, and finally secured with ropes. It was then that I noticed the child, staring out through the rear window, a look of wonder and dread and excitement on his face. A face that in some mystic way matched the face of the deer, which hung out from under the trunk lid. A face of innocence, but innocence marked by the flush of its first encounter with the ultimate realities.

There are two deer hunting seasons in Vermont, one for bow and arrow hunters, who clearly are a breed apart and have their season before what Frank Briggs calls the October–November "centering" date, and the buck season, from the end of the first week of November to about Thanksgiving. All deer may be hunted with bow and arrow, but only the male deer, the bucks, may be hunted with a gun, in November. Despite this, there is an unwritten law that hunters who take up residence in a hunting camp may shoot a doe at the outset of the season and then eat doe meat for the remainder of the hunting season. I came upon this curious fact by accident. I had said something to Frank about hunters bringing plenty of food and drink to their camps at the opening of the season, and he remarked:

> The real hunters, they don't bring meat to the deer camp. They shoot a doe the first day. Or just before the season. That's their camp meat. That's one of the Unwritten Laws, too. But they do bring the booze. They might waste some food, but they don't very often bring back any whisky.

Why a doe, to provide camp meat? And why is the buck the main target of the hunt? There are all sorts of practical reasons, of course. The unsuspecting doe makes an easy target, before the shooting starts; but conservation requires that the female be spared the wider devastation. Beyond that, is there some sort of "gender mystique" at work here? What, for example, is to be made of this conversation: I remarked to Frank, one deer season, that my two immediate neighbors had gone hunting and their wives had gone with them, fully armed and licensed. He replied, "It'd be funny if the wives got buck, and their husbands got doe." I said that as a matter of fact, the wives had gotten buck. He said, "Probably." Or consider this incident: I was having a hot cup of coffee one chilly November night at a roadside diner in Nova Scotia, somewhere between Halifax and Yarmouth. A forest ranger came in, hungry and exhausted. He told the waitress that he had been out tracking a wounded doe, shot by a woman hunter. After several difficult hours, he had managed to locate the animal, and put it out of its misery. He sipped his coffee, and remarked pensively, "I've never seen a woman shoot a doe but it died slowly."

There is, in the hunt, a suggestion of sacred drama, in which the principal actors are the male hunter and the buck. The doe, and the hunter's womenfolk, play a role, but it is important that they play their old, traditional roles, and that none of the taboos be violated. The central motif of the hunt is masculinity in pursuit of masculinity, maleness tracking maleness, maleness invoking death and thereby exulting over death; and in the process making the transition from agrarian provider to hunter-provider. The farmer-turned-hunter crosses over the time boundary that separates the fenced world from the unbounded world. He crosses the boundary from his summer life-style, when he lives as his domestic animals live—free when they are free, milking when they are milking—into his winter life-style, when he must accept the same confinement his cows do. In the transition time, it is essential that he shift his attention briefly away from domesticity and know the freedom of the animals of the wild. As he roams and tracks, he leaves his womenfolk behind. That separation is crucial to the drama. The hunting camp is a men's club. This is how Frank Briggs explains it:

Men might let their wives come up to the deer camp during the summertime, and sorta clean house; they might let 'em come up in the fall, to clean
it out and get things shaped up. They might bring the boys up just before
the hunting season started. But then once the hunting season starts, women
are [he hesitates] not really supposed to be in the hunting camps. I know that my
mother and my sisters never, never went hunting. [He hesitates again, and chuck-
les] My brothers, when they were courtin', they might take their girls out huntin' a
little. But that was—it wasn't so much to hunt, but more courtin' than huntin'.

The Unwritten Law implicitly suggests that men and women should guard
their strangeness; that they should have separate spheres, which alternately
converge and diverge with the moving seasons. Lovers can cross the boundaries with impunity—and may indeed aid the flow of time by so doing. The
men of Fairfield withdraw to the deer camp in November, not because there
is a meat shortage at the local IGA, but because of the unwritten assumption
that a temporary separation of the sexes aids in their communion and has
something to do with the passage of time and the seasons. It is just "a natural
way of doing things." There is a ritual relationship between the sexes, a game
if you will, which these men and women play to demonstrate that they understand nature's sovereign law of seasonal change.

Frank Briggs calls November first and May first the "centering dates" of
the calendar. He explains:

When I was growing up, the farms that were rented always had as their
changing date or expiration date the first of November. Either the first of
November or the first of May, but almost always the first of November. So
you had a kind of natural changeover at that point. We always think of October as a beautiful month, what with the colors of the leaves and all; an' the
leaves are all gone by the first of November; and November begins winter.
Up here the ground freezes right after the first of November, usually, and
the plowing almost always has to be done in October: so again, November is
your orientation toward winter. Then you'd finish up your winter season the
last of April, by fixing your fences, picking up the buckets, pulling the spouts,
and washing and finishing up your sugaring. An' a course the days are
warmer by that time, the May flowers are out. And then the cows would go
out to the pasture around the first of May, and May first was always a centering date in terms of hired help. In other words, they had been there from
the first of November. Or they might begin the first of May. Either the first
of November or the first of May. An' I'm not sure whether there's a written
law or not, but it's an Unwritten Law at least that no farmer could evict a
hired man after the first of November until the first of May. This would more or
less guarantee the hired hand a roof over his head through the wintertime.

Another thing that I think is fairly important to the farmers here: almost all of 'em had mortgages. If you had semi-annual payments, they would come due the first of May, the first of November. By the first of November, the harvest would be in, an' that would be a good time to make a payment. And then almost everybody has one of the two principal payments come due the first of May. The sugarin' would be done, there was a cash crop, and the syrup was sold before the first of May. And this, interestingly enough, was one of the reasons why the buyers—the maple syrup buyers—never set the price for maple syrup durin' sugarin'. They'd wait and see how much was made, and then set the price, usually around the first of May. They knew the mortgages were coming due, and the farmers had to sell it, and they'd be able to buy it for a lower price.

Sugarin' begins somewhere around the first of March. Sugarin' is almost a festival in itself, speaking of festivals. Of course, the sugar is sweet; and it's a sure sign of spring. It was the sweetest time of year for us. We knew the snow wasn't gonna be there much longer. Those first days after Washington's Birthday, as soon as you begin to see the water run down the road, you know that spring is here, an' it's pretty near ready for the sap to run. The spring buds don't start to come till about two months later: so we always figured we had a jump on everybody else's spring, because we sugared.

I remarked that he didn't appear to like the snow too much, and he said:

I dunno anybody that really does. No, snow is a tough problem for the farmer. It meant that—I don't know anything good about snow, really, for the farmer. . . . In the beginning of sugarin', if you had a deep snow, you couldn't work. T'rific to work the horses; t'rific job cutting wood. No, snow isn't much good, really.

I have told how I took a visitor to see a hanging effigy of Jack the Trickster/ Guy Fawkes and found instead the carcass of a slain and gutted deer hanging from that old maple limb, and thereby came by the hunch that the customs that surround the hunt were the connecting link in the matrix of events that mark the November first changeover in the seasons, whose eve is All Hallows Eve. Then I began to take notice of a rash of incendiary acts—barn burnings—that were being reported in the papers. A barn in Milton burned to the ground on Hallowe'en night, the fire set with paper and matches, with one bull lost in the fire, along with all the hay stored there. An open-sided barn in West Milton; a half-finished, two-room summer camp in Colchester; an old farmhouse in Essex Center that had been abandoned fifteen years earlier and not occupied since; a barn in Fairfax; another open-sided barn in Milton, and another in West Milton, this one extinguished soon after it was set simply by touching off the hay with a match; and an unoccupied house in Westford. Suspects were mostly in their teens, ranging upward from sixteen, though one was a mechanic aged twenty-one, and two were farmers from Colchester, both in their thirties, one apparently accompanied by his hired man, a lad of eighteen.

Barn burnings are a common feature of Hallowe'en in this part of the world: usually abandoned barns, and sometimes abandoned houses. Why barns and houses? Are the torchings done in angry anticipation of that long season of confinement to hearth and home, and the stench of the barn? And is fire—barn fire—somehow associated with the winding down of the summer season, the season of outdoor work and freedom? In these barn burnings, is there some reference back to the "hay days" of late summer? Is fire somehow natural to the season of transition? I asked my friend Frank:

> Well, in terms of fire danger, fire hazard, you have the problem of sponta-
> neous combustion in the hay. An' that would be August and September. If
> hay is put in the barn too green, or wet, then it—the moisture, an' the
> greenness, causes the bacteria, which causes the gas, which explodes—and
> you'll quite often find barn fires in toward the end of the haying season,
> along late July and August; sometimes in September.

Or is it just that some aspects of the departing season must face immolation before the new season can begin? Purification by fire is a common enough aspect of year-end rites, ranging from Celtic bonfires to the tamer lighting of candles on the Tannenbaum or Hanukkah-licht, made tamer still in our century by Mr. Edison's marvelous invention.

Of course, immolation can take forms other than burning. Down in Springfield, Vermont, the custom is for the adolescent boys of the town, beginning as early as mid-September, to set out every night and gather pumpkins from every pumpkin patch they can find within a radius of thirty miles or so. They will take them from yards and porches as well, carting them off in blankets, and loading them onto trucks, and the back seats and trunks of cars. They are stored in the local undertaker's garage, I am told, until the glorious coming of Hallowe'en, when all the pumpkins are carted to the top of Elm Hill in a pick-up truck, the tailgate opened, and all the pumpkins go cascading downhill. At the bottom of the hill is upper Main Street, a paradise of plate-glass shop windows. The shopkeepers, knowing what is coming, board them up; but when it is all over, the whole town is ankle deep in orange mush. When a zealous police chief resolves to deter the perpetrators, we are told, he only succeeds in escalating the game.

We asked our friend Frank whether he had played pranks of this sort in his salad days. He spoke in rather general terms, of what others had done:

> Hallowe'en used to be [he hesitates]—in a way it was just as bad [then as now], but somehow or other you had a right to do those things. Pulling doorsteps away from houses, away from porches, and all [he laughs heartily]. I mean, it's a dirty trick, but— [he leaves the sentence unfinished].

"Did *you* ever do those things?" I asked.

> I doubt if I did [laughter of all within earshot]. I might've, but—we never had a Cabbage Night or a pumpkin-throwing. But we used to—we used to have some—well the noisemaking kinds of things. And then pranks. Pulling steps away, or—buggies were free. Somehow or other you'd get hold of a buggy [he hesitates] that was outside of a barn, an', an'—well, they might put buggies up on porches—you know, the horse-drawn surreys or buggies. I 'member—I don't know how the guys did it—it wasn't at home but, uh, there was a buggy put way on top of a schoolhouse. 'Twas a three-room schoolhouse, an' they got the thing settin' way up on the very peak of it. I don't know how.

He is puzzled as he tells me all this. He appears to be silently asking himself, how can what is ordinarily wrong have been so completely right when he was a boy, at that special time of year? Surely he was not puzzled as a child. He understood perfectly well then.

I owe a debt to that little boy from across the street, with his red mask from the Ben Franklin's store. He got me to thinking about Hallowe'en in that Vermont setting. But as my investigation took me away from the cities and suburbs and into the rural areas, it took me away from Hallowe'en as most of us think of it, with very young children going from door to door, gathering lollipops and Tootsie Rolls into their little shopping bags, themselves mischievously sporting costumes, masks, and make-up. Hallowe'en in the countryside is a very different matter. The people who grow the crops and tend the livestock are closer to the life-and-death issues of our very existence than their suburban kin. Suburban children enjoy the festival; country children know its context.[4]

Notes

1.   Ralph and Adelin Linton, *Halloween through Twenty Centuries* (New York: Henry Schuman, 1950).

2.   Ibid., 5.

3.   See, for example, Avon Neal and Ann Parker, *Ephemeral Folk Figures: Scarecrows, Harvest Figures, and Snowmen* (New York: Crown Publishers, 1969).

4.   For a comparative study, the reader might be interested in three earlier essays by the author, "The Form and Meaning of the Festival," *Asian Folklore Studies* 28, no. 1 (1969): 1–16; "Of Talismans and Shadow Bodies: Annual Purification Rites at a Tokyo Shrine," *Contemporary Religions in Japan* 9, nos. 3–4 (1970): 181–222; and "The Grammar of a Rite in Shinto," *Asian Folklore Studies* 35, no. 2 (1976): 17–27.

10. Wishes Come True
Designing the Greenwich Village Halloween Parade

JACK KUGELMASS

The "striking florescence of celebration" in the modern world (Manning 1983, 4) is rapidly transforming both the physical topography of America and the annual holiday cycle of its citizens. Throughout the Midwest, for example, local communities seem almost frenetic in their creation of ethnic theme parks and "historic" pageants and, where appropriate, their rebuilding of habitations and public buildings with Swiss, German, Norwegian, and a variety of other ethnic motifs. Larger cities throughout the country have created "festival" markets and historic districts, and "artists'" neighborhoods have become the hallmark of a thriving city. Chicago, Milwaukee, and Minneapolis all have their Sohos. And, like the East Coast metropolis that dominates both the economic and the cultural life of America, cities everywhere now foster a host of public events to celebrate the cultural diversity of their populations.

This preoccupation with celebrations was already noticeable toward the latter part of the nineteenth century—evidence of the impact of immigrant festive culture on America (Conzen 1989, 73). But its adaptation by Americans of all persuasions is in part a reflection of the search for novelty and experience—hallmarks of consumer capitalism (Manning 1983, 5)—and in part a representation of the modern's notion that authenticity must be found in some other time and place (MacCannell 1976, 3). Little wonder then that the rhetorical modality of these events is so strongly traditionalistic, or that the "rediscovery" of the city among the new commercial class has created virtual simulacra of a nineteenth-century urban gentry.

The very "florescence of celebration" would suggest the existence of some variation in morphology, and it might be useful at this point to outline a preliminary system, which I will describe in more detail below, for categorizing public events. Among the principal types of public events are:

1. Civic celebrations, undoubtedly the most common of public events. These are officially sanctioned and have increasingly become "a distinctive genre of mass communication" that help engender a "we-feeling" among the many and disparate segments of the nation state (Chaney 1983, 120–21). Much like royal pageants and military parades, such celebrations are used by elites to underline the ideal social order of a given community (Cannadine 1983; Da Matta 1984, 219; Warner 1959).

2. "Ethnic" festivals, including social groups based on religion, class, and gender, whose participants wish to claim a place for themselves within the American social and cultural pantheon (see, for example, Wiggins 1982). These events, although semiofficial, may contain elements that do not lend themselves to incorporation into American civil religion (i.e., they may become overly rambunctious or overtly political, such as the Irish Republican Army's participation in New York City's St. Patrick's Day Parade).

3. "Carnivalesque" festivals that shun or are shunned by the official pantheon. Such festivals, which may represent groups that at other times seek to legitimize themselves within the social and cultural hierarchy, deny the legitimacy of that hierarchy. In her studies of the Doo Dah Parade in Pasadena, California, Denise Lawrence argues that these "alternative parades" have become increasingly common since the mid-1970s (1982, 173; 1987, 133). There is, however, considerable evidence that such events were quite common in the past (Bakhtin 1984; N. Davis 1975; Ladurie 1980), and they typically occur alongside mainstream events (S. Davis 1986), particularly among socially marginalized groups (Lipsitz 1990).

This is an ethnography of a "carnivalesque" event, the Greenwich Village Halloween Parade in New York City. In analyzing the parade's evolution and changing structure, I am attempting to explain what the event "has to say," or in Mary Douglas's words, how it "bring[s] out of all the possible might-have-beens a firm social reality" (1982, 36). I conclude by suggesting a connection between the emergence of new expressive forms of, and recent transformations in, the cultural construction of selfhood.

Parades are not easy to document, particularly night parades that attract hundreds of thousands of people, such as the Village Halloween Parade in which most participants wear costumes that have only a thin connection, if that, to the spirits and monsters that we normally associate with Halloween. And there are those intangibles that are so much a part of this parade: the almost continuous blaring music of marching mariachi, reggae, and even klezmer bands interspersed among the other elements of the parade; noise, particularly the cheers from the audience for outstanding costumes and, more typically, catcalls for outlandish transvestites; color—vivid reds, golds, purples, and others intended by their creators to dazzle against the black backdrop of night; and the audience, many of whom are themselves dressed in Halloween costumes and masks. Indeed, squad cars from the local police precinct are sometimes driven by police wearing vampire fangs. The city itself becomes part of the celebration as here and there people display pumpkins and other holiday decorations from their terraces. In Greenwich Village, the home of the parade, whole streets have balconies with puppets of political leaders saluting the crowds below while a huge spider climbs the tower of the public library eerily lit by orange spot lights. What pervades the event is not so much the world upside down (Kunzle 1978) as the world upside down and right side up suddenly juxtaposed. The result is a powerful sense of irony through a collective recognition of the rather easy transposition of order and chaos, when, like in a dream, familiar things can sometimes seem entirely unfamiliar. Halloween is New York's answer to Mardi Gras. And, like its New Orleans counterpart, the celebration "is a way of dreaming with others, publicly and responsively" (Kinser 1990, xv).

To provide the reader with as full an account as I have of the event, to create, so to speak a text out of which much of the discussion will proceed, let me share the notes I took during the 1987 parade, when I tried to record every costumed participant I saw. An hour or two before the parade begins, the marchers gradually fall into formation along West Street just north of West Houston Street. I decided to use the opportunity to record as much as I could while the event was "stationary." Because people arrive at their assigned locations somewhat randomly, my notes are not an accurate description of the order of the parade. But, because I intend to analyze the parade in terms of its content rather than its form, this does not constitute an impediment to my analysis.

The parade begins with its current organizer, Jeanne Fleming, dressed in black and red as a magician and wielding a large baton, followed by Ken Allen, a leading member of the parade's board, dressed as a Mexican god. Nearby are transvestites with huge protruding fake breasts, gaudy skirts and hats, and huge cigarette holders. I try to interview them unsuccessfully. (Most participants are "in character" and the parade is not the time to get a

Fig. 10.1. "Brazilian Caricata." 1991 Halloween parade. Photograph by the author.

"backstage" view.) I begin to follow the "Fashion Police," dressed in white cloaks and white firemen's helmets, who are ticketing people for wearing unstylish clothes. I receive a ticket for my buckskin jacket, which the police attribute to participation in Woodstock and denigrate as "sixties retro."

Walking along West Street, I see a group of mixed gender middle-aged teachers from New Jersey assembling their costumes. They introduce themselves as Gladys Night and the Pits (each member of the group is dressed as a different celebrity pit dog, including Pit Vicious, Dolly Pitton, Daddy Warpits, Rock Pitson, Scarpit O'Hara, Pitter Pan, etc.). Others include a couple dressed in flight helmets, goggles, and bomber jackets with a large-scale silver styrofoam airplane protruding from their front and rear; Vera Carp, a shy transvestite; a man in a white radioactive uniform; Tortilla Flats, a red open truck with a devil growling and a skeleton dancing to the music coming from a trailing mariachi band; the Chrysler Building with jumping stockbrokers (1987 was the year of the stock market crash); a character from "Gilligan's Island"; a monk calling himself the Late Father Barnaby; United Farm Workers with a huge skeleton holding a sign that reads I Ate Grapes; and New Wave Primitives in a car covered in burlap, tinsel twigs, and a Balinese mask. Inside the car, characters have painted faces and are wearing bone earrings and chain necklaces. One group of transvestites, accompanied by a man dressed in a long brown costume with toilet paper dangling from it, explains: "We're out with our date. He's dressed as a turd because everyone knows that all men are shits."

Fig. 10.2. "Moses on Roller Skates." 1991 Halloween parade. Photograph by the author.

Fig. 10.3. "Revenge of the Fuzzy Dice." 1991 Halloween parade. Photograph by the author.

Fig. 10.4. "Saddam Hussein Gets the Electric Chair." 1991 Halloween parade. Photograph by the author.

I see more costumes, including Jesus for Everybody, a group distributing Jesus brochures; a Chinese dragon; a junior high school percussion band; a man wearing a shower curtain and a bathrobe; a woman calling herself Post Industrial Fortune Teller, holding a tray with a lit candle, a jar, and a straw basket containing Chinese fortune cookies; Lady Death; Hershey Bar; a one-man walking Korean salad bar made from painted foam; Pink Pig Floyd; clowns; Indians; a man with a tall green head, which, he explains, is a migraine headache; a Mariachi band singing "La Bamba"; a skull holding a placard that reads More Nukes; a giant tube of Crest toothpaste; Renaissance costumes; Sun Ra from Sweet Basil (one of a handful of advertisements in the parade); a ghoul cocktail party; characters from the *Wizard of Oz;* the Condom Ferry distributing free balloon condoms; The Village Light Opera Group; a transvestite nun; Death as Chicago futures; a man eating a baby and a woman with a sign that reads Eat Me; a pizza with its baker and a family of eaters; a Peruvian band; a graffitied wall with a half-torn poster advertising Visa; an African band; monsters holding human heads; a group dressed as individual cards from a deck that shuffles itself by running to change places; a Caribbean steel band; Sky Tracker; Ghost Busters; Death; a transvestite mermaid; a cowboy transvestite; a family of monsters; a family of clowns; assorted monsters; a transvestite trick-or-treating; a group of men dressed as huge cases of lipstick; a Free Tibet group; an air bubble with a captive couple; white African dancers; African stilt dancers; the Big Apple Corp Gay and Lesbian Marching Band; a fairy godmother; Campbell's Soup; a headless man in a trench coat carrying his head in his hands; male ballet dancers with women's names; a giant can of Raid; a man as a strutting peacock; cardboard penguins; a steel band with Ronald Reagan as the drummer; vampire women; ghouls; Ronald Reagan holding a gun and the Bible; a silver-and-gold brocaded man; Hot 103 FM (an advertisement for a local radio station); a recycling group; two queens and a bishop; Scottish bagpipes; the Loisida Band (the name refers to the Puerto Rican community's colloquial name for their Lower East Side neighborhood); transvestite *Wizard of Oz* characters; a group of Trojaneze lubricated condoms; a man raising money to fight AIDS; Caliente Cab Co. (an advertisement for a Mexican restaurant); and Queen Kong.

In previous years the parade culminated at Washington Square Park with music and various performances, such as the appearance and descent of a spectacular devil on the Washington Square arch. Now, due to changes in the route, the parade stops at Union Square, where musical bands entertain spectators. For many, the Halloween spectacle continues elsewhere at numerous private parties in homes throughout the city; the more daring head to Christopher Street in the heart of Greenwich Village. The Christopher Street promenade is an annual event that parallels the parade, and there are more than a few people—both spectators and performers—who attend this while avoiding the parade altogether. Although the promenade probably preceded the parade, its growth each year demonstrates a certain linkage between the two events. (Greenwich Village has a long, albeit erratic, history of impromptu Halloween celebrations, and there is undoubtedly a link between the recent emergence of such carnivalesque celebrations and the increasingly public nature of gay culture.)[1] The parade, as I shall indicate below, straddles the line between civic festival and carnival; the promenade makes no claim to respectability. On the contrary, it celebrates the irreverent and the lascivious. As New York's gay Mecca and the site of numerous gay-oriented bars and shops, Christopher Street is like an inner sanctum. On Halloween night, the sanctum transforms itself into a public stage, and the city, if not the world, is its audience. Here are my notes.

From Seventh Avenue all the way west to the river, Christopher Street is closed to traffic. The throngs of spectators, which number in the tens of thousands, make entire blocks almost impossible to traverse. There is a physical contact here that is partly ecological—a narrow street and a huge throng—and partly ideological—bodies seem more public than private, to be gazed at, even touched. The event is referred to as "the promenade" because it features transvestites who strut along the street, often in pairs, either acting nonchalant or actively seeking the attention and applause of spectators.

At the corner of Christopher and Seventh Avenue there is a man dressed as Tammy Bakker with gobs of makeup and huge eyelashes, holding a bible, the pages of which are from *Gay American History*. Nearby is Jessica Hahn Dog posing for *Playdog*. In the crowd, I spot characters from the *Wizard of Oz* and a "nun" standing on a balcony sprinkling holy water onto the crowds below. Next to her a man with a huge artificial phallus who is dressed in a bathrobe is sodomizing a transvestite. When he stops, "she" climbs the fire escape begging for more. He goes into his apartment, reemerges simulating masturbation, then throws the liquid contents of a cup onto the crowd. He then hangs from the fire escape, squats, and simulates defecation. Another man pretends to masturbate an electrically lit phallus. A transvestite, dressed like a French courtier, performs fellatio on him. On the opposite side of the street, two bare-chested young men wearing tight blue jeans are exhibiting their lean, muscular bodies by scaling, monkeylike, the fire escape outside their third-floor apartment. The crowd below shouts its approval. When one of the climbers faces the street, people begin to chant, "Show your dick!" One of the men begins to unzip and zip, sadistically teasing the onlookers. Elsewhere, a young man pulls his pants down and sticks his buttocks out the second-story window. The crowd, delighted, demands a repeat performance.

Many who are present at the promenade appear to be passing tourists, often the scattered remnants of the parade seeking a little more time in the spotlight. An "Arab" walks by with a rug protruding from his middle as if he were riding a magic carpet. A group of transvestites is dressed as Girl Scouts. Two Kabuki actors wearing bright silk gowns, their hair tied in knots, pose as a group of Japanese tourists takes their photograph. One man is dressed as a Hasid. I also see a plain white costume with the words "generic costume;" two transvestites dressed as middle-aged, dowdy ladies; and a transvestite nun with metallic hair and a mustache, wearing the Hebrew letters "khay" (a common American Jewish symbol). Toward the westernmost part of the street I spot two young men dressed as grotesque space aliens with flashing red eyes, silver boots, sequined hats, black zippered coats, and long rubber fingers. When I ask them where they are from, they explain with Hispanic accents, "We're not from here. We're from outer space." For the next few minutes we engage in a perfectly absurd discussion about the difficulty of finding parking for space ships in Manhattan, the relative age of space aliens, the time it takes to get from one universe to another, and the best place to eat blood in Manhattan.

From my descriptions we can see that there are some very clear distinctions between the parade and the promenade. Partly because it is framed in space and time and partly because it does have a degree of organization (in theory participants register before the event; in practice many just show up unannounced), the parade is a complex mixture of iconography—some parodic and/or metaphorical join otherwise unrelated domains of experience, others more directly representational or metonymical use one element to stand for something larger. Sometimes metaphor and metonym blend ambiguously. The presence of a huge tube of Crest toothpaste, for example, is as much a celebration of the esthetics of everyday life as a satire on it (fig. 10.5). As Da Matta argues, following from Turner, abstractions and dislocations "bring on a consciousness of all the reifications of the social world" (1984, 214). Completely unstructured and very chaotic, the promenade is purely metaphorical and ludic. Its iconography is entirely of a world upside down. Although I will have much more to say about the two events later, let me conclude for the moment with the rather curious observation that neither event has a particularly close connection to Halloween.

Fig. 10.5. "The Human Clothesline." 1991 Halloween parade. Photograph by the author.

Although Halloween has long been a much-cherished holiday for children in this country, its origins are tied to the British Isles and, especially, to Ireland, where the holiday developed as a blend of native and Catholic beliefs. For the Druids, 31 October marked the end of the year, a time when herdsmen had to find shelter for their livestock for the winter. It also marked a symbolic death, a time when the world of the living and the spirit world were less divided, and the living, therefore, felt compelled to propitiate the dead by offering them food—hence the origin of trick-or-treating (Santino 1983). Irish immigrants brought this holiday to America. Its relegation to the domain of children may reflect a general disenchantment with the world of spirits within modern American culture.

Its recent revival as an American adult festival speaks less to the possibility of religious enchantment than it does to the license the event provides, a type of behavior that has become quite familiar in the 1970s, when the Village Halloween Parade emerged. Moreover, the license is as much a chance to misbehave as it is to display oneself or one's vision of the world, to occupy public attention, which is, as John MacAloon suggests, the most precious of human goods (1982, 262). Through the use of masks, Halloween allows people to transform themselves, to assume personae, to enter a fantasy world with enthusiasm. It offers a time out of time "when we can enter into our experience for its own sake, not for what it produces" (Abrahams 1982, 163). According to Babcock, this fantasy world "does more than simply mock our desire to live according to our usual orders and norms; it reinvests life with a vigor and a Spilraum attainable (it would seem) in no other way" (1978, 32).

For most people, even the relatively innocuous masking for a costume party is a venture well beyond the world of the familiar. But for many of the participants, the time out of time of the Village Halloween Parade provides a public spectacle through which culture takes on a semblance of wholeness, and public rituals, either largely scoffed at as in the case of ethnic parades or ignored as in the case of state rites, seem once again meaningful.[2] Moreover, the profusion of individual identities in postmodern culture, the fragmentation of families through divorce, migration, and single-gender couples, as well as the dislocation of communities through gentrification—a process particularly evident in Greenwich Village throughout the 1970s—has created a need for such productions, for invented traditions that legitimize new social and class formations and give collective expressions to the physical spaces they occupy (Hobsbawm 1983). Community events satisfy the "need to feel part of something" (Bonnemaison 1990, 32). It is precisely the need for new traditions, which became increasingly acute as the economic, social, and cultural landscape of New York City was transformed during the late 1970s and 1980s by a booming Wall Street and its ancillary industries, that has enabled one man's idea to have such dramatic impact on the life of a great metropolis.

In 1973, Ralph Lee, a puppeteer and theater director, rounded up 150 friends and acquaintances and convinced them to march through the streets of Greenwich Village on Halloween night carrying or wearing some of the giant puppets he had designed for his plays. In doing so, Lee began a tradition that was gradually to assume a life of its own, to grow beyond a scale anyone had thought possible. Lee responded by designing ever more spectacular puppets, including a forty-foot articulating snake capable of reaching down to kiss young children in the crowd, a giant Irish sea god riding in a chariot, and a twenty-foot, three-masted ship complete with rats scurrying to abandon it. To help create the proper backdrop, Lee also designed the giant spider, which each year sits atop the Jefferson Market Library, and other creatures that emerged from buildings or otherwise made an appearance during the night's activities. In the early years, the parade lasted no more than an hour. People generally learned about it by word of mouth, or if they happened upon these Halloween revelers on the way home from work. Within a few years the once-intimate parade took nearly five hours to traverse the same route. The length of time was due only in part to the increased number of marchers; it had much more to do with the number of spectators.

To cope with the logistics of large crowds, changes were made, albeit reluctantly: barricades were introduced to separate spectators from participants, a police permit was acquired, and notices were posted by the traffic department banning cars from parking along the parade's route. Eventually the route itself was changed to allow more room for spectators. By 1986 the parade was considered too large an event to hold in the heart of old Greenwich Village—originally the parade began at Westbeth, the subsidized artist cooperative apartments near the Hudson River, wound its way along the narrow streets, and ended up in Washington Square Park. For security reasons, the route was switched so the parade would begin on Sixth Avenue, a bland modern boulevard that could better accommodate the half-million spectators who were coming from all over the metropolitan area to view the parade. It then detoured up Tenth Street—a token reminder of its former route of narrow twisting streets of old brownstones—turned up University and ended at Union Square. In 1987, after considerable pressure from property owners in the Tenth Street Block Association, the Tenth Street route was dropped and the parade was completely restricted to broad boulevards—West Houston, Sixth Avenue, Fourteenth Street. Although the new route is better suited to a parade of this scale, some who recall the early years continually lament the changes. For them, the new route symbolizes the end of a once-intimate and extraordinary ensemble of puppet performances.

With increasing size and visibility, the parade now has to undergo a review by Community Board Two, the local Greenwich Village planning board. In February 1987, I attended the first community board meeting in which the parade's organizers were invited to discuss their plans for the fall. The meeting was used by a handful of opponents to voice discontent about the event's size and its potential impact on an historic district. Despite the testimony from members of the police department, who openly attribute the low crime rate in Greenwich Village on Halloween to the parade, the parade's opponents assumed that the event is a powder keg waiting to explode. They complained, too, about the evolution of the parade, arguing that "it had become political" and that they would "prefer a real Halloween parade, something for children." In order to consider the issues more carefully and to solicit other opinions, the board decided to hold a special open meeting in April at which the parade would be the only issue on the agenda.

When the community board met again, both opponents and supporters of the parade came with reinforcements. For the most part, the parade's opponents were Greenwich Village property owners; the supporters were tenants. As at the February meeting, opponents complained about the changes in the parade, the fact that it had grown too large and that it had become too political and bawdy. Some suggested turning the parade into something else, either a local event or a children's parade. What lay behind much of the opposition, indeed what was a recurrent theme in the complaints, were two seemingly contradictory issues: the nature of the parade's politics, that is its seriousness, and the parade's playfulness, particularly its licentiousness. "We do not want this parade," exclaimed one block association leader. "It's lost its meaning. It's a Mardi Gras. And Halloween is for children. It's not a Mardi Gras!" The notion of a Halloween parade for children in part reflects the earlier dominating presence of giant articulating puppets that delighted young and old. But it also suggests that despite its creator's disavowal of officialdom and city sponsorship, the parade has at its core a coherent vision of civic order. The promenade is very much the converse. Indeed, the very combination of alternative vision and lack of structure makes such an event potentially explosive (Handelman 1990, 55).[3]

Despite their threats, the parade's opponents failed to stop the event. Indeed, one board member who was himself opposed to the parade admitted at a public meeting that an informal poll he had conducted showed neighborhood residents to be overwhelmingly in favor of the parade. The only persistent complaint he recorded was displeasure over changes in the parade's route:

local residents liked the old route of winding streets, and they generally liked to view the parade from the comfort of their apartment windows.

If opposition within the community board proved ineffectual, a much more serious threat was posed by the increasing alienation of the parade's founder from his creation. When I met Ralph Lee in the summer of 1986, he had just resigned as head of the organizing committee and was uncertain whether there would be another Halloween parade. What became clear during the interview was that he had begun to consider the parade a monster of his own creation. It had gotten too big, too much out of his control. Lee had meant the parade to be a ritual-like collective enactment of primitive myth. The giant puppets he saw as part of a pantheistic belief system centered around nature and incorporating ideas and images from primitive religions. Marching through the streets carrying the spirit puppets offered the Greenwich Village community a chance to cleanse itself (the parade was led each year by hags on stilts sweeping the streets with brooms made of twigs).

Lee was particularly bothered by the size of the parade. In 1973, audience and participants were one. But recently the parade had become overwhelmed by spectators. The parade had turned from ritual to theater and, in that sense, it no longer served the purpose he had envisioned for it. Not only were the crowds passive spectators, but they had even become somewhat ominous. The 1982 parade's stage manager recalls what it was like to lead the event and confront masses of people at one major intersection:

> The truck came to a halt. I said, "Please move out of the way." And as the truck inched forward there was a chant that was started in the crowd yelling, "Stop the truck!" I realized that ten thousand people were yelling at me. They wanted to hurt me because I was on top of this truck.

Despite prior concern over the possible impact of Lee's resignation, the event continues to grow. The smooth transition has much to do with the organizing skills of Jeanne Fleming, the parade's current director, who describes herself as a "celebration artist" and "orchestrator of events." Fleming, who has a master's degree in medieval studies, sees a direct connection between medieval carnival celebrations and the Halloween parade. She became involved in the parade as a participant, and began organizing the event after she met Lee in 1982 and he had indicated his desire to let go of it. As Fleming recalls:

> And I said, "You can't let that parade die!" So I said, "Maybe I could help with it." And then I realized I was saying maybe. And I just said, "No, I'll be there. On September first in New York and I'll help you do it." So I did.

By the time Lee resigned, Fleming had already been doing most of the administrative work for the parade for several years, such as generating grants, securing official permits, finding sponsors, and contracting artists and musicians to design and participate in floats. Lee, meanwhile, focused all his efforts on making puppets. Fleming was very much inspired by Lee's work and, at least initially, did not resent Lee's abandoning the administrative work to her. The two shared certain ideas including a sense of the significance of the parade for participants. According to Fleming:

> Parades let people see themselves as a performance rather than as machines. It lets them see the imaginative side of themselves. You can go to a disco and dance and be feeling like you're creating something of yourself out there, but it costs you a fortune to get in and there are social constraints. On the night of Halloween there are no social constraints. People can be as weird, as sweet, as mean, or whatever. They can look into their craziest mind, their deepest desire and realize what that is.

According to Lee:

> The parade charges people up. It warms their insides; energies are allowed to flow between people. The masks in that situation give people permission to play with each other and assume roles that allow them to give vent to things that they might be holding back. The obvious example is the gay people. For them to be able to be out there in the street doing their dream persona is pretty fantastic. And not just them, but if somebody wants to be Ronald Reagan to the nth degree, he can do it, he can act that out or be Nixon or be some witch or guru or whatever you want to be. I don't think people are aware of what they are doing a lot of the time or what they are revealing about themselves. The choices they make as to what their disguises are going to be are heavy-duty choices. For example, a costume years ago, I might have only seen a photograph of it, it was covered with patches of different kinds of fur and sewed on to it was this kind of vegetation. I'm not sure what he was, but it was something from inside himself that was allowed to surface.

Despite this shared sense of the value of the parade for individual self-expression, Lee and Fleming had very different notions about the significance of the parade for the larger community and the city. For Lee the parade was closely tied to his interest in spirits, primitive ritual, and nature. From that standpoint, the Old World charm of Greenwich Village provided an extraordinary setting—a stage upon which to perform:

There are trees on the streets in the Village. Halloween has a lot to do with nature and the changes of the season and the fact that there are all those bare branches at that point is a great backdrop for Halloween. You see a figure against those branches you can imagine yourself in the countryside.

Although Fleming argues that the Halloween parade has special importance because it is "the last event before people shut themselves up in apartments for winter, and that by releasing energy it prevents evil by acting as a safety valve for restless energy," she believes the parade has less to do with reacquainting city people with the power of nature than it does with acquainting them with the very place they inhabit:

Parades let people reclaim urban spaces not just as a place of work but to renew their relationship with the environment. By animating all senses, parades change peoples' relation to the city, letting them look at the city in a new way. Parades allow all different groups of people to get together in public in an important way, crossing all political, economic, religious, ethnic barriers. There are very few events in the city that do that.

The differences in Lee's and Fleming's respective points of view are critical for understanding the radically different perspective each had on the parade's evolution. For Fleming the growth of the parade into a huge spectacle is a sign of its success. For Lee that growth is a sign of failure, because the parade moved increasingly away from the intimate ritual he had devised. By 1987 he simply wanted nothing more to do with the event. According to Fleming:

When Ralph decided to drop out of the parade I begged him to save the giant sweepers. And he wouldn't do it. I promised him I'd hire professionals to wear them, they'd be paid and I'd have a stage manager, you know every assurance he could have had about the costumes. And I said, "You know Ralph, to do that, you're like cursing the parade because I believe in the power of these things." And he said, "I know that it might be happening, that that's a problem, but I won't do it." And that was another real break for me with him. It was a real break of faith with what celebrations are about. With what this parade is about. It was a real spiritual, philosophical break that happened between us."

The "spiritual, philosophical break" was by no means one-sided. Lee was more than just tired by the work involved organizing the parade and the annual transformation of his Westbeth loft into a factory for erecting his giant floats. The fact is that the parade had long since made a "spiritual, philosophical break" with its creator.

In conducting my interviews with people who have designed some of the more impressive costumes and floats in recent parades, I found it striking how little they knew of Ralph Lee or his work. Indeed, sometimes they began participating without ever having seen the parade before. Ross Burman, a fashion stylist, describes missing the parade altogether in his first attempt to see it because he was too busy doing his makeup for his Connie Francis drag routine. Another one of his friends dressed as Veronica Lake, and a female friend came as Marilyn Monroe. Although once in costume there was plenty to do in the Village even without the parade, he found his first venture into the world of Halloween celebrants disappointing:

> We hadn't yet gotten to our conceptual Halloween. It was fun but I felt there was something missing. It wasn't clicking. There were a hundred other people dressed exactly the same way doing exactly the same thing and we felt we weren't reaching a degree of design that we could in creating something for Halloween. So next year we decided we could do something conceptual and there'd be four of us. And we went through everything in the world and we decided on sixties stewardesses. And then we came up with the idea of TWAT, which stood for "transvestites will attempt travel." And we decided to design the costumes in a very sixties sort of way, but sort of update them. I was the funniest, so I was Connie, and we all had names: it was Connie, Barbie, Luvie, and Tippie. And I was Connie formerly of Lingus Airlines. So that's where that went. And we started planning it in August and a friend of mine made the patterns for the costumes for us and basically did the sewing.

The costumes were bright yellow, and each member wore either red, purple, blue, or green stockings, scarf and gloves. "Tasteful" earrings were acquired from wholesalers.

> We wanted to be "conceptual" but not be Lana Turner, Marilyn Monroe, or Jane Mansfield. We wanted to do something that would sort of be Camp and sort of fun and sort of more accessible to people, because we felt that it would be a very accessible thing to be flight attendants where they have not met Marilyn Monroe or Joan Crawford. And as it turned out, we were very well received. It was beyond our wildest dreams that people would applaud us as we walked through this parade and screamed for us. And people recognized us out of costume afterward that we had never met before but would come up to us and say, "You were the TWATs. You were wonderful!" It was incredible.

Fig. 10.6. "Men in Spider Webs." 1991 Halloween parade. Photograph by the author.

For Ross Burman the parade is closer to theater than ritual. The costumes should "make a statement and be conceptual." The statement is spoof and lacks a conscious political intent:

> It just so happened last year when we did the TWAT thing that was when TWA was on strike. So everyone was saying, "Oh, how political of you." But we were . . . like it just happened this way.

Robert Tabor is another young designer whose costumes for large groups—pink flamingos, goldfish, and slices of pizza—have won a good deal of public recognition. Although he suggests that there are some commercial benefits to winning prizes at places like the Palladium (a local dance and concert hall that gives out awards for the best Halloween costumes)—"It's great exposure. People come up to you and take your name down"—he sees the parade more as

> a chance to develop any character, wish, whim that may be inside you. The chance to bring it out, express it and in a sense masquerade your true self as people know you. And it's a chance to really be totally creative, no boundaries whatsoever and just try to in a sense fool, fool the people that know you.

The presence of such costumes and performances has promoted the evolution of the parade from ritual to theater and finally to something akin to a theatrical review or cabaret with the framework of limited time and set space. What we see, of course, is a "folklorization" of an event through communal re-creation (Wilson 1979, 456). Indeed, the parade has come to assume some of the chaotic, ludic quality that characterizes the annual Christopher Street promenade of transvestites on Halloween Eve, and to an increasing degree, one blends into the other. Indeed, many head to the promenade as soon as the parade is finished. At the moment, the principal difference between the two events has to do with the degree of the carnivalesque. The parade is structured linearly in space and framed by time. It ends when the last marchers reach Union Square. And, despite attempts to continue the event with musical performances at Union Square, the crowds tend to disperse quickly; they have come to see a parade, whereas those who choose to party have numerous private options and have little need for it. In contrast, the promenade bursts forth from Christopher Street onto neighboring streets and avenues and has no set beginning or end. There are no walls separating spectators and performers, consequently the sense of structurelessness and *communitas* is much stronger at the promenade than at the parade. The Halloween celebration then is a good example of what MacAloon (1984) refers to as ramified performative type: the parade is spectacle; the promenade is carnival. And there are other performative genres at work here, too.

Although the Halloween festivities may be looked upon as attempts to reestablish "old beliefs" and rites, something that has a certain appeal within postmodern culture generally, the fact is that the entire event—which includes private parties, the parade, and the promenade—in its current form is now a grand urban spectacle and much closer to festival than ritual. As Roger Abrahams notes, "The primary vocabulary of ritual underscores such motives as continuity and confirmation; the transformations put into practice are responsible for maintaining the flow of life. Festivals on the other hand, commonly operate in a way antagonistic to customary ritual confirmation" (1987, 177). Rituals heal rifts in the social fabric; festivals may open wounds, at least for the moment, and often occur at the more stable moments in a group's life (Abrahams, 188). Indeed, were the holiday to occur in the heat of the summer, a traditional time of friction in the city, the explosion some residents fear might very well take place.[4]

Despite the festival quality, there remains a certain ritual component, almost an archaeology of its founding intent. Indeed, Lee's legacy is the continuing benign nature of this event. It is possible, therefore, to divide the costumes into two major categories: those that mythologize and therefore speak to the ritual element of the parade, and those that parody or satirize and reveal the festival element of the parade. I would argue that the two elements are competing, or at the least contradictory, rhetorics that suggest two radically different points of view on the part of participants and, ultimately, viewers. The fact that they occur together underscores the power of the event: festival without ritual is hardly worth the effort. Indeed, it is precisely the resulting ambiguity that gives the event its power.[5] At the same time, each element has its own mode of symbolization. Ritual requires metonymic representation, a part standing for the whole, which lends itself to ready meaning; festival calls for metaphor, a realignment of preexisting categories (see Manning 1983, 26). Mythology is represented metonymically, parody metaphorically. These tropes are keys for understanding the political semiotics of public events; the use of one more than another will push the event toward a particular political direction. Civic ceremonies, for example, rest heavily on the use of metonym; they are fundamentally conservative and derive their authority from common wisdom. Public events that use a good deal of metaphor are those that push against the tenets of conventional understanding.

The Halloween Parade suggests the complexity of a semiotic system. For example, the mythologizing component of the parade consists of Ralph Lee's puppets as well as in the costumes of most of the other participants, including the nonbenign spirits and monsters that appear in the parade. In 1986 Ralph Little, a Trinidadian artist, created a giant demon representing the vices of contemporary culture, particularly drugs. One might call costumes like these "statements" rather than "questions," or "indications" rather than "subjunctions," altering slightly the wording of Victor Turner's evocative formulation (1982, 82). But as their relationship to official culture is by no means univocal, it might be best to see the issue of indication versus subjunction as a continuum rather than an absolute division. The same is not the case for those costumes that celebrate contemporary mythology, particularly the heroes of film, comic books, and television. Of these, *Star Wars* and other sci-fi costumes were the most common in 1987. Some of the more unusual costumes included a group of people wearing white, blood-splattered shirts and black pants, screaming and holding pigeons; they were acting out a scene from Alfred Hitchcock's film *The Birds*. Aside from the last named group, these costumes of popular mythology have a closer fit with the world as known. They postulate nothing new, and so the issue of statement versus question becomes one more of division than continuum.

The satiric and parodic is the component of the parade that is meditative on, and generally more critical of, contemporary culture and values than are the mythological components.[6] Whereas the mythologizing element of the parade props up icons or invents new ones, the parodic is iconoclastic and political. The parodic, for example, was represented in 1987 by the United Farm Workers float led by a huge skeleton and signs suggesting that grapes have chemicals that cause cancer in farm workers. More typically, the critical floats use the rhetoric of satire: giant human roach motels, for example, were a commentary on the pest of urban life, and the three-dimensional mock up of Greenwich Village with giant skyscrapers looming ominously over it was created by a political lobby called Save the Village.

The specific politics of the parade are conditioned partly by the general politics of popular culture, which, as John Fiske argues, work "on the micropolitical level, not the macro level, and . . . [are] progressive, not radical" (1989, 56). But the parade is also conditioned by the political economy of the design community, whose members contribute considerably to the overall quality of the spectacle. Although I do not have precise figures here, it is clear from even a random sampling of outstanding costumes that many of their creators are professionals rather than one-time amateurs. Designers are often independent contractors rather than workers, and their dreams are readily slanted toward the possibility of ownership of the means of production; they are less alienated, therefore, from the labor process. Also, their relationship to work is more complex than in other occupations, so that work and leisure are not entirely in opposition to one another.[7] Because they see themselves as artists or craftspeople, they are likely to use fulfillment or creativity as major factors in choosing the jobs. Moreover, self-expression is a high priority for these designers, and if there is an overall characteristic to their politics, indeed, to their sense of self, it stems from a perception of the world radically divided between those who work to create and those who labor. In the words of Robert Tabor, "The parade brings out creativity. It promotes unleashed creativity for everyone, even if there is no creativity at their jobs . . . It opens up a part of the self for people." Tabor's statement suggests Herbert Marcuse's belief that "art is committed to an emancipation of sensibility, imagination and reasoning" (qtd. in Límon 1983, 38). And it also suggests the tenacity of craft and its peculiar consciousness, both as a form of resistance, despite the bureaucratization of work, and as a political agenda, determined to make an impact on the consciousness of others.

Although there is a tendency for the anthropological literature to see this type of festival as total inversion of the everyday (Babcock 1978), or in a

Marcusean sense a "vehicle for recognition and indictment" (Límon 1983, 31), it makes more sense to place it in the context of Abrahams and Bauman's analysis of festival behavior on St. Vincent and La Havre islands (1987, 195). They argue that the disorder and license of the parade is not the antithesis of the order that is supposed to characterize the rest of the year, "and that many of the people who engage in license during the festival are the community agents of disorder during the remainder of the year." Indeed, Halloween provides a nexus for the urban community, when the forces of order—in this case the commercial and business classes who inhabit the more desirable parts of the city—and disorder—artists and gays—to come together, revealing how closely intertwined, as Raymond Williams suggests, are hegemonic and oppositional elements within culture (Límon 1983, 44).

The design community's participation in the parade has increased the quality and self-expressiveness of costumes. It has also amplified the parodic and, in particular, the campiness of costumes, many of which juxtapose the least likely combinations: blending of genders, as in transvestitism; and blending of species, as in human cocktails, human salad bars, human slices of pizza, giant condoms, gumball machines, fashion police, human poodles. "Camp," Susan Sontag writes, is essentially "love of the unnatural, of artifice and exaggeration" (105). "The whole point of Camp," she argues, "is to dethrone the serious" (116). Camp blends domains that are hegemonically relegated to discrete and mutually exclusive categories, particularly in regard to gender. And it is in regard to gender that the Greenwich Village Halloween Parade dons its most satirical and, in a sense, political costume.

It should be noted, however, that the political issues raised by designers, particularly gay designers, are presented in a masked way—appropriately so, given the fact that this is Halloween, and perhaps, too, because Gay Day has become a more appropriate setting for overt political statements. So camp/parodic is integrated here with the mythological, and the rhetoric of the parade remains ambiguous.

Earlier I suggested a tripartite typology of public events—civic, ethnic, and carnivalesque festivals. Civic and carnivalesque events are similar to Handelman's (1990) typology of presentational and representational events: the former constituting an idealized model of social reality, the latter playing with and distorting reality. My middle category, "ethnic festivals," mediates between the other two categories and contains elements of both. Handelman's typology includes a third category but not a middle one. Instead he posits a category of events that model—worlds unto themselves that may be used to bring about transformations in the real world. Although extremely evocative, there is something awkward about this typology: presentations and representations constitute opposite ends of a continuum; model suggests a separate axis that bifurcates both presentations and representations. It seems to me that presentations that model are typical of revolutionary regimes committed to creating a "new man." Presentations that do not model, for example, the Macy's Thanksgiving Day Parade, are those committed to a preexisting vision of social reality. A similar dichotomy could be made for representational events. The material in this chapter suggests that Lee had constructed a parade that blended the transformational thrust of a model with an event that fits the ethnic festival category of my earlier typology. His discomfort with the parade's evolution hinged on its having moved increasingly toward the carnivalesque side of the spectrum, whereas the model had become overwhelmed by the sheer size of the spectacle. But Lee is not the only one for whom the transformational thrust of the model has significance. Indeed, those at the margins of the social and cultural system are particularly concerned with what Jameson (140) refers to as "authentic cultural productions"—another term, I would think, for model. Given that they are marginalized groups, the models they produce are likely to contain a good deal of oppositional material. They are carnivalesque, and they fall, therefore, easily on the side of representation on the representation-presentation continuum. Given the above typology, one might well expect a rather complex agenda on the part of some people at the Halloween celebration. Let me return to my field notes to illustrate this point.

An hour or so after the parade has ended I am standing on Christopher and Bleecker streets with thousands of other people. In the middle of the intersection I notice a man dressed in a white ballerina costume looking suspiciously like a fairy godmother dispensing wishes with a magic wand. He doesn't pay much attention to me, I suppose, because I'm busy with a note pad rather than a camera; I cannot exchange stardom for a spell. "Do I get a wish?" I ask. "Yes. Anything your heart desires." "I want your phone number." "My phone number?" "Yes. I'm an anthropologist and I'm doing some research on the Halloween parade. I'd like to talk to you." Two weeks later I called Fred to confirm our appointment, and we agreed to meet for brunch at a local bagel shop. Just as I was about to hang up, Fred told me to look for someone with brown curly hair wearing red glasses. Of course, I still had a mental image of someone in a white gown with a magic wand.

At the restaurant, Fred spots me first. Out of costume he looks magically transformed: a tall, slender, good-looking man about forty. We exchange greetings, order food at the counter and head to a table. I learn that the fairy godmother is a playwright who lives in a still not gentrified block in "Alphabetland" (between Avenues B and C). He has been involved in the parade either as spectator or participant for the past ten years. Fred's description of how his costume came together this year revealed the essential self-parody of his humor:

> The costume was designed by someone who's done a lot of work for dance companies. It's sort of a take-off of a ballet dress from the eighteenth century. It was beautiful. Sort of a white satin with glitter and silver sequins. I wore a blond wig with glitter and a wonderful crown like a headdress which actually was from the Snow Queen. I made the wings myself from foam that had been used as packing for a stereo. I used wire and glitter. When I glued the glitter I smiled because I thought, "Yes, there's something so fanciful and frivolous about glitter that it's like the antithesis of being down to earth." They looked kind of frumpy and weren't straight. It looked kind of like I had done a lot of flying around. I liked the bedraggled aspect. I wanted to be slightly frumpy as if I had gone through the mill a bit myself and had still come to the fact that goodness is the bottom line. And I wore white tennis sneakers sort of like yuppie women who go to the office in sneakers. I thought "Well, the good fairy has got to save her feet too." I made the wand from a wood dowel and an aluminum tin foil Christmas tree ornament at the end. My friend Norman has all these costumes in his apartment because he ran a children's theater. It's sad to see all those costumes and realize that it's really the people that make the costumes come alive and not the other way around. Some of the jewels were falling off the crown. They looked sad in the apartment. But once I got it on and I got out there it came alive. I realized it is the spirit of the performer.

Fred talked to me about the loss of two close friends, one of whom had died of AIDS, and how his participation in the promenade was a way for him to emerge from mourning by helping others.

> This year there seemed to be a lot more observers than participants. But even so I must say I was touched by the crowd. I was going up to people with all their façades and defenses and 98 percent of the people just melted. There were three black kids, very very angry teenagers. I went up to them and with my wand I went bonk, bonk, bonk, and they melted. One guy came as a ghoul. I bonked him on the head and nothing happened. I did it again and he just stood there. He wouldn't give me an inch. He was just stubbornly staring me down. So I said, "Oh, come on." And I bonked him. And he melted. A Korean woman came up to me and said, "What does it mean when you bonk them on the head?" I said, "It means

you get your wish darling!" "Oh, she said, "do me, do me." Then another woman dressed as a frog hurled herself at my feet and she said, "Make me into a prince!" I kept going like this (Fred motions with his outstretched arm as if he were waving a wand) but it didn't work so I figured I would try it again. I thought, "Maybe if she wanted to be a princess it might have worked. It's too complicated, I can't deal with it. It's two wishes." I could do it. But I thought she needed to live with it a little longer. Also I thought it was touching. There would be a group of friends and they would say, "Oh, get him. He really needs it." I could tell that this person was really hurting. Whether it was for personal breakup or heartbreak or some physical situation. And they came up to me with such earnestness. Like you know, "Make this better!" And it was a very rewarding thing to hit them with the wand. It seemed to cheer them up anyway.

Fred talked about Halloween, his belief in astrology, and the Christian idea of death and renewal with All Saints' Day following Halloween. His comments revealed the degree to which for him, and for designers and artists and particularly for gay people, the Halloween parade offers a moment for creation, a collective daydream. During Halloween, the skills of labor otherwise used to fashion consumable commodities are suddenly transformed and harnessed through leisure for self, and for collective self-expression. For gay people, Halloween is a moment of utopian wishfulness, a time when their vision of the world has the possibility of moving from periphery to center and capturing, even if only for a few short hours, the hearts of an entire city. As Fred describes his experience:

> Maybe that's mixing up a lot of symbols but it seems like out of negativity is a lot of potential for good. And I just felt like my costume was a lot more successful than the people who were trying to be scary. I felt like there was a magnetism and a magic coming from me. And it was a very rewarding thing to hit them with this wand. It seemed to cheer them up anyway. People have this innate reverence for the power of this mythological figure. And I guess that was what I was thinking of. It was really the power of goodness was really what captivated me about it and also instructed me. I had no idea that I would get such a response going out as some embodiment of merry and goodness. It was really very gratifying. A friend of mine who was with me and is very spiritual, kept saying, "Fred, you're really healing people." And I felt it too. I wish in this world instead of that being a momentary thing it could be a way of living for people. I even had a fantasy of going to midtown dressed as the good fairy. I may even do it. I think there's a magic in Halloween that allows people to suspend things and allows certain fantasies and their own wishes to come true.

Conclusions

Unlike most parades, the Village Halloween Parade makes no claim to respectability. Rather than challenge the city by occupying elite turf and
marching up Fifth Avenue—the typical route of ethnic events—the Halloween parade consecrates its own terrain. And unlike other parades, this dra-
matization of boundaries, in its origins, defined not an ethnic group but a
way of life, particularly a Bohemian, artistic, and, frequently, gay way of life.
One can only surmise that it is not accidental that the stimulus to create this
annual celebration of Greenwich Village culture is a recent phenomenon:
one hardly needs to dramatize the obvious.[8] And, whereas the gay relationship to Greenwich Village is not in dispute, except, that is, through the AIDS
epidemic, Greenwich Village as a Bohemian artist colony is a thing of the past.

In recent years, New York neighborhoods have undergone transformations that are leaving whole sections of the city unrecognizable to their long-
time residents; neighborhoods such as Greenwich Village, long known for
their Bohemian or ethnic character are no exceptions (Zukin 1982). Despite
the high cost of housing in the city in general and in Greenwich Village in
particular, this charming neighborhood of nineteenth-century row houses
has managed to maintain its link to the artist's and writer's colony that once
formed the nucleus of its identity only through Westbeth, a subsidized loft
building for full-time artists. The fact that the parade originated there and
fanned outward through the neighborhood suggests the contentious aspect
of the parade: its attempt to incorporate and consecrate space that in real
life is no longer its own. Outside the narrow spatial and temporal boundaries
of this parade, Greenwich Village has become part of the ordinary workaday
world and not the artists' world of "work as play." Ironically, this is precisely
why the parade grew so quickly, why it found such a ready niche within the
expressive life of a great metropolis, and why it so readily gave voice to
hegemonic as well as oppositional culture. Although intended as a celebration of the spirit of a unique community, in effect, the parade has become
much more than that. It has simultaneously become a celebration of an
emergent mainstream, of the new social classes that have substantially transformed the city and in doing so have destroyed, in effect, the social basis of
the city as a locus for an artists' community.

Finally, let me add something of a purely speculative kind. The general
rise in popularity of Halloween throughout the United States suggests a
transformation in American culture in the individual sense of self. If the
1950s celebrated the nuclear family as the hedge against world apocalypse,[9]

and the 1960s gave rise to oppositionality through a collective youth culture, the 1970s saw the emergence of the New Right and a crass individualism in which the self became increasingly severed from collective obligations. This privatization has taken an interesting twist in regard to popular culture and particularly in regard to gender. With the demise of a procreative imperative, sexuality becomes a matter of choice and life-style (Harris 1982). At the same time, the emergence of transnational cultures is contributing to a "world marked by borrowing and lending across porous national and cultural boundaries" (Rosaldo 1989, 217). The optional is increasingly part of the modern experience. Indeed, the expansion of the threshold of the sexual self is intricately connected to expansion of the self in other domains, and this manifests itself in all kinds of expressive culture, including religious beliefs and practices. Perhaps, then, the popularity of Halloween can be seen as an implicit rejection of a collective self prescribed within the Judaeo-Christian tradition. Neo-paganism offers, if not a world without limits, a self without social encumbrances, then at least a cultural border zone in constant motion (Rosaldo 1989). To understand the roots of that self, clearly one ought to look at the underlying structure of late capitalism. But to see its continual manifestations, all one need do is examine New Age religion. Ultimately, it is within the framework of this emerging New Age culture that we will need to place Halloween to fully understand the position it is assuming within the pantheon of American holidays.

Notes

This chapter was originally published in the *Journal of American Folklore* 104, no. 414 (Fall 1991): 443–65. Research was made possible in part by a grant for summer support from the Graduate School of the University of Wisconsin–Madison. I would like to thank the *Journal of American Folklore*'s anonymous readers for some excellent suggestions, and Marc Kaminsky and Robert Lavenda, with whom I discussed many issues within this article.

1.   Curiously, Denise L. Lawrence, "Parades, Politics, And Competing Urban Images: Doo Dah and Roses," *Urban Anthropology* 11 (1982): 155–76 and "Rules of Misrule: Notes on the Doo Dah Parade in Pasadena," in *Time Out of Time: Essays on the Festival*, ed. Alessandro Falassi (Albuquerque: Univ. of New Mexico Press, 1987), 123–36, makes no link between "alternative parades" and gay culture. As I argue below, even a cursory reading of the Halloween Parade's iconography suggests a significant gay presence. Indeed, many New Yorkers refer to the event as "the gay parade."

2.   See Dean MacCannell, *The Tourist: A New Theory of the Leisure Class* (New York: Schocken Books, 1976), 3, for a discussion of the meaning of tourism for contemporary culture.

3.   The existence of the promenade may have diverted the most blatantly oppositional elements away from the parade, thereby enhancing its benign image to New Yorkers in general. At the same time, the promenade's physical proximity to their residences may explain the negative view of some Greenwich Village inhabitants. The tension between bourgeois notions of order and civility and oppositional behavior is by no means particular to the Greenwich Village Halloween celebration. Lavenda, "The Festival of Progress: The Globalizing World-System and the Transformation of the Caracas Carnival," *Journal of Popular Culture* 14 (Winter 1980): 465–75, for example, discusses the transformation of carnival in nineteenth-century Caracas from a disorganized "rite of reversal" among the lower classes to a "civilized" and highly organized display.

4.   The fear of possible eruption did become acute just before the 1989 parade, due to various acts of violence that had taken place in the weeks before the event. Roving gangs had been "wilding" just north of Greenwich Village, and there was considerable fear on the part of the parade's organizers that they would return on Halloween. Both the organizers and the police were relieved when rain that year kept the crowds to a fraction of what they had expected.

5.   As Abner Cohen, "Drama and Politics in the Development of a London Carnival," *Man* 15 (1980): 65–87, argues, "Culture generally is expressed in terms of symbolic forms and performances that are by definition ambiguous . . . Once the symbols are reduced to either politics or existential issues alone, they become unidimensional signs, lose their potency and hence their social functions." Cohen, "A Polyethnic London Carnival as a Contested Cultural Performance," *Ethnic and Racial Studies* 5 (Jan. 1982): 22–41, argues that both hegemonic and oppositional orientations are present in every carnival in some state of balance: "To the extent that that balance is seriously disturbed, the nature of the festival is changed and is transformed into a different form altogether. If the festival is made to express pure and naked hegemony, it becomes a massive political rally of the type staged under totalitarian systems. On the other hand, if it is made to express pure opposition, it becomes a political demonstration against the system. In either extreme case it ceases to be carnival."

6.   Although this is a more complex issue, particularly in the case of Lee's work, and I shall discuss this at greater length in a future article.

7.   See Stoeltje, "Riding, Roping and Reunion: Cowboy Festival," in *Time Out of Time,* 137–51, ed. Falassi, for a discussion of this issue in rodeo culture.

8.   Two comparable examples come to mind. Denise Lawrence's account, "Parades, Politics," explains the origins of the Doo Dah Parade as a rebellious response to developers encroaching on an artists' enclave in Pasadena. Michael Hughey, *Civil Religion and Moral Order: Theoretical and Historical Dimensions*

(Westport, Conn.: Greenwood Press, 1983), has reinterpreted W. Lloyd Warner's material on the Memorial Day celebration in Newburyport as an attempt on the part of an old elite to assert symbolically a status that at least in economic terms is a thing of the past.

9.   See Elaine May, *Homeward Bound: American Families in the Cold War Era* (New York: Basic Books, 1988).

References

Abrahams, Roger D. 1982. "The Language of Festivals: Celebrating the Economy." In *Celebration,* ed. Turner, 161–77.

———. 1987. "An American Vocabulary of Celebrations." In *Time Out of Time,* ed. Falassi, 173–83.

Abrahams, Roger D., and Richard Bauman. 1978. "Ranges in Festival Behavior." In *The Reversible World,* ed. Babcock, 193–208.

Babcock, Barbara, 1978. "Introduction." In *The Reversible World,* ed. Babcock, 13–36.

Bakhtin, Mikhail. 1984. *Rabelais and His World.* Bloomington: Indiana Univ. Press.

Bonnemaison, Sarah. 1990. "City Policy and Cyclical Events." *Design Quarterly* 147: 24–32.

Cannadine, David. 1983. "The Context, Performance and Meaning of Ritual: The British Monarchy and the 'Invention of Tradition,' c. 1820–1977." In *The Invention of Tradition,* ed. Eric Hobsbawm and Terrence Ranger, 101–64. New York: Cambridge Univ. Press.

Chaney, David. 1983. "A Symbolic Mirror of Ourselves: Civic Ritual in Mass Society." *Media, Culture and Society* 5: 119–35.

Cohen, Abner. 1980. "Drama and Politics in the Development of a London Carnival." *Man* 15: 65–87.

———. 1982. "A Polyethnic London Carnival as a Contested Cultural Performance." *Ethnic and Racial Studies* 5 (Jan.): 22–41.

Conzen, Kathleen Neils. 1989. "Ethnicity as Festive Culture: Nineteenth-Century German America on Parade." In *The Invention of Ethnicity,* ed. Werner Sollors, 44–76. New York: Oxford Univ. Press.

DaMatta, Roberto. 1984. "Carnival in Multiple Planes." In *Rite, Drama, Festival, Spectacle,* ed. John MacAloon, 208–39. Philadelphia: ISHI.

Davis, Susan G. 1986. *Parades and Power: Street Theater in Nineteenth-Century Philadelphia.* Philadelphia: Temple Univ. Press.

Davis, Natalie Zemon. 1975. *Society and Culture in Early Modern France: Eight Essays by Natalie Zemon Davis.* Stanford, Calif.: Stanford Univ. Press.

Dorson, Richard. 1983. "A Historical Theory for American Folklore." In *Handbook of American Folklore,* ed. Richard Dorson, 326–37. Bloomington: Indiana Univ. Press.

Douglas, Mary. 1982. *In the Active Voice.* London: Routledge & Kegan Paul.

Fiske, John. 1989. *Understanding Popular Culture*. Boston: Unwin Hyman.

Handelman, Don. 1990. *Models and Mirrors: Towards an Anthropology of Public Events*. New York: Cambridge Univ. Press.

Harris, Marvin. 1982. "Why the Gays Came Out of the Closet." In *America Now: The Anthropology of a Changing Culture*, 98–115. New York: Touchstone.

Hobsbawm, Eric, and Ranger, Terrence, eds. 1983. *The Invention of Tradition*. New York: Cambridge Univ. Press.

Hughey, Michael W. 1983. *Civil Religion and Moral Order: Theoretical and Historical Dimensions*. Westport, Conn.: Greenwood Press.

Jameson, Fredric. 1979. "Reification and Utopia in Mass Culture." *Social Text* 1 (Winter): 130–48.

Kinser, Samuel. 1990. *Carnival American Style: Mardi Gras at New Orleans and Mobile*. Chicago: Univ. of Chicago Press.

Kunzle, David. 1978. "World Upside Down: The Iconography of a European Broadsheet Type." In *The Reversible World*, ed. Babcock, 39–94.

Ladurie, Emmanuel Le Roy. 1980. *Carnival in Romans*. New York: George Braziller.

Lavenda, Robert. 1980. "The Festival of Progress: The Globalizing World-System and the Transformation of the Caracas Carnival." *Journal of Popular Culture* 14 (Winter): 465–75.

Lawrence, Denise L. 1982. "Parades, Politics, and Competing Urban Images: Doo Dah and Roses." *Urban Anthropology* 11: 155–76.

———. 1987. "Rules of Misrule: Notes on the Doo Dah Parade in Pasadena." In Falassi, *Time Out of Time*. 123–36.

Límon, Jose. 1983. "Western Marxism and Folklore: A Critical Introduction." *Journal of American Folklore* 96: 34–52.

Lipsitz, George. 1990. "Mardi Gras Indians: Carnival and Counter-Narrative in Black New Orleans." In *Time Passages: Collective Memory and American Popular Culture*, 233–53. Minneapolis: Univ. of Minnesota Press.

MacAloon, John J. 1984. "Sociation and Sociability in Political Celebrations." In *Celebration*, ed. Turner, 255–71.

———. 1984b. "Olympic Games and the Theory of Spectacle in Modern Societies." In *Rite, Drama, Festival, Spectacle: Rehearsals Toward a Theory of Cultural Performance*, ed. John MacAloon, 241–80. Philadelphia: ISHI.

MacCannell, Dean. 1976. *The Tourist: A New Theory of the Leisure Class*. New York: Schocken Books.

Manning, Frank E. 1983. "Cosmos and Chaos: Celebration in the Modern World." In *The Celebration of Society: Perspectives on Contemporary Cultural Performance*, ed. Frank Manning, 3–30. Bowling Green, Ohio: Bowling Green Univ. Popular Press.

May, Elaine. 1988. *Homeward Bound: American Families in the Cold War Era*. New York: Basic Books.

Rosaldo, Renato. 1989. *Culture and Truth: The Remaking of Social Analysis.* Beacon Press, Boston.

Santino, Jack. 1983. "Halloween in America: Contemporary Customs and Performances." *Western Folklore* 42 (Jan.): 1–20.

Sontag, Susan. 1982. *A Susan Sontag Reader.* New York: Vintage Books.

Stoeltje, Beverley J. 1987. "Riding, Roping and Reunion: Cowboy Festival." In *Time Out of Time,* ed. Falassi, 137–51.

Turner, Victor. 1982. *From Ritual to Theater: The Human Seriousness of Play.* New York: Performing Arts Journal Publications.

Warner, W. Lloyd. 1959. *The Living and the Dead: A Study of the Symbolic Life of Americans.* New Haven: Yale Univ. Press.

Wiggins, William H. Jr. 1982. "They Closed the Town Up, Man! Reflections on the Civic and Political Dimensions of Juneteenth." In *Celebration,* ed. Turner, 284–95.

Wilson, William A. 1979. Folklore and History: Fact Amid the Legends. In *Readings in American Folklore,* ed. Jan Harold Brunvand, 444–48. New York: W. W. Norton.

Zukin, Sharon. 1982. *Loft Living: Culture and Capital in Urban Change.* Baltimore: Johns Hopkins Univ. Press.

PART III

Material Culture

11. Things that Go Snap-Rattle-Clang-Toot-Crank in the Night
Halloween Noisemakers

CARL B. HOLMBERG

Writing culture takes place in many ways.[1] As a child we write culture in gestures by trying it out, interacting with its material and immaterial aspects. Later we may try to pay attention to the once-ephemeral thrills we thought were lost except to memory by writing that experience as data for analysis. The experience of Halloween noisemakers is no different. I can remember when I was pretty sure I would never say, "When I was a kid," but I am about to do just that—as a reflective step for observing and then interpreting culture. This step is particularly appropriate for the subject at hand, Halloween noisemakers, because many children no longer know the delights of raising a ruckus while shouting "trick or treat!" Go to a five-and-dime store like Kresge, Woolworth, Ben Franklin, Newberry's, or McCrory just before the holiday. You will not find noisemakers any more, not Halloween noisemakers, but I did, once—no, many times—when I was a kid.

It is to stores such as these we shall go to generate a first-person narrative account that will then serve as an ethnographic database for an analysis of the sounds Halloween noisemakers produce. I shall then describe the analysis as an *audeography* of making ritual noise.

When I was a Kid

One of my favorite memories entails going to five-and-dimes throughout the Cleveland, Ohio, area and looking over the Halloween stuff in late September or early October. Usually we went to the new mall called Southgate, where there was a Kresge and a Woolworth store, but if we were in another part of town at that time of year, we took in dime stores there too. It was the mid-1950s and Mom had her own things to look for; she told my brother and me that we'd meet in a bit at the Halloween section, near all the party stuff. The first Halloween I went trick or treating I was Tweetie Bird, the only store-bought costume I can remember wearing. I was pretty young, maybe six or seven; that makes it 1955. I picked it out myself before my older brother could separate himself from the guns in the toy section and razz me and Mom about our stuff.

"All well and good," said Mom, "but what about a noisemaker?" "Noise-maker?" I said. "You remember," she said, "the noisy things the kids had last year when they came to our door." "Oh, yeah." I had been enamored of the costumes and nothing else, but there they were in plain sight: horns, like the kind you got at parties—but with black cats and witches on them (fig. 11.1). I picked one up and blew it. HONK! Mother put her hand on my shoulder and gave me a pleading look. Oops. There were rattles too. One had a nice picture of a witch brewing something (fig. 11.2). I was especially taken by cranks (fig. 11.3), and one ended up in my hand without my realizing it. CRANK! "Carl!" Mom admonished. Another kind was like a tin pan with spoons on each side (fig. 11.4). One was like a bell, but you carried it with the clapper up (fig. 11.5). There were so many of them! Most were orange, black, and white. Odd, some didn't have Halloween stuff on them. There were dancers (figs. 11.6 and 11.7), singers (fig. 11.8), clowns (fig. 11.9), toy soldiers (fig. 11.10), a slide whistle. I picked it up but put it back down, re-membering not to blow on it, but there were snaps! I had to snap a snapper, an owl (fig. 11.11B). SNAP! Oooo, the loudest of all. "I want this one," I said because it had a bird on it, like Tweetie. I really wanted it because it was loud. "Put that clicker back," my brother Al said in his best big brother bossy way. Brothers. Al grabbed a crank.

When we got home and were putting things away, Mom got to the two noisemakers first. She cranked Al's and snapped mine at the same time. C-R-SNAPSNAP-A-N-K! We reached for them but she put them back in the bag and made a big deal about folding the bag neatly closed, like it was a Federal Project. "But Mom!" Al and I complained in unison. She just smiled and put the bag on a high shelf in the closet.

Two days before Beggar's Night (as we called it around Cleveland—an extra night of trick or treating on 30 October characterized by mischief and thus often called Mischief Night as well) I carved my first jack-o'-lantern. I

Fig. 11.1. Horn, circa 1935. Photograph by David Hampshire, Instructional Media Services, Bowling Green State University.

Fig. 11.2. Rattle, circa 1962. Photograph by David Hampshire, Instructional Media Services, Bowling Green State University.

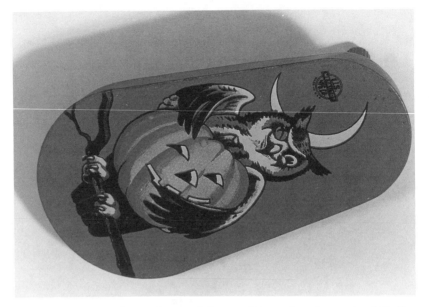

Fig. 11.3. Crank, circa 1962. Photograph by David Hampshire, Instructional Media Services, Bowling Green State University.

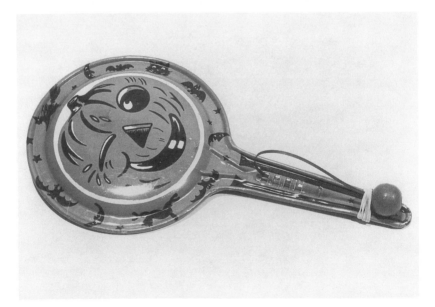

Fig. 11.4. Clapper, circa 1950. Photograph by David Hampshire, Instructional Media Services, Bowling Green State University.

Fig. 11.5. Bell clapper, circa 1965. Photograph by David Hampshire, Instructional Media Services, Bowling Green State University.

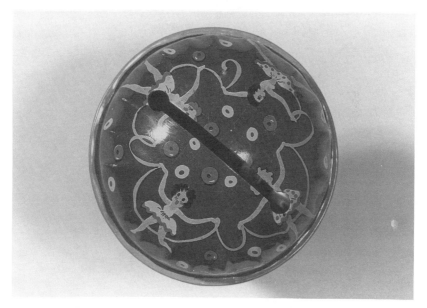

Fig. 11.6. Rattle, circa 1950. Photograph by David Hampshire, Instructional Media Services, Bowling Green State University.

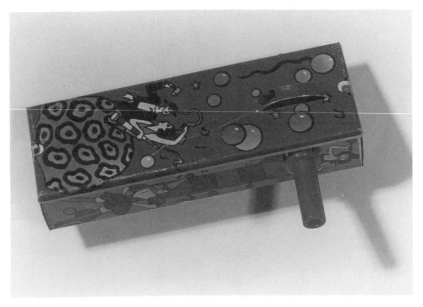

Fig. 11.7. Crank, circa 1968. Photograph by David Hampshire, Instructional Media Services, Bowling Green State University.

Fig. 11.8. Rattle, circa 1947. Photograph by David Hampshire, Instructional Media Services, Bowling Green State University.

Fig. 11.9. Clapper, circa 1970. Photograph by David Hampshire, Instructional Media Services, Bowling Green State University.

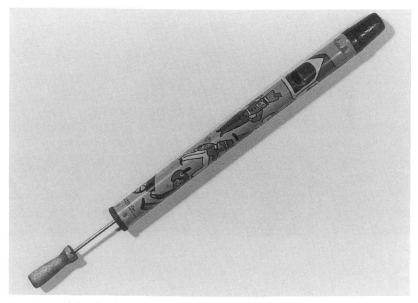

Fig. 11.10. Slide whistle, circa 1950. Photograph by David Hampshire, Instructional Media Services, Bowling Green State University.

Fig. 11.11A. Snapper, circa 1947. Photograph by David Hampshire,
Instructional Media Services, Bowling Green State University.

Fig. 11.11B. Snapper, circa 1949. Photograph by David Hampshire,
Instructional Media Services, Bowling Green State University.

should have copyrighted it. It was a happy face. The next day we got out the rest of the Halloween stuff and put up decorations on the front door and other places in the house. Al made a big dagger with blood on it out of construction paper for the front door. He rigged it so it would fall when you opened the door. Neat. Dad came home just as I found my snapper. I greeted him with a *snap, snap, snap* as I met him at the door. He smiled and took it from my hand and *snapped* it himself. "Carl," Mom said from the kitchen, "*Don't* do that; Daddy's home!" I grabbed it back. Oops. Dad smiled.

The year I was Tweetie I didn't go out on Beggar's Night. Mom said I wasn't old enough but Al was. As he walked out the front door he turned, looked directly at me and *cranked* his noisemaker loudly at me. "Al," Mom warned. He laughed and ran down the steps and out of the yard to meet a group of kids. For the rest of the evening, well after Al returned with a sack full of goodies, we answered the door to sudden bedlams of "trick or treat!" accompanied by all sorts of noise.

Halloween day arrived. I took my noisemaker along with my costume to school for The Party. When it was time, I became Tweetie and started *snapping.* "No, Carl," Miss Davis, the Teacher said ominously, "does anyone else have a noisemaker?" Oops, again. I hadn't realized you weren't supposed to have or use noisemakers at school. A hellraiser was I. *Snappers* at school, for shame. I pocketed it, even when some of the other kids wanted to *snap* it.

Later at home it *was* time, time for trick or treat. I waited until I was on the doorstep and then I turned around, *snapped,* and yelled, "Trick or treat!" Mom smiled and tossed a DumDum lollipop in my bag.

Another mother was walking five of us around the neighborhood. At first it was still twilight but I didn't hear or see any other groups of trick-or-treaters. After a few stops at the closer neighbors it started to get darker; the sun had set and there was a delicious orange glow to the black horizon; above, the pale blue sky almost glowed white. I heard other trick-or-treaters at a distance, in the dark. Is that what we sounded like? Cool. I *snapped* just for the fun of it. No one told me to shush. The others across the street *snapped, rattled,* and *clanged* back at me. I *snapped* again. And again, repeatedly. They did too. So did the kids in my group. Yes. This is it! *Snap!* But as we got closer to the next house, Brian put a finger to his mouth and shushed us. The idea was we were supposed to sneak up to the front door quietly and only then make a racket. That's what we did at every house we could.

We would even hold our noisemakers so they wouldn't make a sound as we walked up to each door. At Mrs. Mills it was a short walk. We stepped onto her porch and stood close together. Each of us wanted to use our noisemaker first, but we magically waited and did it together, yelling, "Trick or treat!" We pointed the noisemakers at one another's faces as much as at Mrs. Mills's door. She was old and it took her a while to open the door. We continued our clamor until she offered goodies to us. She tried to guess who we were and got each of us wrong—on purpose, I thought.

The Kramers had a long, long stone driveway. It was dark with dry meadow on each side. Keeping quiet for that stretch was very difficult for us; it was agony. By the time we got to the front steps, the street looked far away. Later I said that we might not have walked it without Joey's mom present. The Kramers had narrow concrete steps guarded by an ironwork railing. It was, after all, an old farmhouse. We had to traipse single file to the top. Joey's rattle clunked once. We gave him dirty looks. Since we couldn't all get up on the top step together, we had to hold up our noisemakers carefully after we got into position and watch one another so we could begin at the same time. We made our noise and then faced the door and cried, "Trick or treat!" No one opened the door so we kept making noise, but after a bit our arms started to get tired. We looked down at Joey's mom and there instead was a sheet flapping around and beginning to moan. Joanie just about swallowed her voice in fright. Two of us pointed our noisemakers at it and made noise, and then the others joined in. The ghost moaned loudly and ran to the back of the house. We stopped and were quietly stunned. No one had told us that noise drives away spirits, but to our magical intuition of children, it made sense.

The ghost had stood in front of Joey's mom, and there she was again, looking frightened. "Keep it up!" she encouraged us breathlessly. "You don't want it to come back!" We started in again with our noise, really enthusiastically. By the time our arms were getting tired, the front door began to open slowly. The ghost was inside the house now, but the sheet was gradually being dragged off and it was Mr. Kramer, laughing, "Your trick, my treat!" We laughed too as he gave us whole Hershey bars, just about the best loot of the night. The walk back to the street did not seem so dark and frightful, and we had new respect for our noisemakers.

The next morning I got up and checked my loot the very first thing. There in the bag was my noisemaker. Everyone was up so I figured why not: *Snap, snap, snap!* "Carl?" called Mom. "It's time to put that away for another year!" "Yes, Mom," I said after trying to negotiate more noise. *Snap!* I turned it over to her. Well, I still had the candy, and Tweetie hung in the bedroom closet well close to Christmas, but the noise was done for that year.

Over the years, funny things happened.

Bad times came upon us in 1958. I really wanted to be Zorro and get the Zorro costume at Woolworth, but we didn't have much money. That was the year all the giant-sized pumpkins I'd grown had really scary faces. That was the year I was Jack Frost, with a rattle I made myself from a used Calumet baking soda tin with pennies and rocks inside. I used it the next year, too, when I was an Indian; there was an Indian on the can so it made sense. On Beggar's Night a friend loaned me a bell clapper noisemaker with pumpkins and black cats. I took both of them for Halloween. I had to give the clapper back the next day.

In 1960, the last year I went trick-or-treating, I bought a tin-pan clapper noisemaker with money I saved from not buying comic books for two weeks (fig. 11.12). I almost bought a tambourine instead (fig. 11.13), and maybe I should have done so; I broke the tin-pan clapper, I whacked it around so hard. It wasn't the last jack-o'-lantern I made though. In later years I'd go around with the guys, but we didn't trick or treat. It wasn't as much fun either—but I was bigger.

Now I am *that* old: when I was a kid, noisemakers were as much a part of Halloween as candy, costumes and jack-o'-lanterns.

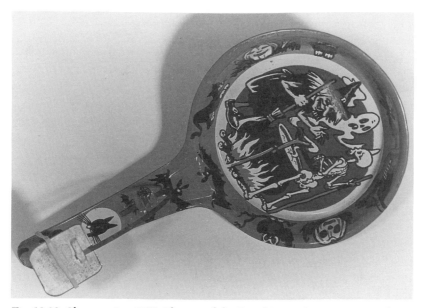

Fig. 11.12. Clapper, circa 1950. Photograph by David Hampshire, Instructional Media Services, Bowling Green State University.

Fig. 11.13. Tambourine, circa 1960. Photograph by David Hampshire, Instructional Media Services, Bowling Green State University.

The Iconography of Halloween Noisemakers

Two problems emerge as we begin to interpret the narrative account of Halloween noisemakers. First, the database for the material component of noisemakers for the present research was limited to twenty-eight Halloween noisemakers, sampled by the process of visiting flea markets, garage sales, and antique fairs for purchases. Many more and a much greater variety were observed throughout childhood and later at fairs, but those photographed here are still quite representative of the domain of Halloween noisemakers.

Second, focusing exclusively on the symbols found on Halloween noisemakers would be at best misleading for discovering their range of cultural significance. Noisemakers are multimedia artifacts that are not only tactile but also produce sound, have shape, and are adorned with symbolic colors and images. Halloween is a season for many senses, with its tasty sweets, its smell and feel of carved pumpkins, and its visions of costumes and candles in the night. Not so long ago it also gave license to children's noisemaking of the kind described above. One is ill-advised to conceive of noisemakers as separate from this seamless lived experience, as if sound were not really a culturally significant part of the holiday. Noisemaking with noisemakers was very much the warp and weft of Halloween for many people, not just myself in Cleveland in the 1950s. Children used noise to announce their presence to one another and at householders' doorways, a practice reminiscent of mumming traditions in other countries.[2]

NOISE ICONICS

Interesting in its own sake, noise appears *visually* on Halloween noisemakers. For instance, a black cat is not merely a symbol of bad luck or of a witch's "familiar." The cat in figure 11.14 has its mouth open, which may very well signify hissing. Cats hiss to warn others not to bother them. If nothing else, it is a danger signal, laden with power. Then again the cat might be howling or yowling. In any case, the visual imagery is audial in nature. Likewise, the dry scuttling of leaves in early fall is represented by bare trees, tree branches, and firewood (figs. 11.2, 11.3, 11.12, 11.13, 11.18, 11.19, 11.20, and 11.21). Leaves litter the streets at Halloween, with all their tactile, olfactory, and audial memories; we love to crunch them under our feet while some may still be in the trees, rattling in the wind. Rattles are isomorphic echoes of the season of dry leaves. Firewood under a cauldron reminds us that it must be collected in rural societies at this time of year for fuel for cold days ahead and for fires to ward off evil spirits.[3] Fire holds special significance for the holiday (figs. 11.2, 11.12, and 11.17). Marian McNeill notes that "the ritual kindling of the need-fire was one of the main ceremonies at the great fire-festivals. It was the most potent of all charms to circumvent the powers of darkness."[4] In Wales "great quantities of straw, gorse, thornwood and other easily ignited materials were carried up to a hill-top, and there set alight at dusk . . . and the bolder spirits leapt" through the bonfire.[5] Firewood also makes sound when collected and when stacked; it also snaps and crackles when it burns.

On the one hand, skeletons are clear reminders of a holiday celebrating death. The skull is a synecdoche for the whole remains (fig. 11.15). Perhaps in their own way jack-o'-lanterns are icons in turn for skulls; they are, after all, hollowed out heads. The entire skeleton interacts with other supernatural beings (fig. 11.12). On the other hand, I have seen noisemakers on which skeletons are shown dancing and gyrating. They are reanimated remains, and their dance evokes sounds of xylophone and bone clatters familiar from classical music such as Saint-Saëns's "Danse Macabre" and from Hollywood movies.

Fig. 11.14. Crank, circa 1947. Photograph by David Hampshire, Instructional Media Services, Bowling Green State University.

Fig. 11.15. Crank, circa 1966. Photograph by David Hampshire, Instructional Media Services, Bowling Green State University.

Bells appearing with crossed broomsticks through a witch's hat (fig. 11.16) may be a vestige of a traditional Celtic assemblage[6] for warding supernatural harm. "Farmers fastened bells that had been blessed on their cows," writes Maymie Krythe. "They also placed crossed branches of ash and juniper at stable doors to keep witches from harming the animals."[7] The bell morphology for the clapper kinds of noisemakers may also be tied to warding off evil. In general, creating noise as a ritual for controlling spirits is related to customs such as exploding firecrackers for the New Year in Chinese culture, firing rifles in Pennsylvania, or banging pots and pans at midnight on New Year's Eve.

Other aspects of the iconics of Halloween noisemakers naturally deserve a more detailed analysis, but perhaps it is enough to have focused briefly on the *visual sound* in their iconics as a stepping stone to the sounds themselves. Sound and its connections to Halloween symbology was never really absent in the forties, fifties, and sixties.[8]

Fig. 11.16. Crank, circa 1946. Photograph by David Hampshire, Instructional Media Services, Bowling Green State University.

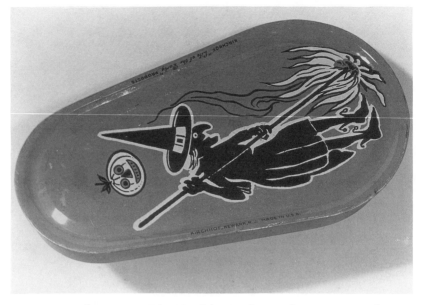

Fig. 11.17. Crank, circa 1964. Photograph by David Hampshire, Instructional Media Services, Bowling Green State University.

Fig. 11.18. Crank, circa 1964. Photograph by David Hampshire, Instructional Media Services, Bowling Green State University.

Fig. 11.19. Rattle, circa 1946. Photograph by David Hampshire, Instructional Media Services, Bowling Green State University.

Fig. 11.20. Rattle, circa 1946. Photograph by David Hampshire, Instructional Media Services, Bowling Green State University.

Fig. 11.21. Horn, circa 1935. Photograph by David Hampshire, Instructional Media Services, Bowling Green State University.

Making Ritual Noise, an Audeography

More important than the visual aspects are the audial aspects of Halloween noisemakers: they make noise. Manufacturers were well aware of the importance of noise for Halloween. The Kirchof Toy Company manufactured noisemakers for various seasons of the year. However, sometimes they struck noisemakers for different seasons from the same mold. A snapper or clicker in the shape of a frog (fig. 11.11A) was also used to make an owl (fig. 11.11B). The owl snapper makes a very penetrating, loud *snap* in comparison to the frog's much weaker sound.

Children love to make noise but are generally discouraged by adults from producing loud or annoying sounds both inside homes and outside in many public places. Halloween during the forties, fifties, and early sixties provided a ritual release from those norms. Trying out noisemakers in a store, at school, or at home invited censure of various kinds. In contrast, adults like my mother broke the indoor rule with impunity, and when my father came home he broke it too, but significantly, Mom assumed it was a child who had.

This inadvertent violation of the indoor norm shadows forth the parameters of noisemaking at Halloween as ritual release. Certainly under most circumstances there are different norms for different people, especially double standards for children and adults. Parents may break the norm just about any time they want, or so it seems to the child. During a former Halloween era, maybe the child could do what grown-ups did with near impunity. Playing with noisemakers was a sign of getting *bigger* or older. At the least it was a series of opportunities to experiment with noise norms, the first of which a child might even have verbalized. Notice how my older brother *cranked* in my face as he crossed the threshold to the outside; he got to go out because he was *older,* and just outside the door was a safe zone for making noise with impunity. The sound was visually aimed at me as a sign of his—an elder's—power. My brother also chose to make the sound as he crossed the threshold from indoors to outdoors. The next night I did the same thing to my mother just after I stepped out the door. Was it merely delight or was it an inversive seizing of power? There was something magically operative to me. Crossing the threshold into a safe zone for noise was a moment of ritual empowerment, marking the past from the future entry into different levels of perceived and unperceived maturation. It was a liminal transition that initiated and enfranchised an individual with new status.[9] The child left the home with its role constraints and entered the liminal space of the street, which during the liminal time of Halloween allowed for role playing and status reversal.

Noise was—and is—suppressed indoors, but outdoors it could be heard throughout the neighborhood, that is, the culturally prescribed area in which trick or treat occurs. My own awareness of the spatial nature of noise at Halloween is clear from the narrative account. Noise defined the liminal space. Children signaled their status reversal to one another by clamoring back and forth at a distance, even when they could not see who answered them. Raucous sound became an audial boundary of liminal space where no physical boundary existed, and using the noisemakers defined this space. This audial boundary communicated their new status to the whole community, not just to themselves. Children also used noise in a more restricted spatial dimension when they stood at someone's front door to announce their disruptive presence by directing the sound at the door. Their silence between the street and the doorstep announced a willing sacrifice to enhance the deferred ritual effects of their noise. Between street and doorstep was a danger zone of sorts, a liminal arena for attaining a desired result in the future.

The performances associated with Halloween noisemakers were an introduction into new levels of culture, and noise was its sign for everyone near and far. The performance of role reversal announced by noise was a kind of ordered disorder. The cacophony of sounds simultaneously gave birth to disorder and to a new world of maturation, especially the taking on of new roles. First children left home with a group of neighbors, later they went without adult supervision, eventually they went perhaps alone.

Precursors of North American Noisemaking

It is no secret that disordered order and noise were associative ingredients for Hallow Eve celebrations in Europe, particularly among the Celts:

> Hallowe'en, the Calends of winter, was a solemn and weird festival. . . . In Scotland, it was a 'night of mischief and confusion,' and its eeriness was intensified by the impersonation of spirits of the dead by young men who went about masked. . . . The boundary between the living and the dead was thus obliterated, and so was the separation of the sexes, for boys wore the clothing of girls and sometimes girls disguised themselves as boys. The general disorder was further intensified by mischievous pranks. . . . The peace of the household itself was disturbed: the door was bombarded with cabbages. . . . A period of disorder in between the old year and the new is a common feature of New Year rituals in many lands. . . . At Hallowe'en the elimination of boundaries . . . symbolize(s) the return of chaos.[10]

Notice how this description of disordered order eventuates in the description of the noise of a door bombarded by cabbages. The description as a whole is clearly that of a liminal holiday appropriate for rural folk celebrating a season between the old year and the new. It also demonstrates the aggressive nature of directing noise and disruption at doors.

Supernatural beings also contributed noise to the season. While witches danced on hilltops with goblins and imps, "the Devil himself played the bagpipes, or castanets made from dead men's bones." As a countercharm, bonfires were lit on hills in merriment, "sometimes to the noise of blowing horns."[11]

In Ballycotton, County Cork, "a procession of horn-blowing youths used to be led by a man called the *Lair Bhan,* whose body was covered by a white sheet, and who carried, or wore, the skull of a mare."[12] One Scottish prank involved two lads, stealthily approaching someone's window with a bottle. "One of them strikes the window with his hand and the second instantly smashes the bottle against the wall of the house. Those inside run to the window convinced that it has been smashed."[13]

These traditions were carried to North America. A householder's front door might be "repeatedly assaulted with bogus calls" by knocking or ringing the doorbell. Americans "considered it fun to make noises with ticktocks on windowpanes."[14] This was the "spool and thread" device many informants from the Midwest and Pacific Northwest told me they used in their childhood, even prior to the 1940s. After the householder first investigated the noise, the pranksters would lie in hiding for some minutes and then repeat the prank ad infinitum, maddeningly waiting at increased intervals to give sign they had left upon hearing the latest imprecations of the man or woman who came to rout them.

The ritualistic nature of Halloween noisemaking was underlined by the fact that the day after Halloween it was no longer appropriate to use Halloween noisemakers. It was time to move on to other experiences. The no-noise norms were suddenly reasserted, as they were in the narrative account. The ritual had a sense of closure to signify that a new year—or at least a new season—and its order had begun.

There may be deeper structures and more latent undertones to Halloween noisemaking. The noisemaking itself may be a vestige of the hunting tradition of prehistoric peoples. Bo Lawergren maintains that musical instruments were originally "closely related to hunting implements or were by-products of hunting." Furthermore, instruments were similar to weapons, sometimes imitated animal sounds, frightened animals to run toward traps, and served as the means of signaling between hunters at a distance. Among the instruments mentioned are percussion that could be scraped or struck, such as bones against bones or spears against other surfaces. Also listed are flutes, which derive from flints and daggers.[15] Halloween noisemakers fall into these primitive types, even the more elaborate versions. The narrative account includes signaling, though it does not have to be explained as some genetic reenactment of hunting rites. Campanelli suggests that the time of year was right for hunting as an additional means of staving off winter hunger. People also stepped up their gathering activities for increased winter store.[16] Perhaps trick or treating as a whole is a vestige of ancient roots; clearly, even today children gather fattening goodies just before the privations of winter, but not so long ago they used noisemakers while on the hunt.

Seasonal rituals with ancient roots must be expected to change over time. Add to that the geographical dispersion of moving from Europe to North America. Even then the celebration of Halloween was not uniform. Regional and local customs were the norm, as opposed to a national culture with clearly accepted national norms. Old forms, such as pranks, became increasingly dangerous in the freer new world. Many communities became alarmed as Halloween tricking progressed to damaged property and hurt children.[17] Perhaps ostensibly as a response to the increasing rowdiness in

Halloween's American celebration after World War II, the use of noisemakers in some communities provided a ritual release and appeasement to the desire for rowdiness. Noise was thus both an unconscious cultural factor for the holiday in its origins and a consciously applied factor in pragmatic North America. Because sound was important in Halloween's origins and in twentieth-century practice, it must be accorded a place of significance along with the visual iconography.

Audeography

Let us call the study of sound icons *audeography*. The analysis just presented is, then, an audeography of Halloween noisemakers. The term is intended to mean fairly much the same as *iconography*, except that it pertains to sounds, their meanings, and their motifs, instead of to objects or images and their meanings and motifs.

The term that would correspond to *icon* would be *aude*, a cognate from Attic Greek meaning "sound" and pronounced aw-day, with the accent on the first syllable. *Audes* may convey relished planes of meaning without the presence of pictures. They may evoke memories and even serve as objects of devotion. The *audes* of Christmas would certainly include carols, jingling bells, chimes, Santa's hearty ho-ho-ho and the ringing of Salvation Army bells. Halloween's *audes* would include noisemakers, particularly bells and clangers, as merry wards and charms against evil. Dry leaves scuttling in the wind; a fire crackling; witch's cackling; ghostly boos and moans; the very few, commercialized and rarely remembered, carols; Bach's "Toccata and Fugue in D Minor"; organ sounds; tritone modulations; and other audial motifs such as screams and maniacal laughter would be *audes* for the season as well. Devotion to *audes* will naturally vary from season to season, but just because the sounds of Halloween are not enshrined at a church as they are for Christmas does not mean that spirituality of some sort does not take place.

Concluding Remarks

Not all regions or communities used noisemakers during the time period. Informants from the Midwest, Pacific Northwest and the Northeast have reported both the presence and absence of noisemakers. Not all the children I saw trick-or-treating possessed or used noisemakers.

Old World and earlier New World traditions suggest that noisemaking involved individually created ways for making noise. Sometimes they were as simple as throwing corn, cabbages, or turnips at someone's door. They could be as elaborate as the spool and thread. Rattles and roarers made from cans were a Depression-era foreshadowing of the kinds of noisemakers later manufactured in the growing consumerism after World War II.

Halloween audeography has changed since the sixties. Perhaps the increased number of local television programs showing various monster movies with their exotic soundtracks created a national sense of scary, if not specifically Halloween-related, sounds that supplanted the earlier and more-limited array of individual sounds. Except for noisemakers, the repertoire of scary sounds available now is clearly more diverse than the postwar era's. Also consider the fact that rock-and-roll subgenres include thrash, heavy metal, and punk, each with their inventories of liminal sounds and experiences to sate unruliness for anyone desirous of it at any time of the year. Now individuals only need to turn on electronic equipment to produce symbols of one's dissonance with life. Ritual unruliness occurs perhaps with greater diversity.

The changes in Halloween noise inscribes three audeographic domains, each with its own significance: (1) *functional* noise, (2) *aggressive* noise, and (3) *atmospheric* noise. Purchasing and using Halloween noisemakers were functional circumstances for children to develop specific and experiential relationships to Halloween and its norms by means of the icons found on noisemakers and by the noise itself. Halloween noisemakers furthermore helped children announce their presence and initiate the trick-or-treat interaction. The role expectation of making noise broke the ice of any shyness when a costume and mask had not. Noisemakers also created and defined the liminal space of Halloween role playing.

In the forties, fifties, and sixties, children stole the license to scare and annoy others with noisemakers. Their noisemaking was *aggressive* and often was particularly directed at adults. Noisemaking as a magical warding behavior was also aggressive, both in its European origins and its North American vestiges. Noisemaking allowed children to take charge of a changing and sometimes ominous world, investing the noisemaking child with a sense of power and control not available at other times.

As the practice of using Halloween noisemakers declined, pranks perpetrated by householders increased. Halloween noise did not disappear but became *atmospheric*. Atmospheric enhancement is something that adults have come to do, not children usually. In fact, because many adults were the aggressive noisemakers of yesteryear, it is of no small interest that they sometimes aggressively direct spooky sounds at trick-or-treaters. The new ritual, if it is appropriate to call it a ritual, is not at all the same. There is no empowerment of children. Adults merely provide an audial environment to enhance Halloween role playing. The activity does not appear to empower adults as a group as did Halloween noisemakers.

Noisemakers still make appearances at New Year's Eve and at birthday parties, two similarly liminal events with customary icons and *audes* of their own. However, the audeography of each holiday would not include aggressive noise of the same qualities or to the same extent as Halloweens past. Noise has atmospheric and functional parameters for those holidays, and perhaps others, but in contrast to them, the iconography and audeography of Halloween noisemakers indicates the aggressive display of power by children who desire the roles of adults but who still live by a magical world view.

Notes

1. See *Writing Culture: The Poetics and Politics of Ethnography,* ed. James Clifford and George E. Marcus (Berkeley: Univ. of California Press, 1986) for an important range of current issues for writing culture. Missing, however, is a fundamental recognition that experience is the first methodology for writing culture. John Dewey recognized the basics of empiricism and experimental methods in raw experience. Children and their experiential viewpoint clearly present themselves as a poetic voice with little politics, so little in fact that noise at Halloween is something adults, not children, do in the 1980s and 1990s.

2. Melvin M. Firestone, "Mummers and Strangers in Northern Newfoundland," in *Christmas Mumming in Newfoundland: Essays in Anthropology, Folklore and History,* ed. Herbert Halpert and G. M. Story (Toronto: Univ. of Toronto Press: 1968), 63–75.

3. Maymie R. Krythe, *All about American Holidays* (New York: Harper & Row, 1962), 251.

4. F. Marian McNeill, *The Silver Bough* (Glasgow: William Maclellan, 1957), vol. 1: 63.

5. Christina Hole, *British Folk Customs* (London: Hutchison of London: 1976), 88.

6. Jack Santino, "The Folk Assemblage of Autumn: Tradition and Creativity in Halloween Folk Art," in *Folk Art and Art Worlds,* ed. John Michael Vlach and Simon J. Bronner (Ann Arbor: UMI Research Press, 1986), 151–69.

7. Krythe, *American Holidays,* 215.

8. Richard M. Dorson, "Material Components in Celebration," in *Celebrations: Studies in Festivity and Ritual,* ed. Victor Turner (Washington, D.C.: Smithsonian Institution Press, 1982), 33–57.

9. See both Arnold Van Gennep, *The Rites of Passage* (Chicago: Univ. of Chicago Press, 1960), 177–88, and Victor Turner, *The Forest of Symbols: Aspects of*

Ndembu Ritual (Ithaca, N.Y.: Cornell Univ. Press, 1967), 93–101.

10. Alwyn Rees and Brinley Rees, *Celtic Heritage* (New York: Grove Press, 1961), 90–91.

11. Krythe, *American Holidays*, 215; Hole, *British Folk Customs*, 87.

12. Hole, *British Folk Customs*, 90.

13. F. Marian McNeill, *Halloween: Its Origins, Rites and Ceremonies in the Scottish Tradition* (Edinburgh: Albyn Press, 1970), 37.

14. Iona Opie and Peter Opie, *The Lore and Language of Schoolchildren* (Oxford, England: Oxford Univ. Press, 1959), 276; Krythe, *All about American Holidays*, 217.

15. Bo Lawergren, "The Origin of Musical Instruments and Sounds," *Anthropos* 83 (1988): 34–37.

16. Pauline Campanelli, *Wheel of the Year: Living the Magical Life* (St. Paul: Llewellyn, 1989), 137.

17. Krythe, *American Holidays*, 217; also see J. Walker McSpadden, *The Book of Holidays* (New York: Thomas Y. Crowell, 1958), 153.

References

Campanelli, Pauline. 1989. *Wheel of the Year: Living the Magical Life* St. Paul: Llewellyn.

Clifford, James, and George E. Marcus, eds. 1986. *Writing Culture: The Poetics and Politics of Ethnography.* Berkeley and Los Angeles: Univ. of California Press.

Dorson, Richard M. 1982. "Material Components in Celebration." In *Celebrations,* ed. Turner, 33–57.

Firestone, Melvin M. 1968. "Mummers and Strangers in Northern Newfoundland." In *Christmas Mumming in Newfoundland,* ed. Halpert and Story, 63–75.

Halpert, Herbert, and G. M. Story, eds. 1968. *Christmas Mumming in Newfoundland: Essays in Anthropology, Folklore, and History.* Toronto: Univ. of Toronto Press.

Hole, Christina. 1976. *British Folk Customs.* London: Hutchison of London.

Krythe, Mamie R. 1962. *All About American Holidays.* New York: Harper & Row.

Lawergren, Bo. 1988. "The Origin of Musical Instruments and Sounds." *Anthropos* 83 (1988): 34–37.

McNeill, F. Marion. 1957. *The Silver Bough* 1. Glasgow, Scotland: MacLellan.

———. 1970. *Halloween: Its Origins, Rites and Ceremonies in the Scottish Tradition.* Edinburgh: Albyn Press.

McSpadden, J. Walker. 1958. *The Book of Holidays.* New York: Thomas Y. Crowell.

Opie, Peter, and Iona Opie. 1959. *The Lore and Language of Schoolchildren.* Oxford: Oxford Univ. Press.

Rees, Alwyn, and Brinley Rees. 1961. *Celtic Heritage.* New York: Grove Press.

Santino, Jack. 1986. "The Folk Assemblage of Autumn: Tradition and Creativity in Halloween Folk Art." In *Folk Art and Art Worlds,* ed. Vlach and Bronner, 151–69.

Turner, Victor. 1967. *The Forest of Symbols: Aspects of Ndembu Ritual.* Ithaca: Cornell Univ. Press.

———, ed. 1982. *Celebrations: Studies in Festivity and Ritual.* Washington, D.C.: Smithsonian Institution Press.

Van Gennep, Arnold. 1960. *The Rites of Passage.* Chicago: Univ. of Chicago Press.

Vlach, John Michael, and Simon Bronner, eds., *Folk Art and Art Worlds.* Ann Arbor: UMI Research Press.

12. Halloween Imagery in Two Southern Settings

GREY GUNDAKER

Of course it is commonplace to say that a holiday and its material trappings mean different things to different people. And although Americans bow to their own diversity with such statements, they also coin comfortably similar accounts of trick-or-treating and costumed wandering that help to stabilize from year to year what Halloween "is." But these glosses can also obscure how people actually interweave the recurring themes of the holiday—ghosts, goblins, things that go bump in the night—with the denser particulars of their own lives. The twists and turns this interweaving takes are richly significant, but also largely unpredictable, based on what a general discussion of the holiday could tell us.

My aim is to briefly explore the emergent qualities of Halloween lore and artifacts as they serve as resources in assemblages composed for different purposes, circumstances, and temporal frames. I will describes two cases, both from the Deep South: first, decorative Halloween assemblages[1] for the graves of children in a predominantly Anglo-American cemetery, and second, Halloween objects incorporated in nonseasonal displays on the exteriors of two African American homes. The focus is on the interrelation of Halloween objects with other components in the assemblages, and how the varied components mutually contextualize one another, the assemblages, and the two kinds of sites.[2] Imagery common to both cases is the jack-o'-lantern pumpkin and the human skeleton. A creative impulse common to both is the use of the ambivalent cultural material of Halloween—the holiday's oscillation between themes of death and celebration—to confront past, present, or anticipated crises. First I will describe both kinds of sites,[3] then close with some additional interpretive remarks.

Halloween in a Cemetery

Home of football's Crimson Tide and the University of Alabama, Tuscaloosa has a metropolitan population of about seventy-five thousand, and a west-central location where the rolling piedmont meets the cotton fields and pulpwood forests of the Black Belt. Protestant denominations—especially Baptist, Methodist, and Presbyterian—dominate the religious lives of white members of the community, most of whom are of British descent.

Memory Hill is one of several cemeteries serving mainly the white population.[4] Its spacious site extends along four-lane U.S. Highway 11 among the fast-food restaurants, strip malls, and motels of the city's northern fringe. Mature, clipped evergreens punctuate gently sloping expanses of grass and curving driveways, bounded to the north by an office and mortuary chapel complex and to the south by a maintenance building and mausoleum, all constructed of red brick fronted by porticos and white columns.

Grave markers in the cemetery follow a standard format: a textured bronze plaque laid flush with the earth on a polished gray granite slab, a bronze vase approximately fourteen inches tall set back-center in the plaque, and embossed inscriptions and emblems with a brassy finish that contrasts with the deep brown bronze background. Although the format is uniform, purchasers have some latitude in adapting it to their tastes and the character of the deceased. Style of lettering and size of names, dates, and epitaphs vary. In addition, purchasers may opt for textured borders resembling stone, oak, or knotty pine to frame the plaque, and choose from emblems such as a car, angel, rosebud, cross, or pair of praying hands. These appear on many markers, with or without an accompanying phrase ("our little angel," for instance). Overall, Memory Hill resembles hundreds of burial grounds around the country—managed by private corporations and offering comprehensive funeral and "burial estate" packages—that have been growing in popularity since the mid-1970s.

Memory Hill came to my attention through a striking Halloween tableau early on the morning of 2 November 1989 while I was idling at a traffic light. About seventy-five feet from the highway, framed between a small live oak tree and a clipped shrub, stood a large inflated jack-o'-lantern, a four-foot-tall ghost carrying a pumpkin, two life-sized black cats, and a rotund teddy bear wearing an orange pumpkin suit, a tall witch's hat, and holding two grinning jack-o'-lantern containers. About twenty-five feet to the left of this group was an upright two-by-three-foot poster, hand lettered in red and blue marker: Happy Birthday Mathew Big #3. What I was looking at was a combination birthday party and Halloween celebration for a dead child (fig. 12.1). Both the poster and the figures invited public reading and appreciation through their flat, frontal alignment with the highway. This arrangement also created a stagelike effect that cast the rest of the cemetery as a backdrop to the Halloween tableau—and a very dramatic one at that, with a monumental white sculpture of praying Jesus looming against the trees. In effect, the poster and tableau reached out toward the land of the living and away from the dead.

At the time the scene was hard to comprehend. Its seemingly contradictory elements—Jesus and witches, pumpkins and clipped yews, the figure of a "lifelike" ghost in a graveyard—resisted any unifying interpretation. The immediate sense I made of it was that the American quest for "authenticity" had gone overboard, that someone had chosen a graveyard for a children's Halloween birthday party in order to provide a "realistic" setting. I wondered if this represented a trend, like the haunted-house tours civic groups offer as fund-raising events. It did not occur to me that the party honored a permanent

Fig. 12.1. Halloween birthday party in a memorial park. Photograph by the author.

occupant of the cemetery. This impression is worth mentioning because, though it proved to be factually incorrect, the nature of the error also points up the compelling immediacy of the display: the way the brightly colored figures helped to construct Halloween as a participatory event and to change the emphasis in grave decoration from semipermanent flower arrangements honoring a past life to temporally located and temporary displays that made the grave site a center of activity in the present.

As it turned out, the Halloween birthday celebration was for a little boy who had died at the age of three months. Invisible from a distance between the pumpkin and the ghost, Matthew's flat bronze marker included the embossed image of a seated teddy bear, a framed color photograph of a chubby baby in a blue suit, and the inscription, "Our precious gift from God" (fig. 12.2).

From Matthew's grave I could see several other bright patches of orange among the multicolored bouquets in the regular rows of bronze vases. In all, there were five graves of children and one of an adult couple decorated for Halloween in the southwestern portion of the cemetery. A few other graves had fall seasonal arrangements of autumn leaves, Indian corn in the husk, and figurines of hunting dogs. Other decorative objects were of the type that also decorate yards and are sold in garden supply stores: colorful

Fig. 12.2. A trick-or-treating Teddy bear, ghost, and jack-o'-lantern for Matthew's party. Photograph by the author.

pinwheels shaped like windmills, daisies, and ducks with rotating wings; plaster angels; plaster and plastic hens, chicks, and roosters; and a cast-cement donkey cart with flowers in the back. Objects illustrating personal qualities of the deceased and their families also rested on a few graves, singly or in addition to other decorations: flags for veterans, a china running shoe, a trophy, a red china lady bug beside the epitaph "our little lady bug."

All told, elements of grave marking at Memory Hill took five interrelated forms: (1) semipermanent, nonseasonal artificial flower arrangements; (2) identity information in writing and emblems on the plaque, or occasionally objects added to it; (3) yardlike decorations; (4) seasonal and holiday arrangements; and (5) commemorations of special dates, through either a labeled object, such as a Happy Birthday balloon, or concurrence of the decorating theme with dates of birth or death.

The graves decorated for Halloween at Memory Hill combined these elements in different, highly personal, ways. Decoration on the paired graves of a husband and wife, sharing one plaque embossed with two open Bibles and a border of roses, consisted of two small plastic pumpkins. The children's graves were more elaborate.

The bronze marker for Dwight, who had died on 16 October at the age of eleven, contained four permanent descriptive emblems and phrases at the four corners: a fish ("daddy's hunting and fishing buddy"), a horse head with a toy van placed nearby ("mama's riding buddy"), crossed bats and a ball ("Nick's baseball buddy"), and a rosebud ("you smell like the roses"). The words "We love you! Together forever" in larger type united these family themes. Dwight's bronze vase held white cloth daisies and a shiny mylar jack-o'-lantern balloon. Clustered at the foot of the vase were small figurines of a praying Teddy bear, an owl, and a black cat jumping out of a pumpkin. Dwight's grave boasted the only real pumpkin in the cemetery. Crisply carved into a toothy grin, it contained the burnt-out stump of a candle (fig. 12.3).

Like that of Dwight, three other Halloween-decorated graves belonged to boys who had died at eleven, an age when Halloween is one of the most acutely pleasurable days of the year. A plastic pumpkin and a bendable, glow-in-the-dark skeleton leaning against the bronze vase joined the more permanent features of Michael's grave: pink roses, a rotary-legged roadrunner pinwheel, a prayerful cement cherub, and praying angels on the bronze tablet (fig. 12.4). "Our beloved son is gone but not forgotten," read the epitaph above an embossed Bible and Michael's name.

Fig. 12.3. A real pumpkin and a Halloween balloon accompany nonseasonal emblems of Dwight's personality. Photograph by the author.

Fig. 12.4. Michael died during the Halloween season. A roadrunner pinwheel, glow-in-the-dark skeleton, and plastic pumpkin mark his grave. Photograph by the author.

The format of the plaque for Charles, also eleven, was almost identical, with the phrase "no one can fill your vacant place" embossed above a Bible and paired angels. Charles's decorations used all the available space in the burial plot. A huge, flat jack-o'-lantern face—with its mouth turned down in a sorrowful grimace—and a streamer-legged skeleton mounted on red posts at the foot of the grave waved in the wind and made the display visible from a great distance (fig. 12.5). Moving closer, viewers got a bird's eye view of a black spider that seemed to creep over a cloud of white cotton.

Lonnie's Halloween decorations were more compact: two pumpkin mylar balloons added to a vase of blue artificial carnations and white lilies, and a white china baby shoe filled with shells on the grass adjacent to the plaque (fig. 12.6).

All the Halloween assemblages at Memory Hill offered deeply moving testimony to the continuing importance of the children to their families, and to Halloween as a special day.

Halloween imagery in the cemetery is also part of the ongoing process that mediates the flow of life through the space, and it indexes the kinds of participation that are allowed within the space, as well as (implicitly or explicitly) the kinds that are questionable or unacceptable. Acceptable participation, including the role of the dead in the cemetery, is not settled or consensual but contested.

Halloween and other grave decorations challenge cemetery rules that attempt to dictate how lively the world of the dead is permitted to be. When families add personal emblems and objects that extend the repertoire of yard decoration to the grave site, they also bring "home" to the deceased family member's space. Seasonal decorations extend this process further, binding the deceased to the annual cycle of living. Birthday flowers and balloons locate points of personal significance in the cycle. On four of the six children's graves, Halloween decorations linked a holiday children especially enjoy with significant dates in the life span: the date of birth for two children, the date of death for two others.

The most important question that remains unanswered by my visually based analysis is how, if at all, the notions of death and the living dead conventionally associated with Halloween fit with families' ideas about the death of their children. Because aspects of the practice of grave decoration, and especially the wording of epitaphs, underscore a conservative Protestant assertion of the open channels between heaven and earth, and an embodied afterlife in heaven where loved ones left behind will soon arrive, my tentative conclusion is that in their families' view, these special children—Matthew,

Fig. 12.5. Charles's grave stands out, framed by a cotton-cushioned spider, skeleton windsock, and frowning jack-o'-lantern face. Photograph by the author.

Fig. 12.6. Blue flowers and orange balloons for Lonnie. Photograph by the author.

Dwight, Charles, and Michael—are indeed alive and in heaven. Further, as their lives and grave sites occasion visits and the purchase and arrangement of decorations, they and others buried at Memory Hill remain viable participants in the family.

The posted rules of the cemetery work against such liveliness, however. Signs limiting cars in the cemetery to "authorized vehicles only" preclude dropping by spontaneously (if visitors heed the messages), and most burial areas are a long walk from the mortuary chapel parking lot. Other signs limit the type and scale of floral and other displays. In 1989, at the time of my first visit, a sign near the entrance bore the following message:

> PLEASE HELP!
> During the mowing season
> *Please* use max. of 2 floral
> Arrangements per grave, in
> order that your burial estate
> can be properly maintained.
> Thank you: The Manager

The Halloween and other decorations I have described flourished at this time, often exceeding the two-arrangement limit and making the cemetery a patchwork of bright colors. When I returned in 1990, I noticed another sign near the main entrance, which limited floral arrangements in "grass cutting season" to the single bronze vase fixed to each marker. Enforcement of this policy had stemmed the visible flow of life through the cemetery considerably. It ruled out not only yardlike decorations but also freestanding sprays and, as I sadly discovered, most Halloween decorations. Indeed, on Halloween morning a large riding mower was roving among the graves, and pitiful tufts of fern and artificial flowers collected prior to the mowing were poking out of the back of a pickup truck parked beside the mausoleum.

Nonseasonal Halloween Imagery on Two Home Exteriors

The Halloween grave decorations I have described so far are exceptional and personal elaborations of a visual repertoire that other members of the community can readily understand, even though only a few of the hundreds of graves in the cemetery had such decorations. The displays on African American home exteriors and surrounding yards to which I now turn are similarly personal and exceptional, yet also largely "readable" in their communities. In obvious contrast to grave decorations, however, the occupants of these homes and yards create their own assemblages. Halloween imagery contributes aesthetically to assemblages and also illuminates how commercially produced artifacts serve functions and accrete meanings that their manufacturers probably did not envision. Further, such uses of jack-o'-lanterns, masks, skeleton figures, and so on show that calendrical time is the most apparent, but not the only, temporal frame relevant to holiday imagery, for themes and objects associated with the holiday also spill over into the rest of year.

SOUTHEAST MISSISSIPPI

Mrs. Ruby Gilmore, a widow in her late sixties, lives in a small southern city in the home she and her husband bought early in their marriage.[5] Since her husband's death, Mrs. Gilmore has augmented her income by recycling glass and aluminum she collects on rounds of residential neighborhoods early in the morning. Inevitably along the way, she also finds useful building material and other objects that have gradually filled her yard from porch to fence. Occasionally she sells this material or uses it to improve her own house. Unfortunately her success in scrap collection also attracts thieves, mainly boys in their early teens and clients of the bootlegger down the street, for whom the scrap presents an irresistible target, especially on Sundays when Mrs. Gilmore is away at church, taverns are closed, and the bootlegger does his best business.

Mrs. Gilmore uses two main strategies to discourage thieves. She bolsters her fence to make it hard for thieves to climb, and she arranges visual warnings in important locations on the property: beside the mailbox, on a line to the front door, and on the roof of the carport. These signs include written messages—Keep Out, Beware of Dog—but also draw on a traditional African American visual repertoire of signs, such as the all-seeing eye, the X or Greek cross, and the figure of a dog: signs that allude to spiritual insight and power.[6]

In addition to thieves, the densely packed scrap in Mrs. Gilmore's yard also attracted an even more destructive form of intruder: the city government. With no official notice and only a few hours informal warning—barely time for Mrs. Gilmore to conceal a few favorite possessions in a ditch—the street in front of her house was blocked off and trucks arrived to haul the scrap to the dump (and to the homes of the cleanup crew, Mrs. Gilmore asserts). Bulldozers scraped the yard to bare dirt, even uprooting a huge climbing rose.

This setback hurt Mrs. Gilmore financially and made her hard work even harder, but it did not break her spirit. She resumed her recycling rounds of the city, though now she keeps choicer scrap out of sight behind white curtains in her carport. She also assembled a new group of protective signs.

Halloween artifacts were among the protective signs in Mrs. Gilmore's yard both before and after the bulldozing. Before the bulldozing, these signs included a stuffed Snoopy watchdog on the roof of the carport, rattles and sounding devices (whose circular shapes can connote transitional zones between material and spiritual worlds), and a complex assemblage drawing on the iconography of traditional African American (and African) burials: small figures, broken vessels, plastic flowers, white and reflective materials, shells, and allusions to water.[7]

At least two Halloween artifacts, commercially produced for holiday use, joined these other objects. One was a plastic monster mask mounted to the house so that its pasty Caucasian visage could confront unwelcome visitors approaching from the south. The other was a life-sized, cutout skeleton with mobile limbs suspended beside a brightly colored windsock near the front door (fig. 12.7). Whenever the wind blew, both these objects took on uncanny life, which—I now realize—is just what Mrs. Gilmore intended.

When I first noticed the skeleton, I did not recognize its protective function. That was 2 November 1989, later in the same day that I had observed Halloween grave celebrations in Tuscaloosa, and near enough to 31 October to mislead me into interpreting the skeleton as seasonal. I said to Mrs. Gilmore: "I see you've got your Halloween decorations up." She shook her

Fig. 12.7. Skeleton beside the front door of Ruby Gilmore. Photograph by the author.

head slightly, gave me one sharp glance of incredulous pity, and turned the conversation to other topics. The skeleton remained in place for another year, until it was hauled away with everything else in the yard.

After the bulldozing, Mrs. Gilmore constructed a more compact assemblage of signs centered on her front porch and entry. It includes a sky blue sword cut from plywood,[8] a painted post to underscore the message that the property is "posted," and plastic red-hot peppers (not visible in photographs). At the base of the post there is a toy clock, which in context imbeds triple messages: an *X* in the path of encroachment, the biblical warning that "ye know not the day nor the hour" but that the "kingdom of God is at hand." Thus, by implication, thieves should remember to prepare their souls to meet God and that God takes a personal interest in Mrs. Gilmore and her guests. Several feet away by the door hangs a small bright orange plastic jack-o'-lantern (fig. 12.8).

Despite their obvious differences, and the differences in objects that accompany them, the skeleton and the jack-o'-lantern play similar roles in Mrs. Gilmore's yard. Both refer to death and spiritual powers, and the jack-o'-lantern adds the red round flash of a stop sign.[9] The connotations of these signs are not necessarily negative. Combined with other objects, such as the

Fig. 12.8. A small jack-o'-lantern hangs over the "posted" sign on the corner of the porch. Photograph by the author.

clock, they also contribute a positive message of divine concern. Thus the assemblage visually restates what Mrs. Gilmore says: "All my protection comes from God. He's all any of us has, and if you trust him, he'll look after you good."

Yard-sign "translations" such as these depend not only on understanding relationships among objects in one yard but also on the fact that similar usages of Halloween material recur across great distances. Nonseasonal jack-o'-lanterns are not as common in yards as Keep Out signs. Nevertheless, they occur intermittently throughout the year at thresholds such as doors, gates, and driveway entrances in black neighborhoods from rural Delaware to Louisiana. In white yards, jack-o'-lanterns seem confined to autumn displays.

SOUTHEAST LOUISIANA

Halloween imagery also appears in the yard of Victor Melancon, a retired auto worker in his mid-fifties, who draws, paints, and creates sculptures from found objects. Like Mrs. Gilmore, he collects scraps and trash around the neighborhood. But unlike her, his motives are noncommercial. Collecting and burning litter each morning is a mission in community improvement for Mr. Melancon.

Scrap metal, clothing, toys, and furniture that he finds in nearby woods and canals become parts of the sculptural assemblages that surround his yard on three sides. These assemblages draw on the same traditional African American repertoire of warning and protective signs that informs Mrs. Gilmore's work. But in some ways Mr. Melancon's work is more aesthetically replete and more focused than Mrs. Gilmore's. Most of his assemblages totter on the edge of explicit figuration, each with its own subtle but distinctive persona. Of course, to some observers Mr. Melancon's collection of objects remains mere junk. But for those aware of his intent, sneaking into this yard would be like breaking through a line of shoulder-to-shoulder border guards.

A hand-drawn jack-o'-lantern hanging year-round on the front door is the image most explicitly associated with Halloween outside Mr. Melancon's home (fig. 12.9). (Recall that the same image appears in the same general location at Mrs. Gilmore's door.) His yard also contains material related to traditional African American grave decoration: pipes, stones, reflective surfaces, whiteness.

Such miniature yard cemeteries do not derive directly from European Halloween traditions. Rather they reflect creolization—the interlacing of previously independent cultural streams—from Europe, Africa, and the West Indies. For example, in the Gulf region of the South, Afro-Haitian Voudou remains an active contributor to emergent creolized forms. The spirit Gede, master of the cemetery, sometimes makes his presence felt in

Fig. 12.9. Jack-o'-lantern drawing by Victor Melancon on his front door in Louisiana. Photograph by the author.

visual tributes that incorporate crosses, skulls, and real or symbolic graves. In her biography of a voudou priestess, *Mama Lola*, Karen McCarthy Brown also points out that because of his graveyard attributes, commercial Halloween decorations appear on altars at celebrations for Gede, like those she attended in New York City.[10]

Creolization also involves tales, freewheeling wordplay, and language change; indeed, the concept derives from these processes under conditions of culture contact. The dynamic nature of creolization is well illustrated by the twists and turns the term *jack-o'-lantern* takes in collision with other terms in Harry Middleton Hyatt's summary of the "ha'nt" type of "hag." Based on his interviews with hoodoo doctors and laymen in the 1930s, Hyatt says this

> spirit of the dead either comes of its own accord to worry someone at night . . . or is sent, usually by a *doctor* . . . It is occasionally called *Jack Mulatta* . . ., a term approximating *Jack-mu-la't'* or *Jack-ma-lantren*, a corruption of Jack O'Lantern . . . [L]antern is pronounced *lantren* or *latren* by uneducated Negroes and Whites. *Jack Mulatta*, a hag or witch carrying a light at night, is identified with Jack o' Lantern . . . Traveling lights are sometimes spirits of the dead . . .[11]

An informant from Tyree Church, Maryland, adds: "What they tell me about a jack-o'-lantern, it's like a ghost, just as ragged as they could be. They carry a light, and they would lead you in the worstest briers and brambles they could find, and all through the water to terrify you."[12] The late Sam Doyle, a noted artist from St. Helena Island, South Carolina, painted a picture of this wandering spirit, showing him with a bright red male body and a Janus-faced head wearing a black hat.[13] A nineteenth-century description is different but equally detailed. The "Jack-muh-lantern" was

> a hideous little being somewhat human in form, though covered with hair like a dog. It had great goggle eyes, and thick sausage-like lips that opened from ear to ear. In height it seldom exceeded four or five feet, and was quite slender in form, but such was its power of locomotion that no one on the swiftest horse could overtake it or even escape from it.[14]

In all probability, Halloween jack-o'-lanterns became incorporated among the warning and protective signs in African American yards because of this rich fund of oral tradition. If this is true, the name of the pumpkin-with-a-face is as important as its appearance in warning unwelcome intruders of the swampy, brambly wanderings in store for them. For the jack-o'-lantern of African American folklore is not a pumpkin at all, though his lamp, mysteriousness, and identification with the dead make him a ripe candidate for creative mixing.

In the yards of Ruby Gilmore and Victor Melancon, objects and assemblages point to spirit presences that are invisible to an uninstructed sense of sight. Because these presences exist throughout the year, it seems appropriate that Halloween images step out of the European seasonal calendar and into a new open-ended time frame as they come to serve new purposes.

I have briefly discussed Halloween imagery in two settings in which, at first glance, ghosts, skeletons, and pumpkins appear to be anomalous. However, in both cases this sense of dislocation marks the creative adaptation of Halloween imagery to deal with special circumstances: the death of a family member and the threat of intruders. The celebration of the Halloween holiday in the predominantly European American cemetery incorporates the dead in the cycle of seasonal life enjoyed by the living by shifting displays usually found in yards onto the family member's grave. In contrast, the use of selected Halloween imagery in African American yards diffuses the particularity of the holiday, as miniature cemeteries and references to spirits find places in yards throughout the year. Both of these forms of adaptation depend upon the ambivalent capacity of Halloween imagery to accommodate notions of life and death. However—most important—in both settings life and death are not polar opposites separated by a yawning gulf. Instead, the graves and the yards construct interlocking worlds and open lines of communication for the living, the dead, and the spirits in between.

Notes

1. See Jack Santino, "Halloween in America: Contemporary Customs and Performances," *Western Folklore* 42 (1983): 1–20, and "The Folk *Assemblage* of Autumn: Tradition and Creativity in Halloween Folk Art," in Vlach and Bronner, *Folk Art and Art Worlds.* 151–69.

2. Referring to "fine art" assemblage, an "artchart" in a recent volume illustrates that assemblage is the longest-running "movement" in American art after World War II, extending unbroken from 1950 to the present. The authors claim that geographically assemblage is "international but especially in the United States." See Robert Atkins, *Artspeak* (New York: Abbeville Press, 1990), 8, 52. The persistence of assemblage while other styles and techniques come and go suggests that assemblages, whether "fine" or "folk," owe something to that same complex (multi)cultural American expressive matrix that sent jazz and creolized dance forms to Paris and proponents of *assemblage* during the early years of the century. On the dialogic relationship of "fine," "folk," and "tribal" art in the assemblage movement, see Henry Hopkins, "Recollecting the Beginnings," in *Forty*

Years of California Assemblage (Los Angeles: Wight Art Gallery, UCLA, 1989), 15–16. Themes from African and African American aesthetics recur across discussions of assemblage. For example, a performance of *Impressions d'Afrique* that Marcel Duchamp attended in 1911 served as a catalyst for his subsequent work. See Octavio Paz, *Marcel Duchamp: Appearance Stripped Bare* (New York: Arcade Publishing, 1989), 10–11. The African American yards I discuss briefly in this paper carry off-beat, punning, and accretive principles similar to those that attracted trained European and American artists to assemblage as a form of visual performance.

3.   A word of caution here—both descriptions and the sense I make of them are provisional, lifted from work in progress and drawn from quite different bodies of data. I encountered the children's grave decorations by chance and what follows depends on photographs and observations from two brief visits to the cemetery. In contrast, I have documented the practice of "dressing" or decorating yards and home exteriors in white and black neighborhoods scattered across twelve states. But I have not studied Halloween or seasonal decoration in detail with either group. Given these limitations, then, my present goal is to draw attention to and invite further inquiry about practices that might otherwise go unnoted.

4.   For a discussion that places Memory Hill Gardens in relation to other cemeteries, see David Charles Sloane, *The Last Great Necessity: Cemeteries in American History* (Baltimore, Md.: Johns Hopkins Univ. Press, 1991), 226.

5.   Because both the homeowners I discuss have mixed feelings about visitors, I have left descriptions of their residences vague.

6.   The pioneer researcher into themes and objects in African American yards is Robert Farris Thompson, *Flash of the Spirit: African and Afro-American Art and Philosophy* (New York: Random House, 1983), 142–58, and "The Circle and the Branch: Renascent Kongo-American Art, in *Another Face of the Diamond: Pathways through the Black Atlantic South* (New York: INTAR Latin American Gallery, 1988), 23–59; "The Song that Named the Land: The Visionary Presence of African-American Art," in *Black Art: Ancestral Legacy* (Dallas: Dallas Museum of Art, 1989), 97–141. Judith McWillie's "Another Face of the Diamond," *Clarion* 12, no. 4 (1987): 42–53, based on extensive fieldwork in the South, also sets yardwork in its larger context. Also see the essay and museum catalog edited by Lizetta LeFalle-Collins, *Home and Yard: Black Folk Life Expressions from Los Angeles* (Los Angeles: California Afro-American Museum); and Grey Gundaker, "Working in the Yard: African American Dressed Yards in the Southeastern United States," *African Arts*, forthcoming.

7.   The literature on grave decoration is extensive. For example, see Robert Farris Thompson, "Kongo Influences on African-American Artistic Culture," in *Africanisms in American Culture*, ed. Joseph E. Holloway (Bloomington: Indiana Univ. Press, 1990), 148–84; H. Carrington Bolton, "The Decoration of Graves of Negroes in South Carolina," *Journal of American Folklore* 4 (1891): 214; and Dor-

othy Jean Michael, "Grave Decoration," *Publications of the Texas Folklore Society* 18 (1943): 129–36.

8.   On sky blue as a protective color, see Thompson, "Circle," 118, 140; Mason Crum, *Gullah: Negro Life in the Carolina Sea Islands* (Durham, N.C.: Duke Univ. Press, 1940), 40, 85; and Rossa Belle Cooley, *Homes of the Freed* (New York: New Republic, 1926), 53.

9.   Actual stop signs appear near thresholds in several African American yards I have visited.

10.   See Karen McCarthy Brown, *Mama Lola: A Vodou Priestess in Brooklyn* (Berkeley and Los Angeles: Univ. of California Press, 1991), 356–57.

11.   See Harry Middleton Hyatt, *Hoodoo—Conjuration—Witchcraft— Rootwork* (Hannibal, Mo.: Western Publishing, 1970), 135.

12.   Hyatt, *Hoodoo,* 135.

13.   See *Baking in the Sun: Visionary Images from the South* (Lafayette: Univ. Art Museum, Univ. of Southwest Louisiana), 134.

14.   See William Owens, "Folklore of the Southern Negroes," in *The Negro and his Folklore in Nineteenth Century Periodicals,* ed. Bruce Jackson (Austin: Univ. of Texas Press, 1967), 146–47.

References

Baking in the Sun: Visionary Images from the South. 1987. Lafayette: Univ. Art Museum, Univ. of Southwestern Louisiana.

Bolton, H. Carrington. 1891. "Decoration of Graves of Negroes in South Carolina." *Journal of American Folklore* 4: 214.

Brown, Karen McCarthy. 1991. *Mama Lola: A Vodou Priestess in Brooklyn.* Berkeley and Los Angeles: Univ. of California Press.

Cooley, Rossa Belle. 1926. *Homes of the Freed.* New York: New Republic.

Crum, Mason. 1940. *Gullah: Negro Life in the Carolina Sea Islands.* Durham: Duke Univ. Press.

Forty Years of California Assemblage. Los Angeles: Wight Art Gallery, Univ. of California, 1989.

Gundaker, Grey. 1993. "Working in the Yard: African American Dressed Yards in the Southeastern United States." *African Arts.*

Hyatt, Harry Middleton. 1970. *Hoodoo—Conjuration—Witchcraft—Rootwork* 1. Cambridge, Md.: Western Publishing.

LeFalle-Collins, Lizzetta. 1987. *Home and Yard: Black Folk Life Expressions from Los Angeles.* Los Angeles: California Afro-American Museum.

McWillie, Judith. 1987. "Another Face of the Diamond: Afro-American Traditional Art from the Deep South." *The Clarion* 12, no. 4: 42–53.

Michael, Dorothy Jean. 1943. "Grave Decoration." *Publications of the Texas Folklore Society* 18: 129–36.

Owens, William. 1967. "Folklore of the Southern Negroes." *The Negro and His Folklore in Nineteenth Century Periodicals,* ed. Bruce Jackson, 144–56. Austin: Univ. of Texas Press.

Paz, Octavio. 1989. *Marcel Duchamp: Appearance Stripped Bare,* trans. Rachel Phillips and Donald Gardner. New York: Arcade.

Santino, Jack. 1983. "Halloween in America: Contemporary Customs and Performances." *Western Folklore* 42: 1–20.

———. 1986. "The Folk *Assemblage* of Autumn: Tradition and Creativity in Halloween Folk Art. In *Folk Art and Art Worlds,* ed. Vlach and Bronner, 151–69.

Sloane, David Charles. 1991. *The Last Great Necessity: Cemeteries in American History.* Baltimore, Md.: Johns Hopkins Univ. Press.

Thompson, Robert Farris. 1983. *Flash of the Spirit: African and Afro-American Art and Philosophy.* New York: Random House.

———. 1988. "The Circle and the Branch: Renascent Kongo-American Art." *Another Face of the Diamond: Pathways through the Black Atlantic South.* New York: INTAR Latin American Gallery.

———. 1989. "The Song that Named the Land: The Visionary Presence of African-American Art." *Black Art: Ancestral Legacy.* Dallas: Dallas Museum of Art.

Selected Bibliography

Abrahams, Roger D. 1982. "The Language of Festivals: Celebrating the Economy."
   In *Celebrations: Studies in Festivity and Ritual,* ed. Victor Turner. Washington,
   D.C.: Smithsonian Institution Press.

Abrahams, Roger D., and Richard Bauman. 1978. "Ranges of Festival Behavior." In
   The Reversible World, ed. Barbara A. Babcock. Ithaca: Cornell Univ. Press.

Babcock, Barbara A., ed. 1978. *The Reversible World.* Ithaca: Cornell Univ. Press.

Banks, M. Macleod. 1939. *British Calendar Customs 2, The Seasons.* London:
   William Glaisher.

Bannatyne, Lesley Pratt. 1990. *Halloween: An American Holiday, An American
   History.* New York: Facts on File.

Bateson, Gregory. [1936] 1958. *Naven.* Stanford, Calif.: Stanford Univ. Press.

Bauman, Richard. 1972. "Belsnickling in a Nova Scotia Island Community."
   Western Folklore 31: 229–43.

Beck, Ervin. 1982. "Children's Guy Fawkes Customs of Sheffield." *Folklore* 95, no.
   2: 191–203.

———. 1983. "Children's Halloween Customs in Sheffield." *Lore and Language* 3: 9.

———. 1985. "Trickster on the Threshold: An Interpretation of Children's Autumn
   Traditions." *Folklore* 96, no. 1: 24–28.

Bennett, Gillian, and Paul Smith, eds. 1989. *The Questing Beast.* Sheffield: Sheffield
   Academic Press.

Best, Joel. 1985. "The Myth of the Halloween Sadist." *Psychology Today* 19 (Nov.):
   14–19.

Best, Joel, and Gerald T. Horiuchi. 1985. "The Razor Blade in the Apple: The
   Social Construction of Urban Legends." *Social Problems* 32 (June): 488–99.

Bossard, James H. S., and Eleanor S. Boll. 1950. *Ritual in Family Living.* Philadelphia:
   Univ. of Pennsylvania Press.

Brody, Alan. 1969. *The English Mummers and Their Plays.* Philadelphia: Univ. of
   Pennsylvania Press.

Buchanan, R. H. 1962. "Calendar Customs, Pt. 1." *Ulster Folklife* 8: 15–34.

———. "Calendar Customs, Pt. 2." *Ulster Folklife* 9: 61–79.

Burns, Robert. 1793. *Poems, Chiefly in the Scottish Dialect*. Belfast: W. Magee.

Carmichael, Elizabeth, and Chloë Sayer. *The Skeleton at the Feast: The Day of the Dead in Mexico*. London: British Museum Press.

Clifford, James, and George E. Marcus, eds. 1986. *Writing Culture: The Poetics and Politics of Ethnography* Berkeley and Los Angeles: Univ. of California Press.

Danaher, Kevin. 1972. *The Year in Ireland* Cork: Mercier Press.

Davis, Natalie Zemon. 1975. "The Reasons of Misrule." In *Society and Culture in Early Modern France*. Stanford, Calif.: Stanford Univ. Press. 97–123.

Dorson, Richard M. 1972. *Folklore and Folklife: An Introduction*. Chicago: Univ. of Chicago Press.

Douglas, Mary. 1966. *Purity and Danger*. London: Routledge & Kegan Paul.

Dundes, Alan. 1989. "April Fool and April Fish: Towards a Theory of Ritual Pranks." In *Folklore Matters*. 98–111. Knoxville: Univ. of Tennessee Press.

Eco, Umberto, V. V. Ivanov, and Monica Rector, eds. 1984. *Carnival*. Berlin: Mouton.

Evans, E. Estyn. 1957. *Irish Folk Ways*. New York: Devin-Adair.

Falassi, Alessandro, ed. 1987. *Time Out of Time: Essays on the Festival*. Albuquerque: Univ. of New Mexico.

Frost, Peter J., Larry F. Moore, Meryl R. Louis, Craig C. Lundberg, and Joanne Martin, eds. 1985. *Organizational Culture*. Beverly Hills, Calif.: Sage.

Gailey, Alan. 1966. "The Folk Play in Ireland." *Studia Hibernica* 6: 113–54.

———. 1967. "The Rhymers of South-East Antrim." *Ulster Folklife* 13: 18–28.

———. 1969. *Irish Folk Drama*. Cork, Ireland: Mercier Press.

———. 1972. "A New Year Custom in South-East Ulster." *Schweizerische Archiv fur Volkskunde* 68: 126–36, 754.

———. "Mummers' and Christmas Rhymers' Plays in Ireland: The Problem of Distribution," Ulster Folklife 24 (1978), 59-68.

Geertz, Clifford. 1973. *The Interpretation of Cultures*. New York: Basic Books.

———, ed. 1971. *Myth, Symbol, and Culture*. New York: W. W. Norton.

Glassie, Henry. 1975. *All Silver and No Brass: An Irish Christmas Mumming*. Bloomington: Indiana Univ. Press.

———. 1982. *Passing the Time in Ballymenone*. Philadelphia: Univ. of Pennsylvania Press.

Gregory, Ruth W. 1975. *Anniversaries and Holidays*. 3d ed. Chicago: American Library Association.

Grider, Sylvia. 1984. "The Razor Blades in the Apples Syndrome." In *Perspectives on Contemporary Legend: Proceedings of the Conference on Contemporary Legend*, ed. Paul Smith, 129–40. Sheffield, England: CECTAL.

Halpert, Herbert, and G. M. Story, eds. 1968. *Christmas Mumming in Newfoundland: Essays in Anthropology, Folklore, and History*. Toronto: Univ. of Toronto Press.

Handelman, Don. 1990. *Models and Mirrors: Towards an Anthropology of Public Events*. Cambridge: Cambridge Univ. Press.

Hernandez, Joanne F., and Samuel R. Hernandez. 1979. *The Day of the Dead: Tradition and Change in Contemporary Mexico.* Santa Clara, Calif.: Triton Museum of Art.

Hole, Christina. 1976. *British Folk Customs.* London: Hutchison of London.

Humphrey, Theodore C., and Lyn T. Humphrey, ed. 1988. *"We Gather Together": Food and Festival in American Life.* Ann Arbor, Mich.: UMI Research Press.

Hunter, Darryl M. "No 'Malice in Wonderland': Conservation and Change in the Three Hallowe'ens of Ann Mesko." *Culture & Tradition* 7: 37–53.

Huntington, Richard, and Peter Metcalf. 1979. *Celebrations of Death.* Cambridge: Cambridge Univ. Press.

Kelley, Ruth Edna. 1919. *The Book of Halloween.* Boston: Lothrop, Lee, & Shepard.

Klavans, Nancy. 1988. "A Halloween Brunch: The Affirmation of Group in a Temporary Community." In *"We Gather Together": Food and Festival in American Life*, ed. Theodore C. Humphrey and Lyn T. Humphrey, 43–51. Ann Arbor, Mich.: UMI Research Press.

Krythe, Mamie R. 1962. *All About American Holidays.* New York: Harper and Row.

Lévi-Strauss, Claude. 1969. *The Raw and the Cooked.* New York: Harper and Row.

Linton, Ralph and Adele. 1949. *We Gather Together: The Story of Thanksgiving.* New York: Henry Schuman.

———. 1950. *Halloween Through Twenty Centuries.* New York: Henry Schuman.

MacAloon, John J. 1981. *This Great Symbol.* Chicago: Univ. of Chicago Press.

———. 1984. *Rite, Drama, Festival, and Spectacle: Rehearsals Toward a Theory of Cultural Performance.* Philadelphia: Institute for the Study of Human Issues.

MacNeill, Maire. 1969. *The Festival of Lughnasa: A Study of the Survival of the Celtic Festival of the Beginning of Harvest.* Oxford: Oxford Univ. Press.

———. 1970. *Halloween: Its Origins, Rites and Ceremonies in the Scottish Tradition.* Edinburgh: Albyn Press.

McDowell, John H. 1985. "Halloween Costuming Among Young Adults in Bloomington, Indiana: A Local Exotic." *Indiana Folklore and Oral History* 14, no. 1: 1–18.

McNeill, F. Marion. 1961. *The Silver Bough* 3, *A Calendar of Scottish National Festivals: Hallowe'en to Yule.* Glasgow: William Maclellan, 1961.

McSpadden, J. Walker. 1958. *The Book of Holidays.* New York: Thomas Y. Crowell.

Moore, Sally, and Barbara Myerhoff. *Secular Ritual.* Assen: Van Gorcum, 1977.

Myerhoff, Barbara. "Rites of Passage: Process and Paradox." In *Celebrations: Studies in Festivity and Ritual*, ed. Victor Turner. Washington, D.C.: Smithsonian Institution Press.

Myerhoff, Barbara. 1978. *Number Our Days.* New York: Simon and Schuster.

Newall, Venetia. 1971. *An Egg at Easter: A Folklore Study.* Bloomington: Indiana Univ. Press.

O'Drane, Mary. 1986. "San Francisco's Gay Halloween." *International Folklore Review* 4: 90–95.

Opie, Peter, and Iona Opie. *The Lore and Language of Schoolchildren.* Oxford: Oxford Univ. Press.

Ó'Súilleabháin, Seán. 1970. *A Handbook of Irish Folklore.* Detroit: Singing Tree Press.

Owen, Trefor M. 1968. *Welsh Folk Customs.* Cardiff: National Museum of Wales.

Pomar, María Teresa. 1987. *El Día de los Muertos: The Life of the Dead in Mexican Folk Art.* Fort Worth: Fort Worth Art Museum.

Richardson, James T., Joel Best, and David G. Bromley, eds. 1991. *The Satanism Scare.* New York: Aldine.

Robertson, Margaret R. 1984. *The Newfoundland Mummer's Christmas House-Visit.* Ottawa: National Museums of Canada.

Robinson, Philip S. 1984. *The Plantation of Ulster: British Settlement in an Irish Landscape, 1610–1670.* Dublin: Gill and Macmillan.

Russ, Jennifer M. 1982. *German Festivals and Customs.* London: Oswald Wolff.

Santino, Jack. 1983. "Halloween in America: Contemporary Customs and Performances." *Western Folklore* 42: 1–20.

———. 1986. "The Folk Assemblage of Autumn: Tradition and Creativity in Halloween Folk Art." In *Folk Art and Art Worlds,* ed. Vlach and Bronner, 151–69.

Sloan, Edward L. 1984. *The Bard's Offering: A Collection of Miscellaneous Poems.* Belfast: Northern Whig.

Paul Smith, ed. 1984. *Perspectives on Contemporary Legend.* Sheffield: CECTAL.

Smith, Robert J. 1972. "Festivals and Celebrations." In *Folklore and Folklife: An Introduction,* ed. Richard M. Dorson, 159–72. Chicago: Univ. of Chicago Press.

Stone, Gregory. 1959. "Halloween and the Mass Child." *American Quarterly* 13, no. 3: 372–79.

Stewart, George R. 1954. *American Ways of Life,* Garden City, N.Y.: Doubleday.

Sutton-Smith, Brian, and Diana Kelly-Byrne, eds. 1984. *The Masks of Play.* New York: Leisure Press.

Sykes, Homer. 1967. *Once a Year: Some Traditional British Customs.* London: Gordon Fraser.

Turner, Victor. 1967. *The Forest of Symbols: Aspects of Ndembu Ritual.* Ithaca: Cornell Univ. Press.

———. 1977. *The Ritual Process: Structure and Anti-Structure.* Ithaca: Cornell Univ. Press.

Turner, Victor, ed. 1982. *Celebration: Studies in Festivity and Ritual.* Washington, D.C.: Smithsonian Institution Press.

Van Gennep, Arnold. 1960. *The Rites of Passage.* Chicago: Univ. of Chicago Press.

Vennum, Thomas, Jr. 1985. "The Objibwa Begging Dance." In *Music and Context: Essays for John M. Ward,* ed. Anne Dhu Shapiro, 54–78. Cambridge, Mass.: Harvard Univ. Dept. of Music.

Vlach, John Michael, and Simon Bronner, eds. 1986. *Folk Art and Art Worlds.* Ann Arbor: UMI Research Press.

Warner, W. Lloyd. 1959. *The Living and the Dead: A Study of the Symbolic Life of Americans*. New Haven: Yale Univ. Press.

Yoder, Don. 1990. *Discovering American Folklife*. Ann Arbor, Mich.: UMI Research Press.

Zeitlin, Steven J., Amy J. Kotkin, and Holly Cutting Baker. 1982. *A Celebration of American Family Folklore: Tales and Traditions from the Smithsonian Collection*. New York: Pantheon.

Contributors

JACK SANTINO is a Professor in the Department of Popular Culture at Bowling Green State University in Ohio. He holds the Ph.D. in Folklore and Folklife from the University of Pennsylvania and has been a Folklife Specialist at the Smithsonian Institution. He has published articles in journals and magazines on many aspects of occupational folklore, and on ritual, festival, and celebration, especially Halloween. His ethnographic film *Miles of Smiles, Years of Struggle: The Story of the Black Pullman Porter* won four Emmy Awards, and he has published a book of the same name with the University of Illinois Press. He was a Fulbright Research Fellow in Northern Ireland 1991–92, where he researched Halloween traditions and the uses of symbols in public.

RUSSELL BELK is N. Eldon Tanner Professor of Business Administration at the University of Utah. He has taught there since 1979 and has had previous appointments at the University of Illinois, Temple University, and the University of British Columbia. His Ph.D. is from the University of Minnesota. He is past president of the Association for Consumer Research (1986), a fellow in the American Psychological Association, past recipient of the University of Utah Distinguished Research Professorship (1986), and has been an advisory editor for the *Journal of Consumer Research*. He has also served on the editorial review boards of thirteen journals, has written or edited twelve books or monographs, and has published more than one hundred articles and papers. His research primarily involves the meanings of possessions and materialism. One prior paper on the meanings of Christmas received the Carl Bode Award for the best article in the *Journal of American Culture* during 1987.

BILL ELLIS is Associate Professor of English and American Studies at the Hazleton campus of the Pennsylvania State University. He is editor of *FOAFtale News*, the newsletter of the International Society for Contemporary Legend Research, and heads the Folk Narrative Section of the American Folklore Society. He has published widely on camp horror stories, adolescent legend trips, and rumors concerning satanic cults and child abductions.

GREY GUNDAKER, a painter and former museum educator, holds degrees in Art from East Tennessee State University, Community Education from Teachers College, Columbia University, and a Ph.D. in Anthropology from Yale. Her interests include vernacular literacies and communication using commonplace objects. Currently, she is studying African-American landscape in Washington, D.C.

CARL B. HOLMBERG, currently an Associate Professor of Popular Culture at the Bowling Green State University, Bowling Green, Ohio, received the Baccalaureate degree in Applied Music from Heidelberg College, Master's degree in Classics and Interdisciplinary Studies from the University of Chicago, and Doctoral degree in Communication Studies from Ohio University. Research interests include New Age culture, horror experience, and social gatherings. Carl is also Executive Secretary and Program Director for the Midwest Popular Culture Association and the Midwest American Culture Association.

PAT JASPER has a Master's degree in Folklore from the University of Texas at Austin. As Folk Arts Coordinator and Field Representative for the Texas Commission of the Arts 1980–84, she has extensive experience and familiarity with Texas folk artists working in all genres of the traditional arts. Ms. Jasper has worked as a consultant to a variety of organizations, including the National Endowment for the Arts, the Texas Historical Commission, the Institute of Texan Cultures, the Museum of African American Life and Culture, and the Smithsonian Institution Office of Folklife Programs. As founder and director of TFR, Ms. Jasper's programming credits include the exhibitions "Art Among Us / *Arte Entre Nosotros:* Mexican American Folk Art from San Antonio" (San Antonio Museum of Art), "Handmade & Heartfelt: Contemporary Folk Art in Texas" (Laguna Gloria Art Museum), and "Texas Folklife / Texas Photography: Focus on Black Tradition" (African American Heritage Museum of Houston), as well as performing arts productions such as *Accordion Kings* (Austin Opera House), *Dance Traditions* (Miller Outdoor Theater, Houston), and *Blues, Boleros and Breakdowns* (Antone's, Austin).

JACK KUGELMASS is Associate Professor, Department of Anthropology, and Director of the Folklore Program, University of Wisconsin–Madison. He is the author of *The Miracle of Intervale Avenue: Aging with Dignity in the South Bronx* (Schocken Books, 1986), editor of *Between Two Worlds: Ethnographic Essays on American Jewry* (Cornell University Press, 1988), and editor of *Going Home: How Jews Invent Their Old Countries* (Northwestern University Press, 1993). He is currently completing a series of essays for a book titled *The Rites of the Tribe: The Public Culture of American Jews* (University of Wisconsin Press) and is collaborating with a group of photographers for a book on New York City's Greenwich Village Halloween Parade to be published by Columbia University Press in 1994.

PHILIP ROBINSON is Head of the Departments of Buildings and Non-Material Culture in the Ulster Folk and Transport Museum, County Down, Northern Ireland. His book on *The Plantation of Ulster* was published in Ireland and the United States, and he is coeditor of a current series of volumes in the *Folk Poets of Ulster*. He has published articles on a wide range of subjects relating to the settlement and cultural history of the north of Ireland.

A. W. SADLER is best known for his writings on Japanese folklore and Japanese folk religion and festivals, which have been published periodically since 1968 by *Asian Folklore Studies*, based in Nagoya. He received his Doctorate from Columbia University in 1958 and has taught comparative religion and folklore at Sarah Lawrence College for more than two decades. He and his wife lived in Vermont from 1956 to 1970 and have made regular return visits. In 1984 they founded their own small press, the Laughing Buddha Press.

CATHERINE SCHWOEFFERMANN has been Director of the Folklife Program and Curator of Folklife at the Roberson Museum in Binghamton, New York, since 1983. She has curated numerous museum exhibitions, presented related public events, and developed model Folk Art in Education programs. Schwoeffermann has worked extensively with ethnic communities in upstate New York and is the author of several exhibition catalogs and articles based on this research.

STEVE SIPORIN is Associate Professor of English and history at Utah State University. He writes about public folklore, Italian Jews, Italian American folklife, Western folk art, and festivals. His book *American Folk Masters: The National Heritage Fellows* was published by Harry N. Abrams in 1992. He was a Fulbright Scholar in Lisbon, Portugal, 1992–93.

MICHAEL TAFT is a folklore and oral history consultant based in Saskatoon, Saskatchewan. He received his Ph.D. in Folklore from Memorial University of Newfoundland in 1977 and a postdoctoral certificate in Folklore from Université Laval in 1978. He has taught folklore at Sir Wilfred Grenfell College, St. Mary's University, University of Regina, and University of Saskatchewan, and has been a Visiting Scholar at University College of Cape Breton. He has authored or co-authored ten books, including *A Regional Discography of Newfoundland and Labrador* (1975), *Discovering Saskatchewan Folklore* (1983), *Tall Tales of British Columbia* (1983), and *Blues Lyric Poetry: A Concordance* (1984). He is a past President of the Folklore Studies Association of Canada, and for the past fifteen years has been the Head of the Folklore Section of the MLA International Bibliography. Currently, he has a major, three-year contract from the Canadian government to investigate mock wedding dramas in the prairie provinces and plains states, and he is a consultant for Western Heritage Services, Inc.

TAD TULEJA did undergraduate work in cultural history at Yale and holds a Master's degree in American Studies from the University of Sussex. The author of *Curious Customs* (1987), an ethnographic survey of North American social practices, he has also published papers on yellow ribbons, Thanksgiving symbols, and the tooth fairy. Currently enrolled in the folklore program at the University of Texas at Austin, he is writing a dictionary of popular Americana.

KAY TURNER is a freelance folklorist living in Austin, Texas. She holds a Ph.D. in Folklore from the University of Texas and wrote her dissertation on Mexican American women's home altars. She recently published an essay for *Niño Fidencio: A Heart Thrown Open* by Dore Gardner (Museum of New Mexico Press), a photography book on the followers of a Mexican folk saint. Turner was formerly the Associate Director of Texas Folklife Resources.

Index